DRAGON IN THE DARK

How and Why Communist China Helps Our Enemies in the War on Terror

By

D.J. McGuire

© 2003 by D.J. McGuire. All rights reserved.

No part of this book may be reproduced, stored in a retrieval system, or transmitted by any means, electronic, mechanical, photocopying, recording, or otherwise, without written permission from the author.

ISBN: 1-4140-1823-1 (e-book)
ISBN: 1-4140-1822-3 (Paperback)
ISBN: 1-4140-1821-5 (Dust Jacket)

Library of Congress Control Number: 2003097696

This book is printed on acid free paper.

Printed in the United States of America
Bloomington, IN

1stBooks – rev. 10/29/03

Table of Contents

Preface: Communist China – With Us or With the Terrorists?................ v

Chapter 1: A Check on American Power – Communist China, al Qaeda, and the Taliban................ 1

Chapter 2: Iraq and Iran – Axis of Evil to Us, Friendly Arms Customers to the PRC................ 23

Chapter 3: North Korea – Terrorist State, Nuclear Power, and Communist Chinese Ally................ 45

Chapter 4: Pakistan, Communist China, and Terrorists vs. India................ 77

Chapter 5: Other Terrorist Issues and the Dangers of Engagement................ 101

Chapter 6: East Turkestan – the Communists' Big Lie on Terrorism................ 127

Chapter 7: Why Communist China Supports Our Enemies in the Terrorist War................ 157

Chapter 8: Cold War II – How to Win It and Win the Terrorist War................ 185

Chapter 9: Conclusion – What the Future Holds................ 215

Works Cited................ 223
Index................ 275
A Note on the Author................ 287

Preface:
Communist China – With Us or With the Terrorists?

On September 11, 2001, nineteen terrorists, backed by Osama bin Laden's al Qaeda organization, destroyed the World Trade Center and damaged the Pentagon. Nearly 3,000 people died, and that was the good news – estimates of the dead had been as high as 10,000. The New York City skyline was forever altered, and the Pentagon had a gaping wound that took almost a year to fix. Another planned attack, likely against Washington, D.C., would have taken hundreds more lives, but the passengers of Flight 93 thwarted the terrorists' plans. Nine days later, as he prepared the nation for war, President George W. Bush sent a message that resonated around the world, to allies and enemies alike, "You are either with us, or with the terrorists."

In the months since, many nations and regimes have taken sides, and some have tried to take both sides. One regime, however, has succeeded in the unusual trifecta of playing the two sides against each other while extracting diplomatic and other benefits from both. That regime is the Chinese Communist Party, currently ruling what it calls the People's Republic of China. It has attempted, successfully, to pass itself off as a friend and ally in the war on terror. Its actions have revealed a very different preference.

For Communist China, the terrorist war is simply another stage in their undeclared cold war with the United States. Just as World War II was another stage in the first Cold War for the Soviets, the war on terror is a stage of Cold War II for the People's Republic. At times – and they have been less frequent than is widely believed – it has sided with us in the war on terror. Far more often, it has sided with the terrorists. The focus on Afghanistan and the Middle East has allowed Communist China's activities prior to September 11 – and in a number of cases, since then – go unnoticed. The West, in particular the United States, would ignore those actions at their peril.

In January 2002, President Bush took the terrorist war beyond al Qaeda to the "axis of evil," indicting by name three regimes for their support of terrorists and development of chemical, biological, and nuclear weapons. Those rogue regimes were Iraq, Iran, and North Korea. Many others have noted terrorist support from Syria, Libya, and even American "ally" Pakistan.

In fact, these nations – Pakistan, Afghanistan prior to the end of Taliban control, Iraq, Iran, North Korea, Syria, and Libya – and al Qaeda all have two things in common. First, they have either taken part in terrorist attacks or supported others that did commit attacks on the United States of America. Second, each and every one listed, including al Qaeda, has won support from or struck deals with the People's Republic.

The support varies among the members of the list, but the record is there, and it is not disputed – all have, in fact, gone so far as to boast of Communist Chinese backing. Despite this, the People's Republic continues to win praise from Washington, D.C. for its "support" of anti-terrorist efforts. Meanwhile, most of Communist China's anti-American impulses and statements have gone largely unnoticed. Many Americans, while concerned about Communist China's increasing strength, still see the People's Republic as an "ally" in the war on terror. It is a dangerous illusion, one that does not take into account the actions Communist China has taken in support of our enemies, and its exploitation of the war on terror in order to achieve objectives that have absolutely nothing to do with terrorism.

This dangerous view on Communist China has led to a number of problems. The military is shifting to a smaller fighting force equipped to handle small, quick actions only, rather than diversifying to enable it to act both where fast, small forces are needed and where large forces are required to deter a major hostile power. The rose-colored glasses on Communist China have also skewed policy towards Stalinist North Korea, and the possibility of the People's Republic replacing its ties to Iraq (and Iran if it falls) with other nations that are rich in oil or have helped terrorists in the past – i.e., Saudi Arabia, the United Arab Emirates, and Yemen.

That was the inspiration for this book: the need to set the record straight on what Communist China has really done in regards to terrorists and states that support terrorism. This book will also put the terrorist war in the larger geo-political picture in Asia and throughout the world, and how it is connected to the cold war the People's Republic continues to fight against us. It will explain why the United States is such a danger to Communist China that it seeks to build ties to terrorist states that wish to destroy us. It will also show why "engagement" with Communist China is not only wrong, but very dangerous to American interests in both the war on terror and the new cold war, from Iraq and Afghanistan to Iran, North Korea, Pakistan, India, Syria, Libya, and throughout the world. Finally, it will provide a road map to win not only the war on terror, but to achieve victory in both.

Communist China's ties to terror are long, wide, and deep. The People's Republic paid upwards of $10 million to al Qaeda for American unexploded missiles in Afghanistan. It signed an economic agreement with the Taliban the day the World Trade Center fell, and hosted Taliban leader Mullah Omar's right-hand man nearly a year after American troops helped to dislodge it from power. It has maintained a longstanding alliance with Pakistan – which helped put the Taliban in power and to this day refuses to take concrete action against terrorists in Kashmir, including al Qaeda operatives – John Walker Lindh first began his anti-American military training with the Harakat ul-Mujahideen, one of the leading Pakistani terrorist groups in that region.

Regarding the axis of evil, the Communists installed a fiber-optic network in Iraq to enable Saddam Hussein to integrate his air-defense network, and according to a German newspaper cited by the BBC, supplied "hi-tech fibreglass (British sp) parts for air defence (British sp) installations." In other words, Communist China has had a direct hand in enabling Saddam Hussein to more accurately target and shoot down American pilots during both the enforcing of the "no-fly" zones and the liberation of Iraq. The Communists even tried to sell missile-launching patrol boats to Saddam; the United States had to buy the vessel carrying the cargo to keep it out of the Ba'athists' hands. The People's Republic has even closer ties to Iran – a recipient of, among other things, two tons of uranium, naval missiles, missile parts, and help in "nonconventional" weapons (read: weapons of mass destruction) from Communist China.

Then there's North Korea, Communist China's fifty-plus-year ally. For all the supposed help the People's Republic has given the rest of the world, in reality, no one has been a better friend to the Stalinist regime than the Communists – arms sales to terrorists, nuclear weapons, and abductions of Japanese and South Korean citizens notwithstanding. In fact, mere weeks after North Korea announced it had violated earlier pledges not to develop nuclear weapons, the People's Republic sold North Korea tributyl phosphate, a chemical used to make both plutonium and uranium in weapons grade fashion.

A nuclear North Korea is bad enough by itself. Taken with its numerous weapons sales to terrorist sponsoring states such as Iran, Syria, Pakistan, and Libya, it is doubly terrifying, except to the People's Republic. Of course, the Communists have largely been in the arms trade with these regimes *themselves*, so one could hardly expect them to be upset at their ally imitating their actions. Communist China even used North Korea to send missile and weapons-of-mass-destruction components to Iran.

All the while, the Communists have insisted they are America's friends. They have even tried to don the mantle of terrorist victim. This comes from their massive propaganda campaign regarding the large Muslim-populated area just north of Tibet, that they call Xinjiang. Many Americans are more familiar with its older Chinese name, Sinkiang. Far fewer are aware that it once went by an altogether different name: the Republic of East Turkestan. The brief independence of East Turkestan ended with the founding of the People's Republic in 1949. The ensuing crackdown against the Uighurs has been vicious. Communist China has done more than simply jail political prisoners in East Turkestan; it has also executed many of them, a leading reason why the People's Republic has executed more people in recent times than the rest of the world *combined*.

Until September 11, 2001, Communist China was more than willing to keep the situation in East Turkestan out of the headlines, for obvious reasons. After the terrible events of that day, as America mourned, the People's Republic sensed an opportunity to put the terrorist label on the entire collection of East Turkestan dissidents, one they grabbed with both hands. The People's Republic was suddenly finding Uighur terrorists all over the region. The Communists even released "statistics" of terrorist activity in East Turkestan – but with no evidence to back up the numbers. Communist China also tried, desperately, to tie East Turkestan dissidents to al Qaeda and Osama bin Laden.

Meanwhile, several media reports out of East Turkestan revealed the Communist claims to be a carefully built collection of lies and half-truths. Contrary to reports out of Pakistan, Egypt, and other Muslim nations, Uighurs were openly supportive of American military action. Given the fact that Communist China itself never came out in support of defeating the Taliban – choosing instead to complain about the presence of American troops in Central Asia and scheme to prevent a "pro-American regime in Kabul" – this was a remarkable, and quite dangerous, show of solidarity with the American people.

It was a solidarity the Bush Administration at first was more than willing to reciprocate, until the summer of 2002. Eager to win Communist "acquiescence" for the liberation of Iraq, the Bush Administration became the first Western nation to label a Uighur group as terrorist – the East Turkestan Islamic Movement (ETIM). What was Communist propaganda in January became United States-backed, and stated, statistics in August and September. Weeks later, reports came out that ETIM was not based in the People's Republic, had likely gone defunct, and according to *Time Asia*, "never carried out operations on Chinese soil." Even a claim that Uighurs had targeted the American Embassy in Kyrgyzstan – the only report of any Uighur targeting the United States in any way, shape, or form – was not confirmed by Kyrgyz security.

Communist China also used terrorism as an excuse to build what it hoped would be a counter to American presence in Asia: the Shanghai Cooperation Organization (SCO), an organization founded by the People's Republic, Russia, Tajikistan, Uzbekistan, Kazakhstan, and Kyrgyzstan. The SCO was supposedly a multinational group against "terrorism, separatism and extremism," but the Communists were hoping it could become their answer to the North Atlantic Treaty Organization (NATO).

The liberation of Afghanistan threw "Beijing's NATO." into disarray. Russia made a noticeable shift toward the United States – although not enough of one to stop being Communist China's largest supplier of military hardware and technology. The SCO itself nearly collapsed. Uzbekistan – Afghanistan's northern neighbor and the strongest post-September 11, 2001 ally of the United States – has been practically AWOL from every major organization event. Meanwhile, the People's Republic is deeply disturbed by the presence of American troops in Central Asia, which the Communists consider their "backyard." Whatever help Communist China may have provided against the Taliban and al Qaeda – and descriptions of said help have been vague at best – was tempered, if not overshadowed, by Communist efforts to prevent a "pro-American" regime to take shape in Afghanistan. Even a border agreement between the People's Republic and Kyrgyzstan, which had nothing to do with the war on terror, helped to spark a nationwide protest movement in Kyrgyzstan that forced the government there to resign *en masse*. In many ways, the war on terror has forced the People's Republic to play defense in Central Asia.

Communist China's support for terrorist states and plans against the United States are no accident, nor or they unrelated. They stem from the same reality: the United States stands in the way of the People's Republic's plans for becoming the dominant regime in Asia and a world superpower. After the Tiananmen Square massacre, the Communists realized that economic growth was not enough justification to maintain their iron grip on power. Rather than choose political reform – a one-way ticket to oblivion for the regime – the Communists chose jingoism as its excuse to silence dissent and remain in power.

This requires the willingness of the rest of the world to accept Communist China increasing regional and global clout at the expense of Asia's democracies and the United States. The People's Republic knew America would not be so willing. Whether it's "reunification" with Taiwan – and Communist China's foreign, domestic, and economic policies are in many ways fixated on snuffing out the increasingly confident democracy there – replacing Japan as the leading regional power, or thwarting India's goals for South Asia, the nation most clearly in the Communists' way is the United States. This is why the Communists continue to support our enemies in the war on terror while pretending to be friend of the United States.

Terrorists and the regimes that sponsored them declared war on us, and began fighting it, long before we recognized it as such. As September 11, 2001 painfully taught us, if you do not realize you are fighting a war, you are losing that war. In the war on terror, this is no longer true; unfortunately it most definitely still is true in Cold War II. However, it is still early enough to fight and win Cold War II if we recognize it for what it is. This will do more than simply ensure freedom for the Chinese people and a more stable East Asia, it will provide tremendous benefits in the war on terror.

President Bush gave this challenge to the world: "You are either with us, or with the terrorists." Communist China has responded by continuing its age-old policy of trying to be both and neither. When it comes to its long-term objectives, the People's Republic has repeatedly chosen the terrorists' interests over our own. It is a fact we ignore at our peril. We are not only in a declared war against terrorism, but also an undeclared war against Communist China. If we are to secure the benefits of victory in the terrorist war, we must also do all we can to win Cold War II. This book will reveal not only why it must be done, but also how it can be done.

DRAGON IN THE DARK
How and Why Communist China Helps Our Enemies in the War on Terror

Chapter 1:
A Check on American Power – Communist China, al Qaeda, and the Taliban

On September 11, 2001, two United States airliners, hundreds of American passengers, and thousands of Americans in the World Trade Center and the Pentagon became part of the worst terrorist attack in American history, and the most painful example of the horrors of war on American territory since Pearl Harbor. The world was shocked, and America was deeply wounded. A terrorist group called al Qaeda, or "the base" inflicted this wound. Its leader, and chief source of inspiration, was Osama bin Laden. Today no is sure if the son of a wealthy Saudi Arabian family is dead or alive.

Osama bin Laden found homes, and operational bases, in a number of regimes. Two in particular – Sudan and Afghanistan – became critical sources for his efforts. After 1996, Afghanistan was both his home and the headquarters for The Base. From then until September 11, 2001, bin Laden trained thousands of terrorists, and as such, provided the manpower for a slew of terrorist cells throughout the world. In the aftermath of the attack, the United States won the sympathies of nearly every nation, and many joined the United States in the fight against both al Qaeda and its hosts in Afghanistan, the radical Taliban regime. Not the least of those supporters were Afghans themselves, both horrified about September 11, 2001 and seething under the brutal tyranny imposed upon them by the Taliban.

Some regimes, however, chose to hedge their bets. A few told the world that an undisputed American victory in Afghanistan was, in some respects, an undesirable outcome. In other nations, academics turned up their noses at the United States, and told Americans that the horrors of September 11, 2001 were their own fault. Officials in some regimes advised Pakistan – Afghanistan's neighbor – that it should not accept any American military on its territory, which, had Pakistan followed the advice, would have severely crippled the battle against al Qaeda.

However, one regime did all of these things at once, and more, to all but broadcast its ambivalence in the war on terror. This included wringing its hands at the possibility of a "pro-American regime" in Kabul, Afghanistan and establishing ties to the Taliban on the very day the United States was attacked. This regime, even as it publicly declared itself willing to help the United States against terrorism, discussed future plans against America, and pondered if the United States was ripe for concessions, or even outright conflict in some way, shape, or form. That regime was the People's Republic of China.

This may come as a surprise to most Americans, and a shock to many others, but Communist China actually has a long and extensive history with al Qaeda, their Taliban allies, and their Pakistani benefactors. That history includes a number of events in which the Communists cooperated with America's first and most hated enemies in the terrorist war, such as:

- Up to $10 million paid to al Qaeda for American unexploded cruise missiles to be reverse engineered
- A recommendation by two Communist Chinese colonels for a terrorist scenario in which the World Trade Center is attacked, and in which Osama bin

Laden is named specifically as someone able to accomplish an attack of that magnitude
- Opposition to United Nations sanctions against the Taliban despite the latter's refusal to hand over Osama bin Laden to the United States for al Qaeda's role in terrorist attacks in the 1990s
- A pact on economic cooperation with the Taliban, signed on the morning of September 11, 2001, mere hours before the World Trade Center fell and the Pentagon was attacked
- A slew of academics after the attack calling it the result of what they called America's "quasi-hegemonic" policies
- A Xinhua press agency video about September 11, 2001, "glorifying the strikes as a humbling blow against an arrogant nation"
- A public demand to Pakistan – a half-century PRC ally – to keep out all "foreign troops," including American forces
- A Communist Chinese technology firm – Huawei Technologies – building a telephone network in Kabul, *after* September 11, 2001
- A large cache of weapons from Communist China, including surface-to-air missiles made in the People's Republic, found by American and allied forces in al Qaeda hideouts in Afghanistan

- Repeated comments opposing the presence of the American military in Central Asia – including a speech by then-Communist Chinese President Jiang Zemin ripping the American troop presence during a visit to Iran
- A similarly unsupportive attitude toward a "pro-American regime" in Kabul
- An invitation to a three-man delegation from the Taliban, led by Ustad Khalil – believed to be Mullah Omar's right-hand man – for a week of meetings with Communist Chinese officials, in September of 2002

The above list reveals a pattern that is disturbing to say the least. For a period of at least three years, Communist China saw the Taliban and al Qaeda not as dangers to international stability, but as tools to be used against the United States. The fact that the People's Republic would still be willing to use the Taliban in such a fashion, even roughly a year *after* September 11, 2001 and more than nine months after the fall of the Taliban, is even more troubling.

The incidents and events described above are, in fact, part of the Communist policy regarding our enemies in the terrorist war that in point of fact did not change either on September 11, 2001 or after it. For Communist China, it is the United States, not the terrorists, who must be watched, restrained, and held back. It is the United States, not the terrorists, who are the danger, for it is Cold War II – the cold war against the United States – not the war on terror, which shapes Communist China's worldview.

In fact, days after the World Trade Center fell, Communist China considered Osama bin Laden and the Taliban not as a danger, but as "some kind of check on United States power." That chilling observation, made by CNN's Willy Wo-Lap Lam, says all America needs to know about just how uncommitted Communist China really is to the war on terror. For those who would disagree, Lam also had this, almost in response: "But many senior cadres, including (then-Communist Party leader and President) Jiang (Zemin) and (then-) Premier Zhu Rongji, have decided it is not yet time to take on the United States" In other words, the supposed alliance of Communist China to the United States in the war on terror is not based on heartfelt support, or a desire to defeat terrorism, or even common interests. It is based on timing, and nothing more.

As for the Taliban militia, it began as a small group of radical Islamic Afghan refugee students in the Pakistani *madrassas*. In 1994, after its members militia rescued a Pakistani convoy from road bandits, the Pakistani military, particularly the shady Inter-Service Intelligence agency (ISI) took notice of the group. With ISI help, including arms, money, and other logistical support, the Taliban had roughly 90% of Afghanistan under its control by 1996.

This sounds a lot more impressive than it actually was. As many who follow Afghanistan closely noted, the Taliban won few major battles. Most of its territorial gains came from deals struck with local warlords – here Pakistan's backing must have been quite a bargaining chip. When the Taliban fell in late 2001, it lost few actual battles, which were mostly concentrated in a few cities. Most of the territory it lost came from those same local chieftains who saw the writing on the wall after the fall of Mazar-e-Sharif, and dropped the Taliban like a rock.

Given the radical Islam the Taliban imposed upon the area they ruled, only three nations were willing to recognize the militia as the government of Afghanistan: Pakistan, Saudi Arabia, and the United Arab Emirates. Because Afghanistan's radical Sunni Islam was of a different theological bent than that of Iran under the Shiite Ayatollahs, even the Taliban's relationship with Iran was frosty at best, and some friction soon came between Iran and Pakistan as well. That may have been a factor in keeping Communist China from joining its longtime ally Pakistan in recognizing the Taliban: the Communists were already selling weapons to both Pakistan *and* Iran by this time.

The lack of diplomatic recognition from the People's Republic did not necessarily mean open hostility. Pakistan's support of the Taliban, coupled with India's support for the local opposition – the Afghan Northern Alliance – provided some fairly good reasons for the Communists to reach out to the radical Islamic regime in Kabul. One of those reasons made its presence felt in Afghanistan in 1996, and in the rest of the world soon afterwards; for that was the year Osama bin Laden left Sudan for the Taliban theocracy.

One of several sons of a Saudi construction magnate, Osama bin Laden made his mark in Afghanistan during the *mujahedin* against the Soviet Union in the 1980s. By the 1990s, he was miffed at American troops in Saudi Arabia, and at the Saudis willingness to rely on them. This led him to decide that the United States was the enemy, and that America's allies in the Saudi royal family were perverting the radical Wahhabist Islam that it was supposed to preserve. He began building an anti-American, anti- royal terrorist group, which took the name al Qaeda.

Sudan seemed an excellent base for Osama at first. Since 1989, it had been under the control of a radical Muslim regime that was engaged in a civil war with the Christian and animist people of southern Sudan – and the Sudanese military was especially vicious in its prosecution of the war. By 1996, however, Sudan, looking to end icy relations with the United States, was making offers to hand Osama over.

Meanwhile, the Taliban were solidifying their control over Afghanistan. For Osama, Afghanistan under Taliban rule must have seemed too good to be true (of course, by 2002, it was just that). Here was a regime with a radical Islam much like his own. Osama could reasonably expect that some financial help to the group would make them, at the very least, grateful enough to be far more helpful – and far less willing to hand him over to the United States – than Sudan was.

Once he came to Afghanistan, he never left until the terrorist war. The Taliban were deferential and helpful to their new "guests," and Osama used Afghanistan to build a massive terrorist training and financing operation. The rest of Afghanistan, already suffering under Taliban rule, were decidedly less than thrilled about the "guests."

By 1998, under the protection of the Taliban, bin Laden was able to engineer two terrorist attacks on American embassies in East Africa, killing hundreds. America responded to the attacks on its embassies with a cruise missile attack in both Osama's current home base – Afghanistan – and his former home base – Sudan. Until 2000, Osama appeared to fade from view. He and his group re-entered the public scene with a dramatic attack on the *U.S.S. Cole*, an American naval vessel docked at the time in Yemen. Within weeks, the evidence pointed to Osama bin Laden and al Qaeda.

After the attack on the *Cole*, Osama appeared to fade away again, until, of course, September 11, 2001. The Taliban was a different story. Its ever tightening grip on Afghanistan was choking the Afghan population. The Taliban banned television and music, demanded that women cover themselves in burqas, and even had a minimum length for men's beards. The situation was so bad that during this period, as a drought ravaged the nation and Taliban leader Mullah Mohammed Omar blamed the dry weather on the people for not following Allah's will, one unnamed Afghan, and few can blame him for wishing to remain anonymous, opined that Allah was really punishing Afghanistan for Mullah Omar himself.

In 2001, however, the Taliban outdid itself in terms of garnering international opprobrium. In an incident reminiscent of Nazi Germany, the group demanded that non-Muslims wear markers on their clothing to reveal their membership in other faiths. Given the Taliban's hatred of non-Muslims, the group's insistence that the measure was for their protection against local enforcers of Islamic law rang pretty hollow. Less damaging to individual freedom, but just as controversial, was the destruction of two four-story tall Buddha statues that were considered priceless historical landmarks the world over. The statues were believed to be at least a millennium and a half old, but to the Taliban, and even more so to their al Qaeda "guests," they were heresy. Their destruction generated outrage the world over.

During this time, the 19 al Qaeda terrorists who would soon be forever known as "the hijackers" were practicing, and waiting. Suddenly, on September 9, 2001, the unofficial but widely acknowledged leader of the anti-Taliban Northern Alliance, Ahmed Shah Massoud was dead, killed by operatives from al Qaeda. Nearly every observer of Afghanistan during the

Taliban era was convinced that the one real threat left to continuing Taliban control of Afghanistan – and thus to bin Laden's protection – was Massoud. Known as the "Lion of Panshjir Valley," Massoud had managed to resist both the Soviets and the Taliban for two decades. He had managed to hang on to northeast Afghanistan against a radical Islamic regime backed both by Osama's millions and Pakistan's political clout. With his death, Osama must have felt invincible.

Massoud died mere hours before the horrific attack of September 11, 2001. The force he had led in life – and which mourns his death to this day – made its presence known that day, too. As America grieved, and turned its eye to the Taliban, it saw someone fire rockets into Kabul. The damage was minimal, but the symbol was there. The Northern Alliance said: we are here, your war is our war, and we are ready to help.

Less than one month after September 11, 2001, the United States – along with a number of its allies – began its effort to help the Northern Alliance liberate Afghanistan. In November of that year, the first major Afghan city – Mazar-e-Sharif – fell to the Northern Alliance. By the end of the year, both the Taliban *and* al Qaeda were on the run, and an interim government was in place to move Afghanistan past the dark cloud of Talibanism.

This is not to say that the situation in Afghanistan is set in stone. The Taliban has been forced from power, but not eliminated. Osama bin Laden's group, meanwhile, has engaged in or backed a number of terrorist acts since Afghanistan was liberated. Whether bin Laden himself is alive or dead is still unknown to this day.

What *is* known, however, is how the rest of the world saw the situation. Few if any regimes were willing to stick up for and/or reach out to the Taliban or al Qaeda during its 1990s heyday. Those few were the aforementioned Saudi Arabia, the United Arab Emirates, Pakistan, and the People's Republic of China.

The beginning of Communist China's ties to the Taliban and al Qaeda are not exactly known, but the first contact of which we do know came in 1998, just after the American cruise missile attack. An unknown number of cruise missile did not explode upon contact. These unexploded cruise missiles became a bonanza for al Qaeda.

Communist China was, as always, eager for whatever American technology they could find and learn how to assemble. After the 1998 cruise missile attack, the People's Republic reportedly paid up to $10 million for some of the cruise missiles (a CIA spokesperson cast doubt on the $10 million figure, but not on the transaction itself). The money was, according to the report, used to finance numerous al Qaeda operations, including possibly the very attack of September 11, 2001, although bin Laden's wealth likely ensured that the attack would have occurred anyway.

The brazenness of the Communists on this matter is breathtaking. They made this deal with al Qaeda just after it blew up two American embassies in Africa and killed hundreds of people, and during the second term of an American administration that was friendlier to the People's Republic than that of any President before it. In fact, President Bill Clinton himself had just completed a well-publicized visit to Communist China, during which he ruled out any American support for Taiwan's campaign for international recognition. It was also a few months after reports surfaced that two major Democratic contributors had handed over satellite technology information to the People's Republic in ways that might have run afoul of United States law but for a well-timed waiver from Clinton himself.

Is this really a move conducted by a regime that is sympathetic to America's interests? Is this the action of a "strategic partner," the term Clinton gave the People's Republic?

Moreover, this would not be the only sign of Communist China finding al Qaeda a useful tool against the United States. In fact, two Communist Chinese colonels were willing to praise terrorist acts sponsored by Osama bin Laden in a possible war against the United States, and they even put it in print.

Less than a year after the 1998 cruise missile deal, two colonels in the People's Liberation Army – Qiao Liang and Wang Xiangsui – wrote *Unrestricted Warfare*, a book describing possible regular and irregular military actions the Communists could take against the United States. The book recommends terrorism as a useful tool against the United States, including an attack on the World Trade Center. As for possibly useful terrorists, the authors recommended none other than bin Laden himself: "Whether it be the intrusions of hackers, a major explosion at the World Trade Center, or a bombing attack by bin Laden, all of these greatly exceed the frequency bandwidths understood by the American military."

It should be noted that after September 11, 2001, the aforementioned colonels were hailed as heroes in the People's Republic.

Meanwhile, in 2000, when Russia and the United States proposed an arms embargo and other sanctions against the Taliban – to be lifted if it handed over Osama bin Laden – Communist China initially opposed the idea. It wasn't until a month and a half after al Qaeda attacked the *U.S.S. Cole* that the Communists dropped their opposition to the embargo.

Then came September 11, 2001, itself, and the immediate aftermath.

No evidence exists that Communist China had any knowledge of the attack on the World Trade Center before it occurred, although they certainly looked at it as a very convenient blow on a hypothetical level, as *Unrestricted Warfare* reveals. However, on September 11, 2001 itself, mere hours before al Qaeda attacked the World Trade Center and the Pentagon, Communist China signed a "memorandum on economic and technical cooperation" – the rest of the world would call in an agreement – with the Taliban. This stunning development was revealed days later, and, of course, immediately denied.

Immediately after the attack, the People's Republic expressed its condolences. However, at the same time these condolences were sent, the academic "community" in Communist China – under the watchful eye of the Chinese Communist Party – rose nearly as one to tell the United States, according to CNN's Willy Wo-Lap Lam, that "its main enemy is not the others but itself." The Communist-run Xinhua News Agency would later produce a video of September 11, 2001. The *London Daily Telegraph* summarized the video's message of that horrible day as follows: "a humbling blow against an arrogant nation."

Meanwhile, in the corridors of Zhongnanhai – the Communist Chinese version of the Kremlin – the Communist cadres were making decisions. Their initial view of Osama bin Laden and the Taliban was best described by Lam: "*countries and elements such as Iraq and the bin Laden group constitute some kind of check on United States power*" (emphasis added). After the events of September 11, 2001, the Communists took stock of the world, and decided that, in Lam's words again, "*it is not yet time to take on the United States*" (emphasis added). In other words, had bin Laden waited until 2030, 2020, or perhaps even 2005, the reaction of the People's

Republic may have been very different. Even as it was, the Communist decision to "cooperate" with the United States came with caveats, restrictions, and a push for concessions.

One of the most critical nations in the war against the Taliban was the former sponsor of Osama bin Laden's host: Pakistan. However, Pakistan had more with which to be concerned than the reaction of the United States and its own people, for it is also a fifty-year ally of Communist China. The People's Republic quickly tried to use this alliance to put its own interests ahead of American interests.

Until September 11, 2001, Communist China and Russia were the dominant powers in Central Asia. The new focus of the United States brought a potential challenge to each. For Russia, which had backed the Northern Alliance for years, the possible loss of influence in Central Asia was less important than winning American support for its Afghan allies, and its battle against the independence movement-turned-terrorist force in Chechnya. Communist China reacted very differently. At first, they demanded that no foreign troops be allowed *anywhere* in Pakistan, putting the Pakistani leadership in the almost untenable position of choosing between its longtime ally – and much larger neighbor – and the rest of the world.

This may seem like a strange way to show support for the war on terror, but for Communist China, the issue of the Taliban and its support for Osama bin Laden was secondary to preventing a loss of geopolitical power for itself. As a result, in the aftermath of September 11, 2001, as everyone else worried about the survival of the Taliban or reprisal attacks from al Qaeda, the Communists wrung their hands with concern over the American military establishing a "pro-U.S. regime in Kabul" or using the war as a pretext to "encircle and contain" the People's Republic.

The Communist Chinese policy toward the Taliban included more than just mere concern at a pro-American government replacing it. Days after September 11, 2001, intelligence officials told the *Washington Times* that two Communist Chinese firms were building a telephone network in Taliban-controlled Kabul. The two firms were Zhongxing Telecom, a Communist-owned and operated firm, and Huawei Technologies – a first with a murky ownership history and ties with Saddam Hussein.

Furthermore, arms made in Communist China were found many times in Taliban hands. The Communist themselves acknowledged the possibility that some of their weaponry that they had sold to Pakistan may have made its way to the Taliban and al Qaeda. One might find it hard to blame the Communists for that, until one remembers that Pakistan received weaponry from the People's Republic long after it had made clear its support for the Taliban.

Meanwhile, the Communists were also insisting that the United States win United Nations Security Council approval before sending in troops to defeat the Taliban, despite a near universal acknowledgement from the rest of the world of America's right to defend itself. Throughout the battle for Afghanistan, the Communists repeatedly looked for concessions for the United States, first in exchange for its support, then as gratitude for essentially keeping its mouth shut.

The concessions the Communists desired focused mainly on two subjects: Taiwan and East Turkestan. The obsession with the island democracy of Taiwan, as previous and later chapters will show, color nearly every foreign policy issue from the perspective of the People's Republic.

Any political controversy, dangerous situation, or imminent conflict – particularly if the United States is involved – is an excuse to attempt to score points against Taiwan.

East Turkestan, about which more detail can be found later in this book, became a critical issue in large part due to where Afghanistan is, and who the Taliban and al Qaeda are. The Communists saw a possibility to give their brutal treatment of the Uighur Muslims in East Turkestan – called "Xinjiang" by the People's Republic – the veneer of anti-terrorism. It is a credit to the Bush Administration that it refused to grant the Communists the public relations victory they needed until the focus shifted from Afghanistan to Iraq. In fact, the United States made a point of refusing to call any Uighur caught in Afghanistan a terrorist throughout the first phase of Afghanistan's liberation.

When the bombs began falling on Afghanistan in early October, the Communists finally began to give ground. Communist Chinese Foreign Minister Tang Jiaxuan told his Russian counterpart Igor Ivanov that the People's Republic would support a coalition government in Kabul, although what Tang meant by that was anyone's guess. Meanwhile, as Lam noted, the Communist military continued to warn against "Washington setting up a pro-U.S. regime in Afghanistan" and "the United States establishing footholds in countries including Uzbekistan and Tajikistan," the latter being the two Central Asian nations that most quickly signed on to the American-led war on terror in Afghanistan.

While the Communists were wringing their hands and hedging their bets, the United States presented carrot after carrot to them, making it clear there would be rewards for stronger support in Afghanistan. That none of them came to fruition is a sign of just how little Communist China actually supported the fight against al Qaeda and the Taliban.

In the midst of the fighting, one Taliban commander even claimed that Communist China was *supporting* his group, although he said the nature of that support "cannot be disclosed." The Northern Alliance also claimed that the People's Republic had funneled arms to the Taliban. Parts of Pakistan's military were also helping their former protégés across the shared border, leading one official to cynically note to the *Washington Times*: "There are two border control regimes: One before sundown and one after sundown."

The claims of Communist Chinese support for the Taliban were forgotten almost as soon as they were made, until November, when the combination of the Northern Alliance and American-led forces pushed the Taliban out of the metropolitan centers in Afghanistan. The Taliban and their al Qaeda "guests" were on the run.

Even as the Taliban was being defeated, and the residents of Kabul danced in the streets to celebrate – the Communists continued their obsessive quest to thwart the rise of a "'pro-U.S. regime in Kabul." As always, keeping the United States out of Central Asia was more important than ridding the region of terrorist and their sponsors. Then-Communist Chinese Party chief and current Central Military Commission Chairman Jiang Zemin himself went to Iran to blast the presence of American military forces in Central Asia.

Of course, there may have been a more immediate reason for the Communist concern about a pro-American Afghanistan – the presence of Communist Chinese weapons in terrorist hands. As noted earlier, the People's Republic admitted to the possibility that some of their weaponry headed for Pakistan may have gone through to Afghanistan, for either the Taliban or al Qaeda. The Northern Alliance, meanwhile, claimed that the Communists were more direct in their support.

After the Taliban and al Qaeda were cleared out of the Afghan city, the American-led forces and their allies began raiding caves and other terrorist hideouts. They made a number of interesting finds. Chief among them were, as CNN's Donald McIntyre put it "more intelligence about al Qaeda, including *large caches of Chinese ammunition – raising the question of how it got there*" (emphasis added).

During 2002, more caches of Communist Chinese weapons were found in al Qaeda and Taliban hideouts, including – chillingly – about 30 NH-5 surface-to-air missiles (the NH-5 is the Sinicized version of the Russian SA-7 surface-to-air missile). This stunning news came just as the FBI warned that surface-to-air missiles might have been smuggled into the United States by terrorists against commercial aircraft. The concern about al Qaeda surface-to-air missiles fired on commercial flights became a disturbing reality in a missile-launched attack against an El Al airliner in late 2002.

If that wasn't enough, last summer, a general in the Afghan interim government made a startling claim – al Qaeda was regrouping in a part of Pakistan that was "basically under the government of China." The general, Brigadier Rawand, also said the Communists "may give al Qaeda the (surface to air) missiles."

Meanwhile, Communist China continued to rail against the rise of the United States as a power in Central Asia. The "pro-United States regime in Kabul" particularly incensed the People's Republic. According to one report, this even led the Communists to invite a Taliban delegation, led by

Ustad Khalil – the right-hand man to Taliban leader Mullah Mohammed Omar – to Beijing for a meeting with top Communist cadres. During this meeting, the Communists apparently let the Taliban delegation know they were still miffed about the presence of United States troops in the region.

Throughout all of this, from the demand that Pakistan not allow any American troops on its soil, through the public rhetoric against American troops in Central Asia, the admonishments against a "pro-United States regime in Kabul," the caches of weapons from the People's Republic in al Qaeda and Taliban hideouts, the reports of the $10 million cruise missile purchase and the economic "memorandum" signed hours before the World Trade Center became forever known as Ground Zero, and the reports of Communist Chinese aid and comfort to the Taliban and al Qaeda *after* they had been knocked off their respective perches in Afghanistan, Communist China continued to claim it supported the United States in the war on terror.

That the People's Republic was willing to even attempt to make that statement was the height of unmitigated gall. That so many are willing to believe and accept it was a sign of just how little was known of all of the information that proved such professions of "support" to be complete rubbish.

One might wonder why Communist China was so determined to preserve its ties to al Qaeda and the Taliban in the face of the American campaign to rid the world of both. The Communists certainly were not willing to *admit* to their links with either group – they denied them, refused to address them, or attempted to explain them away whenever they arose. So clearly they were worried about American reaction to the fact that they were aiding and abetting an enemy of the United States – one that killed 3,000 in a single day.

Certainly, the Communist entreaties to the Taliban and al Qaeda had quite a bit to do with their shared ally – Pakistan. When Pakistan propped up the Taliban in the 1990s, they were certainly hoping that Communist China would eventually come on board. As the Huawei telephone project and the "memorandum" revealed, Communist China was already beginning to move in that direction before September 11, 2001. Whether it would have continued, and at what pace, will now never be known.

But why continue to support the Taliban *after* September 11, 2001? Why attempt to all but order Pakistan not let American troops set one foot in its territory? Why spend more time fretting over a "pro-U.S. regime in Kabul" than worrying about the possible survival of one of the most fearsome terrorist group in the world? Why travel to, of all places, *Iran* and use the trip as a backdrop to blast the American military presence in Central Asia?

For that matter, why hand over $10 million – or however many million it was – to al Qaeda after the 1998 attack, when it was quite clear the United States and al Qaeda were enemies, and would continue to be, even if the war seemed to be a low-level one prior to September 11, 2001?

Additionally, the fall of the Taliban was a major building block to a strong continued American presence in Central Asia, a region the Communists view as their backyard. The fact that a government in Kabul more friendly to the United States makes Pakistan a less-valued ally to Washington – and as such, a less effective lever for the Communists to use against the United States – was probably another critical factor. Furthermore, the People's Republic has in recent years attempted to fashion itself as the new spokesman for the third world. A key part of this act is

19

close ties to Muslim nations – including Iran and Saddam Hussein. This also had a hand in their effort to reach out to the Taliban.

However, these reasons are merely a part of the larger, overarching rationale for Communist China's links to the Taliban and al Qaeda – the common opposition to the interests and objectives of a common enemy – the United States.

The fact is, Communist China saw, and likely continues to see, al Qaeda as a "check" against American power. The same holds true for the Taliban. For the People's Republic of China, the United States is the major obstacle to its efforts at increasing its power in Asia, and expanding its international profile the world over. The constant references to resisting American "hegemony" in Communist statements are no accident. Anti-American regimes and groups will always garner their attention. For the Communists, these groups, even ones that resort to terrorism, are merely tools and allies in Cold War II.

This is why Communist China refused to publicly support the American effort against the Taliban and al Qaeda in Afghanistan (while clamoring for the rest of the world to support its crackdown in East Turkestan against what it claims are terrorists backed by the very al Qaeda who destruction in Afghanistan they can't bring themselves to support). For the People's Republic of China, it is not a war between civilization and terrorism, nor is it a war between the forces of democracy and the axis of evil, nor is it even the "clash of civilizations" that Osama bin Laden and his cronies claim that it is. For Communist China, it is a battle between the American "hegemon" and the "checks" that can be arrayed against it. It's as simple as that.

No Administration was friendlier to Communist China than the Clinton Administration, yet this did not stop the Communists from giving al Qaeda millions of dollars for missiles the President himself ordered fired on that very terrorist group. This is what Communist China did for al Qaeda in 1998. Three years later, it signed a "memorandum on economic and technical cooperation" with al Qaeda's hosts – the Taliban – mere hours before the World Trade Center fell and the Pentagon was attacked. Afterwards, the Communists have steadfastly watched Afghanistan for the rise of a threatening regime, but to them, that threat comes in a regime backed by the United States. This has continued even after the fall of the Taliban and the temporary scattering of al Qaeda.

However, the People's Republic has been able to keep these actions largely out of view. Additionally, it has put out an unending stream of self-praising rhetoric in which it calls itself an ally in the war on terror. So far, it has largely worked. For the most part, Communist China is considered to most talking heads as an "ally" in the terrorist war. Nothing can be further from the truth.

Communist China has been trying to play both sides in the war on terror ever since September 11, 2001. While President Bush dramatically announced to the rest of the world: "You are either with us, or with the terrorists," Communist China has continued a policy that attempts to be both at the same time. The more this is allowed to continue, the more difficult it will be for the United States to win the terrorist war, due to increasing roadblocks put up quietly by the Communists, in the hope that their actions will continue to be ignored by America.

As the United States fights the war on terror, Communist China will continue to fight Cold War II against the United States. To do that, it will look for other "checks" against American power, and from time to time, maintain its ties with old ones. The actions of the Communists during and after Afghanistan's liberation are ominous signs for American efforts to establish a stable successor regime to Ba'athist Iraq. However, it also reveals a critical truth: winning the war on terror will be almost impossible unless the United States also strives to win Cold War II with the People's Republic of China.

America suffered tremendously on September 11, 2001, but it recovered and took action, liberating Afghanistan from the tyrannical regime that had hosted the perpetrators of the horrifying attack. However, the United States must come to terms with Communist China's role in supporting terrorists and/or the regimes that sponsor them, in order to ensure against the possibility of another such attack against the American people. The terrorist war and Cold War II are intertwined in many areas, due in large part to the actions of Communist China. The United States must do whatever it takes to win both.

Chapter 2:
Iraq and Iran – Axis of Evil to Us, Friendly Arms Customers to the PRC

When it comes to terrorism and the Middle East, two regimes stand out for their virulent anti-Americanism and their willingness to support terrorist groups who use random death and violent destruction as their weapons of choice. Their actions have led President Bush to place them in what he called, and rightly so, an axis of evil. These regimes, the first two the president named, are by now well known to the American people: the so-called Islamic Republic of Iran, and the now destroyed Ba'athist regime of Iraq. Together, they provided succor to terrorists in Lebanon, the West Bank, and elsewhere in the Middle East and throughout the world. Meanwhile, both regimes, according to a number of reports, cultivated ties to al Qaeda in recent years. Both harbored well-known desires to acquire nuclear weapons, and made a frightening amount of progress in achieving that goal. Of course, Iran's Islamic regime is still doing all of these.

What is not as well known is that these two regimes shared something else in common – a history of purchases in military materiel and/or technology from the People's Republic of China. These military ties go back to before September 11, 2001, but the Communists made no effort to stop them after that fateful day.

In the case of Iraq, Communist China's history with the Ba'athist regime – including the installation of a fiber optic network from a Communist firm help Saddam Hussein integrate his air defenses – even caused some in the Bush Administration for a time to consider it an "interlocutor" between the United States and Saddam Hussein, hoping the People's Republic could lean on Saddam to hand over his weapons of mass destruction to the United Nations and prevent the recent war. This was, of course, only *after* the Communists tried to use their veto power on the UN Security Council to wring every concession out of the United States they could get in exchange for not vetoing United States-sponsored resolutions on the Ba'athist regime.

As the United States continued to build the case for military action against Saddam Hussein, Communist China decided to send a shipment of patrol craft armed with missile launchers to Iraq in *November 2002*. But for the ship's interception – and purchase – by the United States, those launcher-armed ships could have been used by the Ba'athists against American and allied troops; the effect on the liberation of Iraq can only be guessed.

Iran, meanwhile, has been a constant, and thankful, recipient of Communist Chinese weaponry. In fact, Iran has been a client of Communist China for nearly a dozen years, going all the way back to a delivery of two tons of uranium from the People's Republic in 1991. The most recent reports of weapons from Communist China to the Iranian mullahs was as late as 2003, over a year *after* President Bush gave the regime its well deserved place in the axis of evil.

By that time, both Ba'athist Iraq and Islamicist Iran had established both their tyrannical regimes and their anti-American, pro-terrorist policies in dramatic fashion.

Ba'athist Saddam Hussein led a regime that has brutalized its own people, repeatedly invaded its neighbors, and of course, fought two wars with the United States. This should not surprise anyone, given the combination of the Ba'athist ideology and the cruelly ambitious, bloodthirsty personality of the regime's longtime leader.

When Saddam Hussein took over the Ba'athist regime in 1979, his first act was to call a meeting of Ba'ath Party leaders. As the Iraqi elite sat in stunned silence, Hussein declared that he had uncovered a "conspiracy" against him, and had an underling read out the names of the "conspirators." Those who heard their names met their end quickly. When the meeting broke up, there was no doubt that Saddam Hussein was in charge, and that he had no compunction against killing anyone determined to resist him.

Saddam Hussein proceeded to terrorize and torture the Iraqi people. The United Kingdom released last winter a damning dossier on the torture the Ba'athists use to keep Saddam Hussein in power. Among the numerous acts of repression, the British found "eye gouging," "piercing of hands with electric drill," and "extinguishing cigarettes on various parts of the body, extraction of fingernails and toenails and beating with canes, whips, hose pipes and metal rods." The British also reported incidents of falaqa: "victims are forced to lie face down and are then beaten on the soles of their feet with a cable, often losing consciousness."

That wasn't all. "Prisoners are beaten twice a day and the women are regularly raped by their guards" in the Mahjar political prison. Rape in particular was such a popular repressive tool that at least one member of the Ba'athist "popular army" committed "violation of women's honor" – quite a euphemism – as part of his profession and duty to the Iraqi state.

What would happen if anyone resisted? Regarding protestors, Iraq's military was instructed "to kill 95% of them, and to leave 5% for interrogation."

Even these facts, as frightening as they are, were nothing when compared to the horror Hussein unleashed during the height of the Iran-Iraq war.

Iran's Islamic Republic was founded in the same year that Saddam Hussein came to power. Sensing turmoil in his neighbor, Hussein invaded Iran, hoping he could quickly win the war and establish himself as the leading power in the Persian Gulf.

In 1988 he established himself as something very different. In March of that year, the Ba'athists unleashed poison gas against their own people in the town of Halabja, a town largely populated by anti-Ba'athist Kurds. Five thousand died, and tens of thousands more suffered permanent physical damage or illness.

Including those dead at Halabja, over 100,000 Kurds have died at the hands of the Ba'athist regime of Saddam Hussein.

When the war ended eight years later – Iran having proved far more formidable than Saddam had believed – Iraq was left an exhausted, nearly bankrupt country.

To replenish his treasury, and to feed his dreams of regional grandeur, Iraq quickly won the attention of the world with a blitzkrieg invasion of Kuwait on August 1, 1990. In response to the invasion, the United States demanded Iraq withdraw from Kuwait. When it did not happen, the United States led a broad, multi-national coalition to drive the Ba'athists out. The military action to expel Iraq from Kuwait was so successful that Saddam suddenly faced a popular anti-Ba'athist revolt in Iraq. Sadly, the revolt was brutally crushed by Hussein. In reaction to the brutal crackdown, northern Iraq became a "no-fly zone," which enabled anti-Ba'athist Kurds to take effective control of the region. The rest of Iraq remained under Ba'athist control until the day the liberation of Iraq began.

Under the cease-fire, to which Hussein cheerfully agreed in order to prevent any attempts to remove him from power, Iraq would end its efforts to acquire weapons of mass destruction, and would only be allowed to sell a fraction of the oil it could produce. This oil was part of the supposed "oil for food" program, although the Ba'athists did little to keep up the "food" end of the bargain. Meanwhile, nearly all attempts to ensure the Ba'athists were keeping their word on biological and chemical weapons were undermined by Hussein, so much so that weapons inspectors sent by the UN to enforce the terms of the cease-fire were gone in 1998, not to return for four years.

The Ba'athists predilection for biological weaponry would be bad enough by itself. Add to it ties to al Qaeda, and one is left with a deadly and dangerous predicament; that is exactly what the world faced in Ba'athist Iraq before its end.

According to many reports, Iraq and Al Qaeda cooperated in the formation of a terrorist group of radical Islamic Kurds that not only Talibanized its small sliver of Iraqi territory but, conveniently enough, has fought a slew of battles with the anti-Ba'athist Kurds who controlled much of northern Iraq.

In the fall of 2001, a slew of radical Islamic Kurds – who vehemently opposed the two main Kurdish groups that resisted Saddam Hussein throughout most of the 1990s – came together to form Ansar al-Islam. At first, the group appeared to be simply a bunch of Talibanized Iraqi Kurds, perhaps getting some help from Iran. That changed quickly as more and more Afghan-trained operatives came to the sliver of territory

Ansar al-Islam controlled. More ominously, some Ansar al-Islam fighters captured by the pro-American, anti-Ba'athist Kurds in the area – the Patriotic Union of Kurds (PUK) – told Jeffrey Goldberg of the *New Yorker* – that Ansar al-Islam had another major sponsor: Saddam Hussein. The PUK has also claimed to have tracked extensive radio traffic between the Ba'athist regime in Iraq and Ansar al-Islam. Moreover, in December 2002, the *Washington Post*, reported that Iraq sold Ansar al-Islam the most deadly of the nerve gas agents, VX. Meanwhile, Ansar al-Islam fought bitterly with the PUK almost since its 2001 founding, and it also conducted numerous experiments with the deadly poisonous ricin gas.

In February 2003, Secretary of State Colin Powell noted that "Baghdad has an agent in the most senior levels of...Ansar al-Islam" and that "this agent offered Al Qaida (Cdn sp) safe haven in the region. After we swept Al Qaida from Afghanistan, some of its members accepted this safe haven. They remain their (*sic*) today."

This wasn't the only evidence of Iraq cooperating with al Qaeda. Powell also noted the presence of Abu Musab Al-Zarqawi, a leading terrorist in the al Qaeda network, in Iraq for "more than eight months." After the Ba'athist regime fell, documents were discovered that revealed that Ba'athist regime was eager to cooperate with Osama bin Laden in the spring of *1998*, which was weeks before the terrorist group destroyed two American Embassies in Africa, and years before September 11, 2001.

Meanwhile, the Ba'athist regime became a leading bankroller for Palestinian "suicide bombers" (put in quotes here because they have by design killed hundreds of Jews, not just themselves, by turning themselves into weapons), giving up to $25,000 to the families of those who choose to strap explosives to themselves in an effort to take out as many Israelis as they can while blowing themselves up.

Throughout the Ba'athists' history of invasion, flouting of international law, violation of human rights, and support of terrorism, Communist China has been largely silent. In fact, Communist China has not only routinely supported Saddam Hussein in his efforts to end UN limitations on oil sales and other restrictions to which he himself agreed, it has even violated those limitations when military technology is involved.

In January 2001, the *Washington Times* reported that Communist China was selling missile technology to Iraq – contradicting earlier pledges from the People's Republic that it would stop doing so. Less than a month later, the press revealed that American bombers had targeted a fiber-optic network built for Iraqi air defenses by Huawei Technologies, and ZTE, both firms from Communist China. ZTE is owned by the People's Republic, while Huawei – whose ownership is murky at best – is the leading firm used by the People's Liberation Army during its massive infusion of technology into its military apparatus during the 1990s.

This wasn't Huawei's only business in Iraq. In 2000 and 2001, according to the German newspaper *Taz* – cited buy the BBC – the firm was "supplying hi-tech fibreglass (British sp) parts for air defence (British sp) installations." That information didn't hit the press until over a year and a half after the fiber optic network was reported.

Almost immediately after the news went public, Communist China heatedly denied it. It later announced it would conduct what it called a "serious investigation" of the claims. After all of a week, the People's Republic announced that the "serious investigation" had ended, and that the charges were baseless. Less than one week after that denial, word got out that Huawei had asked the United Nations Security Council for permission to sell the fiber-optic network and other related materiel for well over a year, and that the United States and Great Britain had blocked the Security Council from blocking said permission. Not only did this make the Communists' "serious investigation" laughable, it also blew their back-up cover: that they had no idea what Huawei was doing. Later, the People's Republic quietly admitted that yes, the reports on the fiber-optic network were correct.

As for the network itself, the Pentagon could not say how much, if any, damage it sustained during the February 2001 bombing. A slew of bombing raids in 2002 were focused on hitting parts of Saddam Hussein's air defenses, in large part likely due to the improvements courtesy of the People's Republic. As late as the fall of 2002, Secretary of Defense Donald Rumsfeld could not say just how much damage had been done to the Communist Chinese installed fiber optic network.

As the American military risked life and limb to liberate the Iraqi people and destroy the tyrannical Ba'athist regime before it can terrorize the world with biological, chemical, and even nuclear weapons, their operations, the very lives of American and allied pilots were at greater risk of capture or death, thanks to Communist China. All American soldier and sailors were at greater risk due to the People's Republic.

Meanwhile, the Communist military actually used the February 2001 incident to get a dramatic increase in its budget to help fight American "aggressiveness."

After September 11, 2001, as the United States began preparing to respond to the terrorist attacks in particular, and the war on terror in general, Communist China repeatedly told the United States not to take any military action against Iraq. As the United States tried to win United Nations support for the use of force, the Communists continued to publicly oppose any military action on Iraq – a major concern given its veto power on the UN Security Council. Privately, however, the People's Republic was singing a different tune, quietly putting the word out that the United States could win their "acquiescence" on Iraq in exchange for concessions on East Turkestan – the region called "Xinjiang" by the Communists and home to millions of anti-Communist, pro-American Uighur Muslims – and Taiwan – the island democracy and *de facto* independent state that has long been the obsession of the Chinese Communists.

After the United States did provide one major concession – labeling a likely defunct group called the East Turkestan Islamic Movement a terrorist organization – word leaked out to the media that the Communists never had any intention of vetoing any UN resolution on Iraq by themselves, but that they would join France and Russia if they vetoed any resolution. In fact, Communist China supported a November 2002 Security Council resolution – although just what the resolution meant was a matter of debate.

That was far from the end of the story. In November 2002, Communist China actually attempted to send a shipment of missile launching patrol craft to Iraq. The vessel carrying the weaponry was intercepted by the United States, but in order to ensure the cargo did not get to Iraq, where the Ba'athists could use them against American troops, America had to buy the ship *and* its cargo.

In other words, as the winds of war were blowing around Iraq, Communist China decided it would be a perfect time to send Saddam Hussein patrol ships capable of firing missiles at the American force deployed to disarm and overthrow his regime. Not only were there no consequences for this heinous action, but the Communists, or their intermediary in the deal, got a payoff from the United States in the process.

One might wonder why the Ba'athist regime that controlled Iraq was so determined to attempt to swallow its neighbors and acquire powerful weaponry, including weapons of mass destruction, and why Communist China was so willing to help them out in the weapons department.

In part that is because most are not familiar with Ba'athism, a combination of pan-Arabism and Communism. Essentially, Ba'athism is an ideology based on the tenets that the Arab people should be united under one regime, and that said regime is destined to have totalitarian control over the Arabs. Saddam Hussein tried to grab his own satellite in Kuwait, but was thwarted by the United States. This did not, however, force him to change his ideology or his vision of the future as the maximum leader of the Arab world. It simply forced him to change tactics, and attempt to acquire a deterrent through weapons of mass destruction, particularly nuclear weapons. It should not be forgotten that the Ba'athist regime Saddam Hussein leads has been attempting to produce nuclear weapons for over twenty years, and but for the Israeli raid on the Osirek nuclear facility in 1981, they may have succeeded.

After the 1991 Gulf War, it became clear to Hussein that so long as he continued to survive, not only could he marshal his forces to fight another day, but he could also become a growing symbol for America haters throughout the Middle East. The more he thumbed his nose at UN inspectors and the United States, the more popular he became to America haters in the region, and the closer he was to achieving his ideological dream.

This also led him to fund the families of "suicide bombers" in Palestine, and why he refused to say anything uncomplimentary about Osama bin Laden or al Qaeda. He was always ready to out anti-American anyone in the Middle East, and to equip himself with what he felt was needed to resist the United States, and make gains despite American opposition. With a nuclear deterrent, he could have reached his goal – becoming the strongman in the Middle East – all the more quickly.

As for Communist China, Hussein became more attractive as he became more anti-American. After the fall of the Soviet Union, Communist China has continuously been searching for allies in Cold War II – or to use its favorite phrase, the battle against American "hegemony." Some of the most fertile ground for such an appeal can be found among the corrupt rulers in the Middle East. Iraq's anti-Americanism in the 1990s made it a very useful "check" for Communist China against the United States.

Additionally, as Communist China is forced to maintain white-hot economic growth to keep up with its population, sources of petroleum are critical. Reaching out to the Ba'athist regime, had it survived, would have ensured the Communists a critically needed supply of oil.

Finally, Communist China also saw Iraq as an easy way to distract the United States from Eastern Asia, in particular the aforementioned Communist international obsession – Taiwan. For a number of reasons, from the need to feed the rampant nationalism they use as an excuse to remain in power to their fear of the continuing survival and growth of the island democracy, nearly all Communist foreign policy, in some way, shape, or form, depends on the effect upon the "rebel province" of Taiwan. A stronger anti-American Iraq meant a relatively weaker United States, and it certainly meant a less attentive United States where Taiwan is concerned. In light of President Bush's statement that the United States would do "whatever it takes" to keep Taiwan free, tying down the United States with other foreign policy problems remains a top Communist priority.

Given this, it should come as no surprise to anyone that Communist China was so willing to sell arms to Saddam Hussein, and that the People's Republic went out of its way to publicly blast the United States every time it has tried to reign him in.

When compared to this history with Iraq, Communist China's insistence of support for the United States in the war on terror rings pathetically hollow.

While Iraq garnered the most attention over the last ten years, its neighbor to the east, Iran, has a longer history of supporting terrorism, in large part because it reached for the anti-American mantle about a decade earlier than Iraq did. Communist China has also supported Iran with the sale of weaponry.

Iran's history with anti-Americanism and terrorism is more extensive, largely because the mullahs have been at it since 1979, far longer than the Ba'athists in Iraq. In fact, the combination of terrorist support and anti-Americanism, best personified by the Ayatollah Khomeni, was so strong that the Ba'athists next door tried, and to some extent succeeded, in passing themselves off as supporters of the United States by comparison.

The Islamic Republic of Iran came to being in 1979, when the royal Shah left for exile in Egypt and never returned. The anti-Americanism of the new Iranian regime became dramatically evident with the seizure of the American Embassy on November 4 of that year, which turned 50 Embassy staffers into hostages. The hostage standoff lasted until the day Ronald Reagan was inaugurated as President of the United States.

Meanwhile, Iran's mullahs, having whipped their own people into both an anti-American frenzy and petrified silence on domestic issues – both of which were far less spontaneous than was first thought – decided to try spreading their radical strain of Islam to the rest of the Middle East.

In Lebanon, Iran created and supported "militias" to battle the American peacekeeping contingent there. A resulting terrorist attack in 1983 killed nearly 200 American Marines, and led the United States to pull out of Lebanon entirely. During the 1980s, terrorist supported by Iran seized a number of Americans and held them hostage. This was quite profitable for Iran during the 1980s, winning it military hardware from the United States in exchange for the hostages' release (this is now known as the Iran-contra affair).

During the 1990s, regional issues appeared to dominate Iranian foreign policy – in particular the 1991 Gulf War and the rise of the Wahhabist, anti-Shiite Taliban (the Iranian mullahs are Shiite). This led many to believe the regime may have shifted away from its virulent anti-Americanism and terrorist supporting actions of the past. Nothing can be further from the truth. While Iran did oppose the Taliban, they chose anti-American Gulbuddin Hekmatyar to be the recipient of their support. Hekmatyar, who made no secret of his deep hatred for the United States, was the only prominent Afghan besides Mullah Omar to oppose the American-backed liberation of Afghanistan. He has since joined with Mullah Omar, the Taliban, and Osama bin Laden against the post-Taliban government currently in place in Kabul, and Iran, according to reports, is still backing him financially.

Iran also has become a major player in post-liberation Iraq – much to the chagrin of the United States. Through anti-American radical clerics in

Iraq, Iran is even now trying to undermine American efforts to build a stable Iraqi government. It scored one major, and bloody, victory in the death of pro-American Shiite cleric Ayatollah Abd al-Majid al-Khoei.

Iranian aid to terrorists – such as Hezbollah, the terrorist group that just suggested to its homicide bombers to expand their anti-Western campaign to the world at large, i.e. the United States – has yet to stop. In fact, a shipment of Iranian weapons destined for the Palestinian Authority itself – whose leader Yassir Arafat has links to the terrorist al Aqsa brigade – was discovered by Israel at the end of last year.

Iran even has ties to al Qaeda. According to German authorities cited by *Die Zeit* magazine, Iran has been a host and staging ground for al-Tawhid, and al Qaeda linked organization that has "arranged false documentation for more than 100 al Qaeda fighters who escaped from Afghanistan during the war." They have also, according to the same report, helped bring Hezbollah and al Qaeda together to "move gold and diamonds from Karachi to Sudan, via Iran," in order to finance further terrorist operations against the United States and its allies.

It has also been an open secret that Iran has been striving to become a nuclear power. In fact, just last December, the United States released evidence that the mullahs were secretly building two large nuclear facilities. One of the plants was believed to be for enriching uranium, while the other was presumed to be a "heavy-water" plant, which can make plutonium. Iran insisted that the facilities were only for "peaceful" purposes, i.e., energy, and even had the cover of International Atomic Energy Agency (IAEA) inspecting its nuclear program, but IAEA knew nothing about the inner workings of these facilities.

More ominously, Iran is looking to Stalinist North Korea for help in its nuclear weapons development. According to Japan's *Sankei Shimbun* – cited by the South Korea's Yonhap News Agency – the two axis of evil members are in talks for an agreement to "promote joint development of nuclear warheads." The deal will also include the mullahs buying North Korea's most advanced ballistic missiles.

Meanwhile, the situation inside Iran has, ironically, allowed for a greater dissent to its rule than that of the late Ba'athist regime in Iraq. Like Communist regimes, Iran goes through the motions of "elections," in which only candidates approved by the mullahs are allowed to win. During the 1990s, however, the Iranian people began to push for real political freedom beyond the right to choose among Ayatollah-backed candidates. The result at first seemed a victory for the forces of reform with the election of President Khatami in 1997. However, Khatami was found to be lacking on two fronts – he had little power, and what power he did have, he was far less supportive of true reform than the people who voted for him were.

More troubling for the United States, Khatami still adhered to the anti-American foreign policy that made Iran infamous. Support for anti-American terrorists has not abated during the Khatami regime. Neither did the repression against the Iranian people; in fact, one could argue the situation became *worse* with Khatami in power. During the Khatami regime, a slew of newspapers were closed down for opposing the mullahs, and a number of journalists and politicians were arrested for the same offense.

The combination of popular frustration at the Iranian regime, and the continued hostility between the United States and Iran has produced a mass resistance in Iran that is pro-democracy and pro-American. Though there has been little reporting of it, the mass anti-Islamic movement has spread nationwide. Last December, the largest demonstrations since the 1979 overthrow of the Shah swept through Iran.

The widespread dissident movement has exposed the Islamic Republic of Iran as an ideologically hollow regime. In response, the mullahs have used repression and rabid anti-Americanism to remain in power, resulting in brutal tyranny at home and increased violence abroad.

For Communist China, Iran represented something else – yet another "check" to employ against the United States in Cold War II, and as such, a worthy recipient of military weaponry.

Prior to September 11, 2001, Communist China and Iran already had strong military ties going back roughly a decade. In 1991, the Communist sold two tons of uranium to Iran, thus effectively giving birth to the mullahs' nuclear weapons program. Communist China also helped Iran with its secret nuclear plants.

In late 2000, the United States charged Communist China with helping Iran advance its ballistic missile program. In response, the People's Republic denied aiding Iran's missile program, but also announced a supposed tightening of military exports. Despite being faced with the international equivalent of "I didn't do it, but I'll never do it again," the Clinton Administration, following its policy of "engagement" with the Communists, decided to waive sanctions that United States law would have otherwise triggered against the particular firms and agencies involved. Instead, Clinton only imposed sanctions on the Iranian firms and agencies.

Less than a year later, two more firms owned by Communist China found themselves on the receiving end of economic sanctions from the Bush Administration, which made clear that its view of "engagement" did not necessarily extend to weapons sales to terrorist states. The United States would not disclose just what in particular led them to hit the firms the sanctions, but an unnamed official chillingly noted that the violations involved the Chemical Weapons Convention – the international treaty designed to control the production and proliferation of chemical weapons.

That wasn't the only help the People's Republic gave to the mullah-led Islamic regime in Tehran. Less than two months after September 11, 2001, the *Washington Times* discovered that Iran was building a new air-defense system, or to be more accurate, having an outside firm build it for them. Who was this outside firm? It was the China National Electronics Import and Export Corporation, a major Communist-owned electronics firm.

In 2002, numerous Communist efforts to improve Iran's military and/or add to its weapons stockpile came to light. Among them was more military aid to the mullahs that were called "nonconventional" – i.e., chemical, biological, or nuclear – by Deputy Under Secretary of Defense Lisa Bronson. Bronson did not go into detail on which firms the Communists used to move Iran forward, but within a month of her comments, the Bush Administration hit two more firms from the People's Republic – the Liyang Chemical Equipment Company, and the China Machinery and Electric Import and Export Company –with sanctions. Communist China responded quickly, denying everything, as usual, and calling the sanctions "unreasonable."

Communist China's support for the Iranian military also includes naval missiles, which were delivered in January 2002, the same month President Bush put the Islamic regime in the axis of evil.

Last spring, all doubt about Communist China's coziness with the mullahs in Iran vanished once and for all when Central Military

Commission Chairman Jiang Zemin, who at the time was also Communist Party chief and People's Republic President, visited Iran. While in the Islamic Republic, Jiang – who according to some experts still runs Communist China's foreign policy, from his perch as Central Military Commission Chairman – publicly blasted American policy in Central Asia, just months after the United States had pushed the Taliban out of power in Afghanistan.

Jiang made his feelings known in a meeting with Ali Akbar Hashemi Rafsanjani, who served as President of Iran during the 1990s, and has grown more powerful since handing the post over to Khatami: "Beijing's policy is against strategies of force and the United States military presence in Central Asia and the Middle East region."

In fact, according to the sources of one analyst – CNN's Willy Wo-Lap Lam – Jiang's trip to Iran was part of "countering Washington's alleged 'anti-China containment policy.'" This despite the fact that no one in the Bush Administration had ever mentioned "containing" Communist China in any way, shape or, form.

It didn't take long for the deeds to reinforce the words. Roughly a month after Jiang's anti-American comments in Iran, more firms from Communist China came under sanctions imposed by the Bush Administration for military aid to the mullahs, this time largely involving cruise missile parts. Two months later, the United States imposed sanctions on eight Communist firms – by now some were being sanctioned more than once – for even more arms sales, including biological and/or chemical weapons components.

The biggest action against the Communists came in the summer of 2003, when President Bush cancelled over $100 million in export contract from the Communist-owned firm Norinco. Norinco had long been exporting numerous consumer goods to the United States, but it was also exporting ballistic missile steel to Iran.

Norinco wasn't alone, however. In late 2003, Middle East Newsline reported that Communist China shipped components for missiles and weapons of mass destruction to Iran – sending them via North Korea to steer clear of its own "export controls." It was the most dramatic example of how far the Communists were willing to go to help Iran.

Meanwhile, Communist China has never said anything remotely critical of Iran's terror sponsorship and support. In fact, the Communists have expressed solidarity with Iran on one of the mullahs' biggest excuses for sponsoring terrorist groups: Israel. The Communist Chinese Ambassador to Iran, for example said the following on the subject: "China supports a multi-polar world, is critical of Israeli killings and believes peace in the Middle East will not be achieved without materialization of the rights of Palestinians including withdrawal of Israeli troops from occupied territories." Not one word sprang from the ambassador's mouth about the victims of Iranian sponsored terror in Israel.

Given the current instability of the Iranian regime, which is growing day by day despite the lack of notice from the rest of the world, many would wonder why Communist China would be so willing to openly tie itself to the repressive, terrorist backing mullahs. Of course, internal repression would never be a problem for the People's Republic, whose modern leadership depends on the justification of the events of June 4, 1989 as the rationale for maintaining its grip on power.

However, there's more to the links between Communist China and Iran, a lot more. Iran's history of anti-Americanism certainly caught the attention of the People's Republic. As with Ba'athist Iraq, this makes Iran a very useful "check" against American "hegemony." Not only is Iran an ally upon which the Communists can count in Cold War II, it can also be a source of petroleum, and a distraction for the United States in its role as *de facto* defender of Taiwan. This reads a lot like a carbon copy of the reasons Communist China is close to Iraq, and that is no accident. The very things that drew the People's Republic to Ba'athist Iraq also draw the Communists to its 1980s enemy.

There may be one more aspect to Iran that would win it support from the Communists. Like Communist China in 1989, Iran is grappling with a younger generation looking for political change after seeing the ideology of the tyrannical regime fall flat. For the People's Republic, a brutal crackdown and rampant nationalism, as explained in more detail in Chapter 7, has been enough to keep the Communists in power. For Iran, the same combination is proving somewhat less successful. The fall of Iran would not only reveal to the Middle East that radical tyranny in the name of Islam is a failure; it could also give hope to the dissident movement in Communist China. The Communist leadership would certainly want to do anything possible to prevent that from occurring. In fact, with Ba'athist Iraq regime out of the picture, there is every reason to believe Communist China will be drawn *closer* to Iran.

Ba'athist Iraq fought and lost two wars with the United States in thirteen years. However, Iraq's military force, such as it was, was better than it would have been were it not for help from the People's Republic. Iran, meanwhile, is a regime on the brink, facing an increasingly restive population that is demanding change, divided within itself on how to respond, and finding the Islamic radical ideology that brought it to power falling flat throughout the country. All that holds the regime together is a willingness to survive, and a virulent hatred of the United States. The few friends it has left in the world are the terrorists it continues to sponsor – including Hezbollah, which recently announced plans to expand their murder-suicide bombing campaign beyond Palestine – and Communist China, which still considers Iran a valued friend and arms customer. The People's Republic has made Iran's military more proficient, thus lengthening the lifespan of the regime, and the lifeline for anti-American terrorism.

There is no better evidence of just where the Communists stand in the American war on terror: with whoever suits their interests. Increasingly, that is not the United States, but rather the most muscular "check" against the United States.

To date, few have been willing to take note of Communist China's aid and comfort to Iran and the formerly Ba'athist Iraq. Most still see the East Asian Communists and Middle Eastern terrorist sponsors as not connected. The facts tell a different story. While Iran does not need Communist China to survive – and the help of the People's Republic may not be enough anyway – the Communists made it clear with their actions that their words of "support" for the United States against the forces of terror are lies.

The Communist Chinese aid and comfort to the formerly Ba'athist Iraq and Islamicist Iran are the first, but far from the only, examples of how the People's Republic sees the terrorist war – as yet another phase in Cold War II against the United States, and nothing more. The actions of the Communists have made the war on terror more difficult to win, at the cost of more blood and treasure for the United States and its allies.

The time has come to call Communist China to the carpet on these actions. American servicemen and servicewomen are at greater risk due to its anti-American policies. Any talk of "engagement" with Communist China must take these facts into account – and then die a quick death. The People's Republic has made clear through its actions that "checks" against the United States are more important than an end to terrorism. While the United States must continue to fight the war on terror, and fight it to a victorious conclusion, it must respond in kind with "checks" of its own against the Communists.

Whatever one may think of the term "axis of evil," Iran and the late Iraqi regime earned their places there; Iran continues to earn it every day. As the next chapter will reveal, North Korea's place is also well deserved. Any regime that has dealt with these regimes should raise eyebrows throughout the world. Americans are already up in arms – and rightly so – for various European links to the Iranian mullahs and the Iraqi Ba'athists. Communist China's actions, largely because they are not as well known, have yet to generate the same outrage. That will change when the news spreads, and hopefully, so will American policy towards the People's Republic.

Until we are prepared to treat Communist China as we treated the Soviet Union, we will likely find the war on terror to be both longer and bloodier. Communist China is not an enemy of terror; it is an enabler of terror. Unless the United States recognizes this, victory in the terrorist war, to say nothing of Cold War II, is far from certain.

Chapter 3:
North Korea – Terrorist State, Nuclear Power, and Communist Chinese Ally

When President George Bush placed Iran, the now nonexistent Ba'athist regime of Iraq, and North Korea in his axis of evil in January 2002, the last of the three received little notice. The focus on Iraq was most prominent, given the recent history of the United States and Iraq during and after the Gulf War of 1991. Iran, as well, had a larger spotlight shone on it, thanks to the Islamic regime's hostility to the United States that goes back more than two decades. Stalinist North Korea, however, has been an American enemy for longer than both Iraq and Iran *combined*. It is in many ways *more* dangerous than the other two, and has a history of arms deals with *both* of them. It is also one of Communist China's oldest and longest allies.

The fact that North Korea is the most dangerous member of the axis of evil may sound strange, given that North Korea has not been in the spotlight as a major sponsor of terrorism. There is no better evidence that looks can be deceiving. While North Korea does not have ties to Middle Eastern terrorists – they *do* have links – especially involving sales of military weaponry and weapons parts – to other terrorist states. Chief among them are none other than Iran and Iraq. North Korea also has ties to terrorists from Eastern Asia and has in fact been one of the leading terrorist entities itself in the region.

Secondly, unlike Iran and Iraq, North Korea is already a nuclear power, and likely became so specifically to prevent anyone from taking military action against it, or to make others think twice about letting it collapse under the weight of a spectacularly mismanaged economy and self-imposed isolation. Thus, the prospect of weakness in Pyongyang now has more people worried about how the Stalinists would react than hopeful that the people they imprison might soon become free.

The final issue that makes North Korea so dangerous is Communist China. North Korea has very few friends; Communist China is its oldest, and vice versa. After the fall of the Soviet Union, the Stalinist regime in Pyongyang has relied almost entirely on its Communist ally and neighbor. The People's Republic has used its ties to North Korea to pressure democratic South Korea on behalf of both itself and the Stalinists. Communist China has also ruthlessly rounded up and sent back across the border any North Korean refugee it can find, leading many to seek escape to South Korea through democratic embassies in the Communist Chinese capital of Beijing. Communist China has even served as a model to North Korean leader Kim Jong-il's plans for economic "reform" – a model he may have followed a bit too well: his first appointment as head of a special economic zone on the border with the People's Republic was arrested by the Communist Chinese for corruption and tax evasion before he could ever assume the post.

In effect, North Korea is where Cold War II and the terrorist war intersect. Sadly, few are willing to discuss bringing the Stalinist regime down, either by war, if necessary, or the combination of isolation, containment, and support of dissidents. Either course of action would have to take into account Communist China's longtime support of North Korea, and its rise as the leading supporter of anti-Americanism throughout the world. Most discussions of American military options against the North focus on the Stalinists' nuclear deterrent as a chief obstacle. The Stalinist alliance with Communist China is just as important a reason why policymakers in Washington are shying away from any talk of liberating the regime, with or without military force. In fact, without that alliance, North Korea would likely not be in existence today.

The regime that calls itself Democratic People's Republic of Korea began under the protection of the Soviet Union at the end of World War II. In August of 1945, as the United States was dropping two atomic bombs on Japan to force them to surrender, the Soviet Union suddenly declared war on Japan, and moved into the Korean peninsula from the north. The United States entered the Japanese colony from the south. After the end of the war, the two superpowers agreed to divide Korea at the now famous 38th parallel, and each helped build a local government in the areas they controlled.

North Korea, as it became quickly known, was led by Communist guerilla Kim Il-sung, a fervent Communist who was determined to rule over all of Korea. On June 25, 1950, he started the Korean War with a massive invasion across the 38th Parallel.

The rabid aggression shocked the world, and President Harry Truman pushed for the United Nations (UN) to condemn the North. Thanks in large part to the Soviet Union's refusal to sit in the Security Council – in protest of the People's Republic of China being shut out of the UN – America's efforts to resist the North won United Nations endorsement.

Meanwhile, on the ground the North was quite successful in the first stages of the war, until General Douglas MacArthur's landing at Inchon reversed the momentum in spectacular fashion. Pyongyang was liberated on October 19, 1950, and soon the liberation of all Korea seemed likely.

Stalin and Kim both begged Communist Chinese leader Mao Zedong to stave off imminent disaster. Mao, busy trying to consolidate his year-old People's Republic, demurred, until it became clear that no one else was going to stop the fall of North Korea. In November 1950, Mao changed the course of world history.

The day after Thanksgiving, 1950, hundreds of thousands of Communist Chinese "volunteers" attacked the United States/UN lines just shy of the Yalu River. The mass of humanity pushed the anti-Communist forces to roughly the same position as the 38th parallel. Pyongyang was back in Communist hands, as was Seoul – the capital of the South – for a brief period. MacArthur publicly called for the bombing of Communist China to get them out of the Korean War. President Truman, in a move both widely hailed and derided at the time, fired MacArthur. Given what we know at present about the Stalinist regime, and its recent behavior over the last decade, Truman's decision to keep the war limited is just as controversial in 2003 as it was in 1951. After two years of near-fruitless negotiations, an armistice was signed in 1953, with the two sides roughly controlling the same territory they had when it began.

At the time, this was treated as a victory, understandable given that the South had almost been entirely lost. The survival of North Korea was not seen to be as important as the survival of the South. Thousands of American troops remained in South Korea along the demilitarized zone (DMZ). They are here to this day. Across the DMZ, Kim Il-sung isolated his regime from everyone except the Soviets and Communist Chinese.

This wasn't much of a problem for Kim himself, although like every other Communist regime, his people suffered horrifically. There were signs of how Kim treated his people even before the war "ended" (no peace treaty was ever signed) when over 50,000 North Korean prisoners of war – nearly half the number captured by the United States and its allies – chose to *stay* in South Korea. Still, the mass depravity of the regime, and the family that ran it, towards its own people did not come into focus for most Americans until the 1990s, when the fall of the Soviet Union forced the Stalinists' hand.

Meanwhile, North Korea, established itself as a both a supporter of terrorism and a terrorist state in the 1970s. The first victims were, to the surprise of no one, South Koreans and Japanese.

In 1970, members of a Communist terrorist group that called itself the Japanese Red Army hijacked a Japanese airliner and ordered it flown to North Korea, where they claimed asylum. The Stalinist regime treated the terrorists as heroes, and has given them safe haven until this very day, despite numerous demands by Japan to have them handed over for trial.

That was nothing compared to what North Korea had in store for the Japanese people. Beginning in the 1970s, North Korea began running a massive espionage operation in Japan "to gain intelligence, money and influence in Japan…and in South Korea, through Japan." Among other things, the spy network sold drugs for the Stalinist regime back home, and tried to ensnare Japanese politicians via blackmail.

Starting in 1978 – and this is just based on what the North was willing to admit –North Korean spies began kidnapping Japanese citizens living in beach communities. According to Kim Jong-il, thirteen Japanese citizens were taken between 1978 and 1983, including a girl no more than thirteen years old and a couple taking a night stroll on the beach. All were spirited off to Kim Il-sung's version of paradise.

Some of the kidnap victims were apparently taken to train North Korean spies in Japanese language and custom. Others were taken, according to one Japanese Red Army member, to be married off to Japanese men living in North Korea, to create a society of "Japanese revolutionaries." According to Ahn Myong Jin, a former North Korean spy who has since defected to the South, some were taken just because they happened to stumble across spies returning to North Korea. Ahn said thirteen year-old Megumi Yokota was kidnapped for this reason.

It took over two decades for Kim Jong-il to admit to Japan – in particular to Japanese Prime Minister Junichiro Koizumi – that a baker's dozen of Japan's citizens were abducted. According to Kim, eight of the thirteen abductees had died. However, for all of the "deceased" except Megumi Yokota, all evidence of their deaths, i.e., their bodies, were conveniently washed away in a flood, and no DNA evidence of them can be found. As for Megumi, she had killed herself, leaving behind a daughter that, of course, was not allowed to leave.

One Japanese Member of Parliament who has worked with the families over the years called the account of the deaths "lies pasted on lies." A relative called the North's explanations "laughable." It is easy to see why – the Stalinist regime said another kidnap victim died of heart disease, in her twenties. Meanwhile, dozens of other families are pushing for information regarding *their* missing loved ones, and no one in Japan is willing or able to rule out that they were kidnapped also.

Kim himself claimed no responsibility for the abductions, claiming it happened during his father's reign and basically without his knowledge. While it certainly occurred when Kim Il-sung was in charge, Ahn, the defector, noted that the younger Kim was head of intelligence when the Japanese were kidnapped, making it very unlikely, at best, that he was unaware of what the North Korean spies were doing.

North Korea returned the five admitted survivors, but this did little to soothe Japanese anger over the fate of the supposed dead. All five – two are married couples and one is now married to an American, Charles Robert Jenkins – have children in North Korea. North Korea forced the children to stay behind, under the Stalinists' watchful eye, while their parents returned home. Even Mr. Jenkins – whose family insisted was also kidnapped – was forced to stay.

The North Korean kidnappings are the most dramatic example yet of just how far outside the normal standards of human decency the Stalinist regime had acted, is acting, and continues to act. They took at least thirteen people from their homes and families, told no one about it for over two decades, insisted eight had died, and then turned the screws on the remaining five by treating their children as hostages. Through it all, Communist China refused to issue even the slightest condemnation of the kidnappings orchestrated by its Stalinist ally.

Japan is not the only nation to suffer the loss of citizens at the hands of North Korean kidnappers. South Korea has hundreds of citizens listed as missing, and that does not include the hundreds of prisoners of war who have not been returned. After Kim's stunning admission on the Japanese kidnappings, the South Korean government vowed to press North Korea on the fate of its missing.

Kidnappings, hostages, and shielding hijackers; all in all, this would be an impressive performance for a regime aspiring to be a terrorist state. However, this is not all North Korea has done during its fifty-odd years of existence. It has also employed mass murder to achieve its aim of reunifying Korea under Stalinist rule by terrorizing South Korea and every

South Korean: from the average citizen all the way up to inhabitants of the South Korean Blue House – the South's version of the White House.

In 1974, the Stalinists attempted to assassinate South Korean President Park Chung Hee. They missed him, but killed his wife. Not content with this, in 1983 they planted a bomb in Burma that killed a visiting delegation of seventeen South Koreans. The delegation included four South Korean cabinet members. Four years later, a North Korean spy with a Japanese passport – part of the aforementioned espionage network, planted a bomb on a South Korean airliner in the Middle East. The bomb exploded the plane in midair, killing 115.

When the Soviet Union collapsed in 1991, an economic lifeline for North Korea ended. It didn't take very long for Kim Il-sung's "paradise" to become the complete dystopia that is typical of Communist regimes, even with major support from Communist China. The spectacular mismanagement led to a massive famine that has killed anywhere from two to three million in the past decade, while at least 250,000 more fled for – of all places – the People's Republic. The famine brought North Korea rare sympathy from the rest of the world, and multiple promises of economic and food aid.

Kim Il-sung, and his son Kim Jong-il, began using the collapsed economy as one more instrument in its war against political dissent and independent thought. As always, the suffering people were the casualties: in a population of roughly 23 million, between two to three million – over one in thirteen at least – died from starvation.

This was seen first hand by one of the Western volunteers invited by the North ostensibly to help the regime feed its people. Norbert Vollertsen, a physician working with German Emergency Doctors, took the Stalinists at their word, went to North Korea, and actually donated a skin graft to a North Korean burn patient. The Stalinists were so impressed with his support of the regime, and the donation itself, that it gave him a "friendship medal" and allowed him unfettered access throughout North Korea. What he saw completely sickened him. Vollertsen specifically cited the World Food Programme (WFP) as one whose aid is repeatedly swiped by the Stalinist regime to feed its political sycophants: "when the WFP cars are gone, all those North Korean defectors told me that the food is collected and then sent to the government storehouses."

Those defectors did not just tell Vollertsen. A former bodyguard of Kim Jong-il revealed this tale, "all food aid was snatched by the military and the ruling elite." According to another defector, "officials used elaborate tricks, like putting on distribution shows for international monitors. But the aid was routinely confiscated from the poor afterwards." As Vollertsen himself noted, "The North Koreans are so sophisticated in this manipulation and propaganda. When they want you to think the food is going to the people, they will present you 100 children who are well conditioned. When they want to get some more food, they will present you 100 skinny and starving children."

The reports were so widespread that the food donors to North Korea, namely the United States, began insisting on more accountability in the distribution of food. As the Stalinists continued to ignore American concerns, the United States pulled out of the donation racket.

North Korea never even bothered to rethink its attempts to turn food into a political weapon and literally starve its dissidents to death.

The famine has led to hundreds of thousands of North Korean refugees in, of all places, Communist China. It is here, in the northeastern region of the People's Republic (known outside Asia as Manchuria), that the Communists in Beijing first reveal where their real sympathies lie: with their fellow Communists in Pyongyang.

The hundreds of thousands of North Korean refugees who crossed the Yalu River are desperate for just about everything, especially a stable food supply. The Communists would prefer that the People's Republic host no refugees, and in deference to the Stalinists, they have sent back any refugee they can find. This remains true to this day, despite the numerous reports from dissidents and others who have chronicled North Korea's torture of "repatriated" refugees. The United Nations High Commissioner on Refugees has pleaded with the Communists not to send the refugees back, given that "execution is likely" for those forcibly returned. The words fell on deaf ears.

Even without such claims, forcing back hundreds of thousands to a regime with the almost unique combination of political repression and economic calamity would be unconscionable: unless, of course, the regime kicking the refugees out had its own history of mass starvation (the "great leap forward" of 1958-61) and suffocating political repression (roughly the norm in Communist China, but particularly bad during the "anti-rightist campaign" of the 1950s and the Cultural Revolution of 1966-76). To the rest of the world, North Korea is a pariah dictatorship. To Communist China, it's the closest copy of itself left in the world.

The practical result of this is a community of nearly a third of a million people forced into hiding, deprived of any legal standing (such as it is in Communist China) or possibilities for a normal life (such as *that* is in Communist China). Reports of Korean refugee women sold as wives or sex slaves in Communist China are rampant, and driven in large part because they have no recourse – outside of being forced back to the repressive, famine-wrecked Stalinist "state."

Those refugees who can actually make it to a major city – almost always the Communist Chinese capital – are forced to make dramatic dashes for the embassies of democratic nations to escape the choice between non-person status and Stalinist victimization. Communist China's determination to please its North Korean allies goes so far as to violate the sanctity of these properties, challenging widely accepted international concepts of sovereignty itself. The first dramatic example of this came in the Japanese consulate in the northeastern city of Shenyang. Communist Chinese police entered the Japanese consulate and seized five refugees. After nearly three weeks of demands from Japan for the refugees', the Communists finally yielded to international pressure and allowed the five to leave for South Korea.

When two other refugees, father and son, tried to get to the South Korean Embassy in Beijing, Communist police breached the diplomatic barrier again. They captured the father and, according to one report, "pushed and punched six South Korean diplomats" in the process. South Korea, as expected, was furious, and the Communists soon returned the father and let the pair flee to South Korea.

While both incidents ended in the refugees escaping to freedom, they revealed just how far the Communists were willing to go to protect North Korea. In fact, early least year, the Communists announced a joint "manhunt" with North Korea to comb the countryside and send back any North Korean refugee in Communist China. After the escapes via embassy began an almost daily occurrence, the People's Republic cracked down with barbed wire, armed guards, and a more determined effort to find and root out the networks that preserved hope for the Korean refugees in Communist China. As a result, the embassy dashes fell dramatically, and several activists helping the refugees found themselves in front of Communist judges, in Communist jails, and/or expelled from the People's Republic.

This is not the only recent instance where Communist China has chosen North Korea over the rest of the world, or even the most well known. For that, one must look at the Communists' reaction to North Korea's nuclear weapons program.

When the North Korean economy fell into a complete morass early in the 1990s, whispers of a North Korean collapse became louder and more widespread. Kim moved quickly to prevent it by going nuclear. In 1993, the North announced it was withdrawing from the Non-Proliferation Treaty, which it had signed only six years earlier, and would attempt to become a nuclear armed state. Given the North's history of terrorism against South Korea, and its fealty to Japanese terrorists, this announcement rattled the rest of the world. The United States nearly attacked North Korea in response.

The following year, as Kim Il-sung died and his son Kim Jong-il took over, the Stalinist regime signed on to the then highly praised, and now deeply scorned, 1994 Agreed Framework. Under this agreement, the United States, South Korea, and Japan agreed to built two light-water nuclear power plants in Korea – on the assumption that the nuclear fuel used in them would be more difficult to turn into weapons-grade nuclear material than the nuclear power plants the North ostensibly said it was using to provide energy for its people. Until the new plants were built and on line, the United States and others would send North Korea annual supplies of fuel oil for energy consumption. By 2002, the amount of aid sent to the Stalinists pursuant to the agreement was worth over $95 million annually.

In exchange, North Korea agreed to "freeze" its nuclear weapons program, and to have its "frozen" program inspected by outsiders, namely the International Atomic Energy Agency. It also agreed to disband its nuclear weapons program in future years.

For eight years, as more nations joined the Agreed Framework's North Korean power plant program – also called the Korean Peninsula Economic Development Organization (KEDO) – the amount of aid sent to North Korea cleared $1 billion in fuel oil alone. Meanwhile, North Korea repeatedly threw up obstacles to the IAEA inspections, insisted that they not begin until KEDO had completed a "significant portion" of the plants, and threatened to pull out of the accord altogether.

Despite this fudging of the Agreed Framework, the Clinton Administration refused to demand that North Korea adhere to the 1994 deal, to say nothing of the Nuclear Non-Proliferation Treaty. The construction continued, and so did the effort at "engagement" with North Korea. When the George W. Bush Administration came to power in 2001, it was united on one thing regarding the North – the regime could not be completely trusted. Beyond that, however, disunity reigned. The result was somewhat tougher rhetoric against the North, with no change in substance to back it up.

This continued despite reports of the Stalinists violating the 1994 agreement coming to light through the press. In March, American media, and former CIA official Robert Walpole, reported that the nuclear weapons program was continuing, and may have already produced a couple of nuclear weapons.

Then, last October, North Korea admitted to having violated the 1994 agreement with its enriched uranium program, but only after being confronted with evidence of such by American officials. Moreover, the

Stalinists declared themselves "not bound" by the accord they signed and blamed the United States for it all. They insisted that they were "entitled" to nuclear weapons, a bald-faced rejection of the Non-Proliferation Treaty that they themselves signed in 1987. Days later, South Korean intelligence reported that the North already had at least three nuclear weapons.

The North then demanded a "nonaggression" pact in exchange for ending a nuclear program they had already promised never to continue.

The Stalinist regime also told the American officials who confronted them that they had "more powerful" weapons. Most suspect they meant chemical and biological weapons by that. Reports prior to the admission had North Korea possessing "a stockpile of 2,500 to 5,000 tons of chemical weapons." South Korean intelligence later reported that the Stalinists had 4,000 tons of biological weapons.

In response, the United States weakly continued to probe for the revival of parts of the 1994 agreement in order to maintain "dialogue" with the Stalinist regime, before deciding to stop the fuel oil shipments to the North that were part of the deal. Meanwhile, Japan also toughened a bit, eventually, insisting the nuclear program be halted before it would even consider "normalization," i.e., official diplomatic recognition, with the North. As it did regarding the Japanese kidnap victims and their families, the Stalinist regime turned them down cold.

In April of 2003, North Korea decided to enter talks with only the United States and Communist China. The idea that these talks were a triumph for American diplomacy was quickly demolished when the Stalinist regime used the talks to announce that they were already a nuclear power, and that they were reprocessing the Yongbyon plutonium. As an added bonus, the North threatened to add the nuclear weapons to its international arms bazaar. The talks collapsed in just over a day. Communist China had the audacity to call the fiasco "a good start."

What is the result of the North's nuclear endeavors, in the face of repeated insistence from the United States, South Korea, and Japan to remain a non-nuclear state? In addition to the nuclear weapons they already have, the Stalinists could, according to the CIA, add one plutonium weapon a year until 2005, and from that date, make roughly *fifty* plutonium bombs plus one uranium-based bomb annually.

Of course, throughout the entire eight-year period that the Agreed Framework was supposedly working, Communist China never criticized its Stalinist ally whenever it dragged its feet or turned its back on prior commitments. As one would expect, the aftermath of the "nullification" of the 1994 deal was no exception. As news of the North Korean nuclear program shocked the world, Communist China repeated age-old platitudes about "de-nuclearization of the Korean Peninsula" as if blame could be spread equally for the North's near-decade long dishonesty, and the need for "dialogue" to resolve the issue. The only warning they came even close to issuing was for the *United States!* The Communists insisted that the matter be resolved "peacefully."

The People's Republic has issued no direct condemnation of Pyongyang's nuclear ambitions. In fact, less than two months *after* that the North's October 2002 announcement, the Communists sold to their Stalinist allies tributyl phosphate, a chemical used in making weapons-grade plutonium and uranium. This has enabled the Stalinists to move ahead their timetable for mass nuclear weapons production, and sent a clear signal to the rest of the world just where the Communists lie.

In fact, the Communists did little or nothing on the subject until April, except join Russia in calling for the United States to open diplomatic relations with North Korea – the very thing the Stalinists were hoping to pry out of the United States with its ridiculous antics – while at the same time pushing boilerplate policy of maintaining a nuclear free Korea, boilerplate rendered hollow by the tributyl phosphate sale.

In April, of course, Communist China offered to host talks among itself, North Korea, and the United States, the talks that ended with the Stalinists declaring themselves a nuclear power.

Meanwhile, Pakistan – one of Communist China's other allies for over 50 years – was reported to be one of the major suppliers of North Korea's nuclear weapons development. Unbelievably, the so-called "ally" aided North Korea's nuclear weapons program as recently as July of 2002. No condemnation of Pakistan came from the People's Republic.

Most would agree that nuclear weapons would be quite scary by themselves. However, without a delivery system (namely a missile) or a willingness to hand them off to terrorists, nuclear weapons are not quite as dangerous. Unfortunately for the United States, its allies, and the rest of the world, the Stalinist regime has both ties to terrorist states *and* a burgeoning missile program. In fact, the missile program itself has been a source of numerous arms deals between North Korea and Iran, Pakistan, and according to a recent report, the late, unlamented Ba'athist regime in Iraq.

The North Korean missile program made its most dramatic splash, literally, in August of 1998. That month, North Korea tested a medium range Taepodong One missile. In the missile test, North Korea launched the missile, sent it directly over Japan, and landed it in the Pacific Ocean to Japan's east. The test shocked Japan and the United States, both of whom refused to believe the North's assertion that it launched a satellite into space with the missile. More ominously, North Korea is also working on a long-range Taepodong Two missile, which, when deployed, would be able to strike the United States. The Clinton Administration projected that by 2005, "North Korea will be able to hit any United States city with a nuclear warhead." Given that the North likely already has three nuclear warheads – and has boasted of "more powerful" chemical and biological weapons – this news is all the more unnerving.

While the North has boasted of a self-imposed moratorium on testing since 1999, it has been more than able to continue developing the long range Taepodong Two. Why? Air Force Lt. Gen. Ronald Kadish had this chilling answer: "During a conflict, the North also could attempt to strike United States and United States interests with ballistic missiles, if North Korea's leadership were attacked directly *or was facing imminent destruction* (emphasis added)." In other words, if a mass protest ever comes to Pyongyang, the Stalinists would use the missiles to threaten us into letting them – or maybe even helping them – crush it. In fact, North Korea has already played the missile card after the normalization talks with Japan failed so spectacularly. Within days of the talks ending at an impasse, the Stalinist regime threatened to resume missile testing, quite an unnerving announcement given that the 1998 test had the missile literally arc over Japan.

The combination of nuclear weapons and the development of long-range missiles would certainly be enough to prove that Stalinist North Korea has earned its place in both the axis of evil and in being listed as a terrorist state. However, the Stalinists also have a history of arms deals – including missile parts and gunboats – with nearly every anti-American regime in the Middle East – the former regime in Iraq, Iran, Syria, and Libya.

Even states now considered "friendly" to the United States have found North Korea an acceptable partner in the weapons trade. Communist Chinese ally Pakistan, the original supporter of the Taliban and its leading ally until September 11, 2001, has long been a recipient of the North's missile program. In fact, the North received critical Pakistani help on nuclear weapons largely in exchange for the missile aid from Pyongyang to Islamabad. Pakistan is not only a nuclear-armed state with long-standing ties to the People's Republic. It is also an open supporter of terrorism in the disputed province of Kashmir, currently divided among Pakistan, India, and Communist China, which has a piece Pakistan gave to it in the 1960s. While Pakistan only claims to give "moral support" to the terrorists in fighting Indian control of its part of Kashmir, a number of reports have shown more substantial Pakistani involvement.

Meanwhile, Yemen, a state on the Arabian Peninsula with a heavy al Qaeda contingent – including the bombers of the *U.S.S. Cole* – has also been on the receiving end of the North Korean missile industry – as a customer, not a victim. The government of Yemen began a tilt toward the United States after September 11, 2001, but that didn't stop the regime from placing an order for Scud missiles from the Stalinist regime. In fact, Yemen actually had the audacity to attempt to defend the missile purchase last August – despite promising over a year earlier to stop buying North Korean weaponry – and had a shipment of Stalinist Scuds planned for December delivery. The Spanish Navy intercepted the ship before it got to Yemen, but after the Yemeni government demanded its release, the United States allowed the vessel, Scuds and all, to sail on to its intended destination.

Less than two weeks after the Scuds were released, the *New York Post*, citing an Israeli source also quoted in the Israeli newspaper *Ha'aretz*, reported that the Scuds themselves were not meant for Yemen at all, but actually destined for none other than Ba'athist Iraq. It was a stunning revelation. North Korea may very well have attempted to sell missiles to its fellow axis of evil regime more than a month after the United Nations had put Iraq on notice about weapons of mass destruction, as American troops were pouring into the region for the liberation of the country.

That wasn't the only report of North Korea sending missiles to Saddam Hussein. Last fall Tokyo Governor Shintaro Ishihara insisted to the Japanese media: "It is absolutely clear that North Korea is supplying parts of Scud missiles to Iraq…(The North) has made those parts in the course of developing its Taepodong missile and is still making them. The Japanese media and Foreign Ministry know it but just don't say so." This was the first report of a North Korean arms link to Ba'athist Iraq – although reports regarding the Communist Chinese military complicity in the North Korea-Iraq arms sales came about a week and a half later – and was completely buried by the North's admission of its violations of the 1994 Agreed Framework.

Regarding the other members of the axis of evil, reports of North Korea's trade with Iran go back years. In fact, the United States tried to get North Korea to end missile sales to Iran and Pakistan in 2000. North Korea demanded $1 billion to end the arms trade. This brought talks on the subject to a quick and decidedly unsuccessful end.

The following year, according to unclassified CIA reports, the Stalinist regime also sold "ballistic missile-related equipment, components, materials, and technical expertise to countries in the Middle East, South

Asia, and North Africa." Among these nations were the aforementioned Iran and Pakistan, plus Syria and Libya.

United States Undersecretary of State John Bolton also cited North Korea's sales of "ballistic missile-related equipment, components, materials, and technical expertise" to "notable rogue state clients such as Syria, Libya and Iran." Other reports noted that Iran has acquired gunboats from North Korea as well, most recently in December of last year. In fact, the shipment reached Iran just one day before the Yemeni Scud missiles were seized.

Meanwhile, last July, the Stalinist regime sent its number two official, Kim Yong-Nam, to Libya and Syria, to discuss missile sales. In Syria's case, that included contracting the North to build the latest Syrian Scud missile (Version D) as well as buying numerous Scud C missiles. Intelligence reports also put a number of North Korean missile experts in Libya, to help Moammar Gadhafi build a missile with a 1,000-mile range.

Finally, according to Japan's *Sankei Shimbun* – cited by the South Korea's Yonhap News Agency – the North Korea is not only in talks for an agreement to sell Taepodong 2 missiles to Iran, but also looking to "promote joint development of nuclear warheads" with the Islamic regime. Such news should frighten everyone.

Communist China has yet to say anything to North Korea recommending they stop the missile sales and other parts of the terrorist arms bazaar. Not that this should surprise anyone, given the Communists' own flourishing trade with Iraq, Iran, and others. In fact, as mentioned earlier, Communist China used North Korea to send missile and weapons of mass destruction components to Iran, hoping the world wouldn't notice. Meanwhile, the People's Republic is also allowing the territory it controls to serve as a transit *between* North Korea and its terrorist state customers, including Iran and the former regime in Iraq, under the eye of People's Liberation Army (PLA) Lieutenant General Xiong Guangkai, deputy chief of staff and head of military intelligence.

It should be noted that this is the same General Xiong who made a thinly veiled threat to incinerate Los Angeles if the United States came to the defense of Taiwan from a Communist invasion. This could explain quite a bit behind the Stalinist regime's nearly obsessive focus on nuclear weapons. The fact that Xiong is handling this issue for the People's Republic should give all Americans, particularly those who support "engagement" with the Communists, a good deal of pause.

Of course, that would also require a major reassessment of our relationship with Communist China – something those who support "engagement" with the People's Republic are also hesitant to do. This refusal to recognize the existence of Cold War II led directly to a decision that allowed North Korea to get away with sending over a dozen missiles to a supposed ally in the war on terror, leading one critic, *National Review Online* Contributing Editor Michael Ledeen, to say that our enemies and our allies in the war on terror "don't think we're serious."

Why would a regime do so much to aid anti-American terrorists and threaten the security of America's allies? Without the hard currency from its arms trade, and without having nuclear weapons to scare the free world, Kim Jong-il would have a much more difficult time maintaining his iron grip on North Korea, including massive, horrifying accounts of violations of human rights – none of which, of course, has earned the Stalinists any criticism from its Communist Chinese allies.

The first accounts of human rights abuses in North Korea, as expected, have come from the dissidents who managed to get out. Soon Ok

Lee was one of them, sent to prison by the Stalinists for her opposition to the regime. The accounts she gives of prison life – or to be more accurate, prison death – is not for those weak in the stomach.

Soon Ok Lee and other defectors have noted that births in North Korean prisons are not allowed, but that several women in the prison were pregnant with "Chinese" fathers – a possible sign that they were refugees sent back by Communist China. As the North would not do surgical abortions in its prison, Stalinist prison guards resorted to other tactics – beatings and tortures to induce miscarriages. If that didn't work, some newborn children were simply left to die in the cold or be eaten by dogs.

Soon Ok Lee also saw political executions and prisoner tortures. Human rights groups have confirmed her shocking accounts, including the sickening treatment of newborns. There are also accounts of despicable torture, forced abortions, arrests of entire families – children included – and prison labor conditions that kill thousands.

Communist China had nothing to say about any of this. Of course, a regime with a "one child" policy leading family planners to murder a newborn baby in her parents' home and political prisoners executed in the area it likes to call "Xinjiang" would not be expected to get too upset about the human rights violations listed above.

In every situation – be it nuclear weapons, arms sales to terrorists, the refugee crisis and human rights abuses from torture to forced starvation – Communist China has had the opportunity to choose between North Korea and the free world. It has sided with its Stalinist ally every time. Despite this, numerous officials and commentators from the United States and its allies have suggested using Communist China to "turn the screws" on its North Korean allies to end its provocative behavior.

The naiveté behind this has been breathtaking. Communist China is in many cases, particularly regarding weapons sales, committing the same actions as North Korea. In fact, as noted earlier, Communist China is even facilitating North Korea's arms sales to terrorist states. Clearly, the People's Republic does not have the same definition of terrorism, let alone the same attitude in dealing with it, that the United States and its allies have.

The idea that Communist China would be willing or able to restrain the North in any aspect of its behavior is ludicrous. While Communist China may be "embarrassed" from time to time about the North's actions and statements, it sees North Korea as no free nation sees it. To Europe, the democracies in Asia, and the United States, North Korea is a "hermetic" pariah and a paranoid, repressive dictatorship. To the People's Republic, North Korea is a useful "buffer" against South Korea, Japan, and American "hegemony." This means that North Korea can, as many Eastern European regimes did vis a vis the Soviet Union, use its "buffer" status to maintain the support of the major Communist power through thick and thin. The result of what happened when the Soviet Union no longer defended those regimes – the Revolution of 1989 and the end of the U.S.S.R. in 1991 – is certainly *not* going to encourage the Communist regime in China to push its satellite toward responsible behavior now, unless it could get something in return, such as a ham-fisted attempt last fall by then-Communist President Jiang Zemin to extract American concessions on Taiwan during the summit in Crawford.

In fact, the real Communist attitude towards North Korea was laid bare by Willy Wo-Lap Lam, CNN, who reported that the People's Republic "still thinks Beijing and Pyongyang should maintain a 'lips and teeth' relationship, and that any attack on North Korea – even a limited offensive to wipe out its nuclear installations – would be a challenge to Chinese power and even sovereignty."

Given that, why should it surprise anyone that Communist China has little incentive to push North Korea into dropping policies that in many cases it is also conducting, particularly toward terrorist states?

Communist China and North Korea are so close that when Kim Jong-il finally began to realize the mess that his economy had become, he chose Communist China – not Japan, South Korea, the United States, or Europe – as a model for economic "reform."

After a couple of years of examination, Kim created his first attempt to move away from his father's Stalinist disaster – a "special economic zone" in the city of Sinuiju, on the Communist Chinese border. Rumors of a freewheeling capitalist zone in the city of Sinuiju ran rampant – there was even talk of an elected city council.

What came of it all? At first, the North seemed to be on the right track, it chose Yang Bin, a Chinese-born Dutch citizen who made millions in the gray area of "private" business in Communist China. Just to make sure no one within North Korea had any ideas, the Stalinists announced that Sinuiju would have a wall built around it to keep ordinary North Koreans out.

It took less than a month for the wheels to come off. Yang's first announcement – that all foreign media would have free access to Sinuiju, had to be retracted in less than a day. More ominously, North Korea found out it had followed the Communist model – one rife with corruption and thievery – a little too closely. Communist China put Yang under house arrest for tax evasion, and his company's stock was suspended from trading amid reports that its profits were widely inflated. Things went from bad to worse quickly, as it became known where Yang had set up shop in Communist China – the thoroughly corrupt, triad-ridden Shenyang.

The selection of one of Shenyang's leading "private" entrepreneurs by North Korea to run its "special economic zone" said quite a bit more about the Stalinists and their plans than they wanted to be known. It was also the ultimate "Freudian slip," revealing just how close Communist China and North Korea truly are.

Sadly, many in the United States, Japan, and South Korea believe a "dialogue" is still possible with North Korea.

South Korea and Japan were the other original signatories to the 1994 Agreed Framework, made their own attempts to thaw relations with the Stalinist North. President Kim Dae-jung at first, drove South Korea's effort almost by himself. Kim Dae-jung was a former dissident during the 1970s and 1980s when the military ruled South Korea, and when he won the Presidency in 1998, and soon launched what he called a "sunshine" policy with the Stalinist North.

This came despite a rather dramatic incident, highlighting the Stalinists reliance on spreading terror and mayhem, from two years earlier. In 1996, a North Korean submarine ran aground, in South Korea. Over twenty Stalinist commandos were loose in the democratic South, and thirteen South Korean soldiers died in the effort to hunt them down. It was a dramatic reminder of North's kidnapping and plane exploding hi-jinks from the 1970s and 1980s.

Undaunted, Kim Dae-jung pressed on with his "sunshine"policy. It appeared to bear remarkable fruit in the summer of 2000 when Kim Dae-jung flew to Pyongyang to meet with Kim Jong-il. It was the first ever summit between North and South Korea, and it won South Korea's Kim the

Nobel Peace Prize in December of that year. At summit end, the two Kims agreed to "a commitment towards reunification and (to) allow reunions of families separated during the Korean War." Of course, by this time, the crown jewel of the apparent North Korean thaw – the 1994 Agreed Framework – was already a sham.

South Korea's efforts at increasing "sunshine" with the North moved along slowly, and not without major bumps in the road. Efforts at family reunions, allowing Korean relatives separated by the 1950s war to see each other for the first time in nearly five decades, led to a few meetings for selected families, but for the most part, the North's intransigence on the issue was a disappointment. It was, however, the least of Kim Dae-jung's problems regarding the Stalinist North.

In the summer of 2002, a North Korean naval vessel crossed the Northern Limit Line, the sea border between North and South Korea, and fired on a South Korean ship sent by the navy to ward it off. Four South Korean sailors died in the gunfight, which at first the North tried to blame on the South. South Koreans were enraged at the action, and Kim's "sunshine" policy, already, under fire for its lack of results outside of the few family reunions, took a major hit. Things went from bad to worse when Kim, just days before the end of his term, was forced to admit to sending North Korea *$100 million* via the firm Hyundai just prior to the 2000 summit, giving credence to the impression that the event that won him the Nobel Peace Prize had been bought.

The end of the 1994 nuclear accord dealt Kim and his "sunshine" policy another blow. All the accomplishments of his policy – which one newspaper, *Chosun Ilbo*, bluntly dubbed: "if we were patient and generous then North Korea would reform and open up" – seemed washed away by the

Stalinists' "missile exports, clandestine nuclear weapons development, and now the scrapping of the 1994 Geneva Agreed Framework, the last safeguard." The North's nuclear weapons boast did nothing to improve the state of affairs.

Despite all of this, and according to some people, perhaps *because* of the nuclear weapons issue, democratic South Korea remains the most dovish United States ally regarding North Korea. In fact, during recent elections in South Korea, many vented their anger at the *United States* for its reaction to the Stalinists. In hindsight, many South Koreans likely saw a far more hawkish American policy than actually existed in Washington. One other factor that certainly didn't help was the complete silence from the Administration on the desirability of a unified, democratic, anti-Communist Korea, which has kept the plight of millions of North Koreans trapped in the starving, Stalinist regime out of the discussion to this day.

The aforementioned election brought another "sunshine" supporter to the South Korean Presidency: Roh Moo-hyun. A former human rights lawyer, Roh firmly believes, and has said several times, that Kim Jong-il is planning to reform North Korea, and if he received aid and assurances that the United States would not end his regime, he would abandon his nuclear ambitions. The fact that the Stalinist-in-chief effectively had exactly that in 1994, and instead chose to start a uranium weapons program, has, for now, not moved Roh one bit.

Meanwhile, Japan has had its own problems with Stalinist North Korea. In late 2001, a North Korean vessel entered Japan's "economic zone." When Japan sent naval ships to investigate, the North Korean boat fled, then sank as the Japanese navy pursued it. The Stalinists insisted it was a "fishing vessel," but Japan thought otherwise, and announced it would raise the vessel. At this point, Communist China decided to become involved – and condemned *Japan* for wanting to raise the ship. Japan raised the ship anyway, and found, according to the BBC, "a Russian surface-to-air heat-seeking missile, portable anti-tank grenade launchers and machine guns." How these items can be of use on a fishing vessel was never explained by Pyongyang.

The weapons Japan found on the boat clearly pointed to it as a spy ship. Some now believe it was part of the aforementioned massive Stalinist espionage operation in Japan, and it might have been sent either to drop off or pick up more Stalinist agents working there.

Before that news came to light – although it more confirmed Japanese suspicions than anything else – Koizumi met with Kim Jong-il for his one-day summit, which was almost immediately dominated by the aforementioned kidnapping issue. Talks on diplomatic "normalization," i.e. formal diplomatic recognition and the exchange of ambassadors between Tokyo and Pyongyang, were also overshadowed by the fate of the abduction "survivors" and their families.

As for the United States, the "conventional wisdom" still refuses to even consider the possibility of "regime change" in North Korea, despite the fact that it would not only end a regime that is tyrannical, terrorist, and selling arms to terrorist states, but also pave the way for Korean unification under the banner of freedom, and thus ensure greater support for the United States in South Korea.

However, few appear willing to advance such a policy within the corridors of power – although several outside those corridors have suggested "regime change." Most policymakers simply accept the existence of North Korea as a given. In fact, the possibility of an Asia without North Korea simply does not command the imagination of many of America's political elite. This ensures that the people of North Korea, while earning the unending sympathy of the world, will have little outside support should they mount an effort against the regime. The dissidents that are in North Korea are almost completely unknown unless and until they can escape to the South.

The major unspoken reason for this is Communist China itself. The North's position as a Communist Chinese "client state" at least partially protects it from a military attack. However, in some cases, this has led supporters of a diplomatic solution to think the Communists can be used to restrain their Stalinist ally. As noted above, the idea that the People's Republic would be willing to do so, given its interests in Asia, is foolish at best.

And what if Communist China does in fact get the North to make various pledges about nuclear arms, or weapons sales? How could we trust that the North would keep their word, or that the Communist Chinese would be willing to hold them to it? Why should we believe a regime that has violated promise after promise on weapons of mass destruction? Because a regime that violated promise after promise on arms sales to terrorist states asked it to do so? Only those who trust Communist China to honor its word – all broken promises to the contrary – would expect it to able, or even willing, to force Stalinist North Korea to honor theirs.

If North Korea as a nuclear state selling weapons to terrorist states is a danger to the world, Communist China – a nuclear state that also sells weapons to terrorist states – is certainly just as much a danger. A policy that opposes one should oppose the other as well. That is another impediment to a sober reexamination of policy toward North Korea. Given their similarities, how can one support ending the North Korean regime, no matter how long it takes, without supporting the same end for Communist China, no matter how long *it* takes? The confusion and weakness on North Korean policy has one unspoken, but very obvious source: the insistence on "engagement" with Communist China.

North Korea is a major focal point in both the war on terror and Cold War II. As the most prolific terrorist state this side of the Middle East, and the most prolific arms seller *to* the Middle East, its role in helping sustain America's enemies and sponsors of terrorism require a far tougher policy than the current emphasis on a diplomatic solution. The weapons sales to Yemen reveal an agenda that won't simply vanish when the regime most known for their anti-Americanism and support for terrorism go away. The American reaction to it reveals something more worrying – a war against terrorism severely restricted by an unwillingness to recognize and deal with Cold War II against Chinese Communism and its allies.

Throughout its entire bloodthirsty, arms-dealing, famine-wrecked reign, the Stalinist regime of North Korea has had one continuous ally and loyal friend – Communist China. It is time the rest of the world treat Communist China for what it really is, an ally and supporter of one of the most violent and terrifying regimes on the face of the earth. To do otherwise would allow our enemies in Cold War II more time to further their anti-American aims while we look the other way. It will also ensure that our enemies in the terrorist war have that much longer to rely on their chief suppliers of armaments: Communist China and Stalinist North Korea.

The United States and its allies must deal with Stalinist North Korea, if not by direct military action – given the North's nuclear ambitions and stash of weapons of mass destruction, caution on that option is understandable – then by a combination of isolation and support for North Korean dissidents to bring the regime down. Victory in both the war on terror and Cold War II require no less.

D.J. McGuire

Chapter 4:
Pakistan, Communist China, and Terrorists vs. India

To many in the United States, the war on terror began on September 11, 2001. The fall of the World Trade Center galvanized the American people for the battle against al Qaeda and their hosts in Afghanistan, the Taliban. A major boost to the campaign came when the Taliban's chief sponsor – Pakistan – announced it would help us dislodge the Taliban and fight al Qaeda. For most Americans, Pakistan had declared itself an ally in the war on terror.

The reality, sadly, is more complicated. Pakistan not only was a major supplier and supporter of the Taliban prior to September 11, 2001, they also have supported other terrorists in the eastern part of the country. Unlike the Taliban post-September 11, 2001, these terrorists are still supported by Pakistan to this day, despite the brutal attacks on Pakistan's rival and neighbor – India – over the disputed Kashmir region. The Pakistanis have insisted for years that they only give "moral support" to the terrorists – whom they call "freedom fighters" – but reports have revealed evidence of more substantive backing from Islamabad.

Kashmir has garnered little attention in the war on terror, but the situation there is vital to the battle against al Qaeda. Osama bin Laden himself has cited Kashmir numerous times as an example of the "clash of civilizations" between the Muslim and non-Muslim worlds, and several al Qaeda operatives have been in the disputed region, including John Walker Lindh, the now infamous "American Taliban," prior to his capture.

Kashmir also is of vital importance in Cold War II. Pakistan and Communist China have been allies for nearly half a century. Pakistan even handed a small part of the disputed Kashmir over to the People's Republic in the 1960s. In fact, when the United States first began the Cold War I initiative to Communist China during the Nixon Administration, they worked through Pakistan to build the framework for Nixon's trip to Beijing in 1972. The coziness with Pakistan disturbed India so badly it tilted toward the Soviets in the latter stages of the first cold war. Today, India continues to see Communist China and Pakistan as two parts of the same problem, with an important twist: many in the maturing Indian body politic see the People's Republic as the most important threat, not Pakistan.

India, as a victim of terrorism both in and due to Kashmir, has also been a strong ally in the battle against the Taliban. In fact, like Russia, India was supporting the Northern Alliance for years prior to September 11, 2001. Before that terrible day, India was also moving rapidly toward closer relations with the United States and her allies in the Middle East, including Turkey and Israel. The battle against the Taliban – and the Pakistani aid in that regard, may have hidden the growing India-United States ties from public view, but it did not stop them.

Since the fall of the Taliban, Pakistan is slowly reverting to its pre-September 11, 2001 ways. Attempts by military dictator Pervez Musharraf to maneuver against his chief non-Islamic political opponents led, in part, to a Parliament in which radical Muslim anti-American representatives actually held the balance of power for a time. Meanwhile, anti-American, pro-bin Laden either seized or shared power in the districts bordering Afghanistan, making the battle against al Qaeda *and* the Taliban that much harder.

India, meanwhile, held an election in Kashmir that was so clean that the allies of the governing Bharatiya Janata Party (BJP) lost power for the first time in decades – while terrorists killed nearly 800 voters and political figures whose only crime was a willingness to participate in local democracy.

Communist China, meanwhile, has made no secret of its support for Pakistan in disputes between the two, although they have attempted to reach out to India in recent years. The Communist support for Pakistan, and Pakistan's support for the al Qaeda-backed terrorists in Kashmir, is yet another example of how Cold War II and the war on terror are connected, in ways that are detrimental to the United States, world liberty, and the effort against worldwide terror.

For India the terrorist war and Cold War II are already one and the same. For this and other reasons – chief among them its democratic history and its military links to Israel and Turkey – India is easily a better fit as an American ally in the 21st Century than Islamist-tainted Pakistan.

India and Pakistan were both part of the British colony of India prior to World War II. Before and during the war, support for independence among Indians grew under the leadership of Mahatma Gandhi. With Gandhi pressuring for independence in India, and the British electorate becoming increasingly weary of the cost of empire – especially after the devastation of World War II – the United Kingdom (UK) decided to de-colonize India in 1947.

However, while India would be free, it would also be divided. In reaction to Muslim concern over life in a Hindu-majority India, the UK carved up the colony into three nations. Pakistan, the nation ostensibly for Muslims, was created out of the northwest, plus a small portion in the east called Eastern Pakistan (now Bangladesh), while Kashmir was preserved as a small principality with an unusual dynamic: a Muslim majority populace governed by a royal sovereign of Hindu faith. The rest of the former colony became the Republic of India.

The first few years after independence were, by all accounts, very ugly. Hindus in Pakistan and Muslims in India left their homes – not all voluntarily in a massive, double ethnic cleansing took place. Pervez Musharraf himself was born in India, while Indian Home Minister L. K. Advani – widely considered the second-most powerful Indian behind Prime Minster Atal Behari Vajpayee – was born in what is now Pakistan. Naturally, this massive population movement, and the violence that caused and accompanied it, led to some ruffled feathers.

The situation in Kashmir was its own, unique, conflagration. The monarch leader of the principality threw in his lot with his fellow Hindus in India, making Kashmir an India state. One can certainly assume the Muslims were less than pleased with that idea – a promised referendum on the subject was never held. In response, Pakistan took roughly half of Kashmir for itself. It was the first of several wars between the two neighbors over Kashmir, which is now carved in two by a makeshift "border" between Indian and Pakistani military forces known today as the Line of Control.

At this time, both India and Pakistan were new nations struggling to lead their peoples in the twentieth century. Over the next fifty-odd years, the two took very different paths. Pakistan quickly earned an ally in Communist China, and alliance that has grown and continued to this very day. During the 1960's, Pakistan cemented the alliance by handing over a piece of Kashmir – a piece still claimed by India as its own – to the People's

Republic. This came less than a decade after the Communists took nearly 40,000 square miles from India in a 1962 border war.

This series of events brought India and the United States very close. In fact, in 1962, India and the United States nearly reached an agreement on military cooperation, and during the 1960s, the two nations conducted joint military exercises.

There were a number of reasons for this friendliness. Both nations had democratically elected governments, and while India's Congress Party dominated election after election, that was due more to a popular government and a weak opposition than anything else. Another major reason, of course, was opposition to Communist China. Few remember this today, but both the United States and India fought wars with the People's Republic within ten years of each other. The United States and its allies were well on its way to liberating North Korea when Communist Chinese leader Mao Zedong sent in hundreds of thousands into the battlefield in 1951-2. Combining brutal determination and a complete lack of concern for human life, Mao's troops suffered tremendous casualties, but preserved the Stalinist regime of Kim Il-sung with the armistice of 1953. Less than a decade later, in 1962, came the aforementioned Communist border war with India. To this day, India has repeatedly demanded the lost territory back. Meanwhile, the People's Republic has insisted it is entitled to nearly 100,000 *more* square miles inside India.

As such, the two democracies shared a number of interests, and remained friendly for two decades. All the while, India faced Pakistan eye to eye over the Line of Control.

A dramatic change came in the 1960's, when the United States began to use Pakistan as an intermediary between itself and Communist

China. President Richard Nixon in particular had hoped to take advantage of growing hostilities between the Soviet Union and the People's Republic to split the Communist world in two. From a worldwide geopolitical perspective, it was quite a success. From a South Asian regional perspective the result was less cheerful. India, noticing the movement in Washington, responded with a shift of its own – toward the regime with whom Communist China was having its increasing problems: the Soviet Union.

As the United States moved closer to Communist China during the 1970s, democracy in Pakistan hit a severe snag. A populist movement led by Zulfikar Ali Bhutto was deposed by a military dictatorship in 1977. The resulting regime quickly established its pro-American credentials when the Soviet Union invaded Afghanistan in 1979, offering aid and comfort to the anti-Communist *mujahedin*. Meanwhile, India, while remaining ostensibly neutral, continued to tilt toward the Soviets.

Dramatic events in the 1980s reshaped the India-Pakistan dynamic. In 1988, the leader of the Pakistan military government – General Muhammed Zia Ul-haq – died in a plane crash. The Pakistani military quickly lost the confidence of the nation as a government, and Bhutto's daughter – Benazir Bhutto – became Prime Minister. Meanwhile, in Kashmir, the anti-Indian groups began to consistently use terrorism as a weapon. The Pakistan leadership, both civilian and military, pledged "moral support" for the terrorists in public, and probably a good deal more support in private.

During the 1990s, Pakistan's politics became a revolving door for both Bhutto and her lead rival, Nawaz Sharif. Between 1988 and 1999, both were elected Prime Minister, twice, and forced from office, also twice, on charges of corruption. Until 1999, however, the major dynamics occurred outside the struggling state.

It began with the end of the first cold war. Suddenly, a major reason for the warm relations between the United States and Communist China had ceased to exist. More importantly, Washington saw India's ties to post-Soviet Russia in a far better light than its ties to the old Communist regime. One year after the Soviet Union disappeared, in 1992, the Afghan Communist regime fell, removing a major source of American-Pakistani cooperation. Within a couple of years, Pakistan helped put the Taliban in power in Afghanistan, beginning the chain of events that led to September 11, 2001. India, for its part, responded by joining Russia in supporting the anti-Taliban Northern Alliance. All the while, the terrorism in Kashmir continued apace against India, with "moral support" from Pakistan's military.

Meanwhile, India was also making a dramatic change in its domestic politics – the rise of an anti-Congress opposition. Founded as a largely Hindu nationalist party, the BJP became the largest party besides Congress in India. By 1998, it won control of the Indian Parliament as the leading force in a multi-party coalition, under the control of BJP veteran Atal Behari Vajpayee. The rise of the BJP moved India in a dramatically different direction. First and foremost, the BJP marked Communist China, not Pakistan, as India's top security threat. Second, the BJP established India as a nuclear weapons state.

When India dramatically became a nuclear power with a May 1998 nuclear test, many felt it was designed to send a message to Pakistan, which conducted its own test within days. What wasn't quite as noticed was the words of Indian Defense Minister George Fernandes. Soon after the nuclear tests, Fernandes called Communist China – *not* Pakistan – India's number one international concern.

The Indian government had good reason to feel this way. Subsequent reports out of Pakistan found Communist Chinese fingerprints all over Pakistan's nuclear weapons program and its missile development. Since India conducted its own test first, most blame it more than Pakistan for the nuclearization of the continent, including. The most representative comment on the matter came from then-President Bill Clinton: "Although Pakistan was not the first to test, two wrongs don't make a right. We have no choice but to impose sanctions pursuant to the Glenn Amendment as required by law."

Such an analysis is incomplete – to say the least – because it fails to take into account one important player: the People's Republic of China. In bordering both Pakistan and India, the People's Republic is an important power in South Asia, and from India's perspective, a very hostile one. While India is certainly less than thrilled to know that Pakistan has nuclear weapons, the idea that a nuclear-free Pakistan was worth the price of not having its own nuclear deterrent in the face of Communist China's nuclear arsenal is, at best, difficult to argue.

Unfortunately, the Clinton Administration did not see things that way. A combination of historical bias favoring Pakistan and the coziness toward the People's Republic that characterized the Clinton Administration for most of its eight years led the United States to immediately impose sanctions on India. Pakistan got its share of sanctions as well, but Clinton's statement made it clear it had more sympathy for Pakistan's supposed need to go nuclear. The Communist threat to India was all but ignored.

The year 1999 was the most eventful for the subcontinent. That year, a major influx of guerilla forces and terrorists infiltrated Indian-controlled Kashmir. The Pakistani government – under control of Sharif – denied any involvement. Few believed them. The incursion began in May, just after Vajpayee's BJP government lost a confidence vote. Perhaps Pakistan assumed the caretaker regime would be too weak to respond. If so, it was a spectacular miscalculation.

In a matter of two months, Vajpayee became immensely popular for standing up to the incursion, and driving them back. In July, the incursion was over. Weeks later, Vajpayee easily won re-election. By October, Sharif himself was gone, replaced in a military coup by General Pervez Musharraf – later reported to be the mastermind behind the incursion into India. However, the Kashmir terrorism continued.

Musharraf's seizure of power turned off the United States, even during the Clinton Administration. However, it was President Bush who began reorienting American foreign policy in South Asia – much to benefit of India and the United States.

Prior to President Bush's inauguration, India had also been reaching out to America's allies. In particular, Israel and Turkey found common ground with India during the 1990s. For Israel, an alliance with India made a great deal of sense – like the Jewish democracy, India was a victim of terrorism based in territory led by a duplicitous regime that refused to acknowledge just how intertwined it was with the terrorists, and both were targets of Osama bin Laden and al Qaeda. Turkey, the only Middle Eastern majority-Muslim nation with a functioning democracy, also saw potential for cooperation. After September 11, 2001, this anti-terrorist triumvirate acquired an even greater urgency for closer ties – particularly India and Israel.

Meanwhile, President Bush moved the United States closer to India than any Administration since the Kennedy era. In the Administration's early days, as it was discussing its proposed missile defense, it found strong opposition from both friend and foe. India, however, was quick to supporter of the idea, and the issue became an opportunity to build closer ties between between Washington and New Delhi. It was an opportunity Vajpayee and President Bush quickly seized. In July of 2001, General Hugh Shelton, then Chairman of the Joint Chiefs of Staff, said military ties between the United States and India – frozen since 1998 – were back on. In the weeks before September 11, 2001, the Administration announced it would work to lift the sanctions imposed upon India for the 1998 tests.

September 11, 2001, of course, brought the United States closer to Pakistan. It did *not*, however, keep the United States from building closer ties to India. Days after the attack, the sanctions against India were lifted. As 2002 dawned, India and the United States signed new pacts on anti-terrorist cooperation and the sharing of military information. In May of that year, for the first time since the 1960s, the United States and India conducted joint military exercises.

The United States movement also encouraged allies, particularly Israel, to follow suit. In one of the most remarkable ironies in geopolitics, Israel began talks with India on the sale of Israeli-made PHALCON air radar systems. Just a year and half earlier, Israel, reacting to last-minute objections from the Clinton Administration, cancelled a contract to sell the systems to Communist China. Needless to say, the People's Republic was not happy with the news.

Still, in the aftermath of September 11, 2001, India suffered for not being a state bordering Afghanistan. That geographic fortune fell to Pakistan, which suddenly was in a position to win United States concessions on a slew of issues (Communist China, meanwhile, took the time to demand that Pakistan not allow *any* foreign troops on its soil).

However, India did what it could, offering the United States whatever military facilities it needed for staging grounds. India certainly had its own interests at heart – al Qaeda was active in Kashmir as well as Afghanistan, and India was a major supporter of the Northern Alliance well before September 11, 2001. Thus, while Pakistan provided the vital territory needed to help liberate Afghanistan, India not only backed the action, but also had a far longer history of opposing the Taliban than Pakistan.

In fact, when the Taliban did fall, Pakistan and Communist China immediately began to worry about the new government in Afghanistan begin to close to India. The fact that a major sponsor of terror had fallen from power seemed to be of little importance to either of them – though that should surprise few given the fact that Pakistan itself had helped bring the Taliban to power in Afghanistan, while the Communists spent more time worrying about who would replace the Taliban than the danger of either the radical Islamic group itself or its al Qaeda "guests."

Then came the event that linked the American and Indian wars against terror together in a dramatic fashion, one in which Pakistan's attempt to disguise itself as a foursquare ally in the war on terror collapsed.

On December 13, 2001, five Pakistanis attacked the Indian Parliament in New Delhi with a car bomb followed up by a hail of gunfire. None of them survived, but they took nine Indians with them. The attack stunned the Indian people, and that says quite a bit, considering that by this point the terrorists had killed 35,000 Indians since 1989.

A year later, the terrorists struck again. They murdered three women – all from a village the Indian side of the "line of control." What was their crime? It was refusal to wear head-to-toe covering burqas, as demanded by the terrorists in posters plastered all over the village. The terrorists threatened to shoot all who disobeyed, and they did just that to two of the victims – the third was beheaded.

The evidence largely pointed to terrorist groups based in Pakistan, where President Musharraf and previous leaders made no efforts to stop them from planning terrorist attacks on Indian targets. In fact, according to intelligence officials from India and the West, cited by the *Washington Post*, Pakistan's Inter-Service Intelligence (ISI), the same military branch that helped put the Taliban in power, gave "weapons and other logistical support" to one of the terrorist groups – Jaish-i-Muhammad, whose founder and leader, Masood Azhar, had ties to both the Taliban and al Qaeda. In fact, according to those same sources, ISI was with Azhar even has he set about consolidating Kashmir's terrorists in 2000 to form Jaish-i-Muhammad.

After the December 13 attack, India immediately demanded that Pakistan to crack down on the terrorists. Musharraf responded by hitting the road – straight for Communist China, to meet with his allies. After returning home, Musharraf pledged to crack down on the terrorists, sort of. Then he backed off. After more acts of terror in Kashmir, Musharraf again pledged to crack down, before backing off again.

Meanwhile, more evidence and reports came out that revealed the Pakistani terrorists in Kashmir were receiving help, and had received it for many years, from al Qaeda and the Taliban. John Walker Lindh, the "American Taliban" captured in Mazar-e-Sharif, told authorities that he had served with al Qaeda and the Taliban in Kashmir. Reports out of the region had al Qaeda and Taliban operatives slipping across the Line of Control into the Indian-controlled section. As news of the al Qaeda and Taliban presence hit the press, Musharraf had the gall to criticize India's military buildup to stop the terrorists from killing any more of Indians, and said he would have to build up his own forces in response, taking them *away* from the anti-Taliban effort on the Afghan border.

In other words, Musharraf was al Qaeda's enemy in western Pakistan, but in eastern Pakistan, he would, at the very least, demand any Indian efforts against al Qaeda and its friends cease, and stopping India was more important than defeating al Qaeda. Pakistan's duplicity in the terrorist war has only few equals – one of them being its longtime ally Communist China.

In fact, Pakistan was so determined not to let the war on terror interfere with its Kashmir campaign that in the aftermath of December 13, 2001, it even asked the United States, privately of course, to pull out of military bases that the United States and its allies were using to find and battle the scattered Taliban in the war on terror. Luckily for the United States, and for everyone else in the war on terror, the request came as the United States was preparing to shift functions from the Pakistani bases to those in Afghanistan, Uzbekistan, and Kyrgyzstan.

It should be noted that the most recent reports about al Qaeda and the Taliban in Kashmir came less than a month before provincial elections ordered by the Vajpayee government to help ease the tension in the region. The BJP government bent over backward to ensure the elections were fair, despite the fact that it came at the expense of its own political allies – the National Conference Party. Meanwhile, Pakistan made a point of deriding the elections. Terrorists cast their own ballots with violence – killing 800 voters and candidates. In the end, the election was widely agreed to be fair, and the National Conference lost power. The coalition government now in power is considered to be the most Muslim-friendly in many years. The terrorists responded by firing grenades on the coalition leader's home just before he was about to take power.

Through it all, Pakistan never followed through on its pledge to focus and crack down on the terrorists. Pakistan was holding its own elections while India was holding its Kashmir vote. Unlike in India, however, Pakistani President Musharraf barred to leading opposition figures – the aforementioned Bhutto and Sharif – from running. While Musharraf, who took power in his October 1999 coup promising to root out corruption in Pakistan, may very well have been working from honorable motives, the result may have been, at least in part, to greatly aid the anti-American Islamic parties, who joined as a coalition and elected enough members of parliament to become the balance of power in the elected body. As it turned out, Musharraf managed to marginalize the anti-American group in parliament, but he could not stop them from winning a region bordering Afghanistan – just where Taliban and al Qaeda members could hide from Pakistani and American troops. He even struck a deal with them in another province bordering Afghanistan.

Throughout this tumultuous time, through the terrorist attacks in the 1990s, through September 11, 2001 and December 13, 2001, through the pledges and the backtracks, Pakistan's best friend in the entire world –

Communist China – offered not one word of criticism of Pakistan's "moral support" for the terrorists.

This should surprise no one, for Communist China was more than simply a diplomatic ally – it was a major arms supplier and nuclear enabler of the military dictatorship.

As recently as 2001, nearly three years after Pakistan become an acknowledged nuclear power, the United States Central Intelligence Agency reported that the People's Republic was violating its earlier pledges not to aid another nation's nuclear weapons program. The beneficiary of this aid was none other than Pakistan. The Pakistanis also won support from the Communists for its missile development. Communist China even agreed to build a major commercial port for Pakistan – which seemed innocuous enough, until one analyst noted that the People's Republic "has a history of piggybacking military cooperation onto commercial ventures."

The situation was so obvious that in 2000, just as it was prepared to leave office, the Clinton Administration nearly imposed economic sanctions on Communist China for its weapons sales and aid to Pakistan. After the People's Republic pledged to stop selling weapons and military technology, Clinton backed off, and decided to impose sanctions on Pakistan alone. Less than a year later, reports revealed that the Communists had gone back on their word.

Meanwhile, the Communists' lead East Asian ally – Stalinist North Korea – began an even more dangerous exchange with Pakistan. In effect, North Korea, which was miles ahead of Pakistan on missile technology but well behind on its supposedly suspended nuclear weapons program, and Pakistan agreed to aid each other in the area where one was less advanced then the other. The Stalinists helped the Pakistanis develop long-range missiles, while Pakistan helped the North move forward on its uranium nuclear weapons program.

But didn't September 11, 2001 change everything? Didn't it reveal to the world that dealing with regimes like North Korea was, at best, an unwise course of action? Not to Pakistan, it didn't. In fact, Pakistani assistance to North Korea's nuclear weapons program continued as late as *July of 2002*, nearly one year after September 11, 2001, seven months after the December 13 attack on the Indian Parliament, and roughly half a year after the President labeled the North an axis of evil regime. Pakistan's actions revealed just how *little* its view of the world changed after the attacks on the World Trade Center and the Pentagon.

Meanwhile, in March of 2002, Pakistan signed two defense pacts with Communist China, one on "defense cooperation" and the other on "defense production." The agreements revealed, once again, where the Communists' sympathies really lie in the war on terror.

There are two reasons why Pakistan is able to pull the wool over so many eyes, despite the fact that the new government in Afghanistan greatly reduces the need to rely on the Pakistani regime. The first one is the reservoir of good will Pakistan has built up in Washington from the first cold war – and protected ever since. For many, Pakistan, while being the nation that helped prop up the Taliban for years, was also the regime that helped stave off the Soviet occupation of the same country for nearly a decade. Pakistan also has a long history of military ties with the United States, including arms sales, which might also explain a greater desire on the part of many in Washington to give Pakistan a pass.

In many respects, India – whose opposition to Communist China and Pakistan shifted it toward the Soviet Union in the 1970s and 1980s – suffers the reverse of this effect, although not nearly as much today.

The other reason for Pakistan's inflated reputation comes from the affliction that has affected so much in the terrorist war and Cold War II: the fallacy of "engagement" with Communist China. The cooperation between Pakistan and the People's Republic would worry a number of American policymakers – and to be fair, many are worried. However, those who support "engagement" do not see the danger inherent in such closeness between Communist China and Pakistan. The best example of this was the aforementioned reaction to India's decision to become a nuclear power in 1998. Those who blasted India for its nuclear tests that year, up to and including Clinton himself, saw *India* as the threat to regional stability. The notion that Communist China – the conqueror of Tibet and aggressor in a border war with India that lost the world's largest democracy roughly 40,000 square miles – would be a threat in any way shape or form, let alone an immediate threat to India's security, is largely a foreign one to supporters of "engagement."

For these reasons, Pakistan has been able to, in effect, fight half a war on terror, if that. Since December 13, 2001, Pakistan has basically refused to deal with the terrorism in Kashmir. Musharraf himself has said Pakistan could never be expected to abandon its "moral support" for Kashmir terrorists. This Pakistani assertion – it can find al Qaeda in *western* Pakistan in conjunction with the new Afghan government, but not in *eastern* Pakistan where the target is India – is worse than a laughable contradiction. It provides the one opening al Qaeda needs to regroup, rearm, and prepare for more terrorist attacks against the United States and its alliance, right under the nose of an "ally" who refuses to even acknowledge their existence, let alone lift a finger to stop them. According to recent reports, al Qaeda has already made its presence felt in Kashmir, on both sides of the Line of Control. The willingness of Pakistan to ignore their presence is the opportunity Osama bin Laden and his henchmen desperately need, and one we cannot afford to let them have.

Will President Musharraf ever be willing to take on al Qaeda in Kashmir? The record so far is less than encouraging. Even before September 11, 2001 and December 13, 2001, Musharraf has had a role in Kashmir. In fact, as commanding General of the Pakistani armed forces during the 1999 conflict – and as *The New Republic* called him, "the chief architect of (the May 1999) Kashmir offensive" – one could say he had *the* role in Kashmir. With that record, it's difficult to say if Musharraf would be willing to respond to American and allied pressure to clean up his side of the Line of Control. The minimal pressure applied to him earlier this year was certainly not enough.

Either way, the United States and its allies must make clear to Pakistan that terrorism is terrorism – whether in New York City and Kabul or in Kashmir and New Delhi. If he responds, Kashmir would be a more peaceful place, and al Qaeda would lose on important hideout. If he does not, then he will reveal his true face, in which case the United States will have to recognize that it cannot rely so heavily either on him or his country.

As for India, the warming relations between it and the United States cannot be underestimated for its ramifications in both the terrorist war and Cold War II. Regarding the former, the growing ties between the United States and India have a number of benefits. First of all, it has brought supporters of the new, anti-Taliban government in Afghanistan closer together. As the need to rebuild Afghanistan grows – and given Communist China's recent overtures to the Taliban and blasts against American military presence in Central Asia, that need is certainly unlikely to shrink – the closer ties to India will greatly help the United States advance its interests both in Afghanistan, where a peaceful, stable, and popular government is an imperative, and in the region-wide battle against al Qaeda.

Close ties to India also provide valuable geopolitical insurance for the United States should the worst happen in Pakistan. While the possibility of civil war or chaos seems remote, it is universally known that there are already large parts of Pakistan, particularly in the areas bordering Afghanistan, where the government in Islamabad his little or no control. Meanwhile, the al Qaeda and Taliban operatives currently in Kashmir have near impunity on the Pakistani side of the Line of Control. Thus, in Kashmir, India's enemy is, in part, America's enemy as well.

The growing relationship between the United States and India gives even greater impetus to the ties between Israel and India. In many respects, India and Israel face the same problem – terrorists attack their people from an area outside their control, while their opposite number – Yassir Arafat for Israel, Musharraf for India – goes back and forth between promises to crack down and rhetoric demanding concessions along with excuses the acts of terror. For Israel, India's friendship provides a crucial ally in its battle to maintain its legitimacy as a sovereign state and worthy member of the community of nations.

In these areas, India and United States working more closely together has been a sizeable advance for the war on terror. However, the effect on Cold War II will likely be even greater for several reasons, some of which few have even noticed.

India's rivalry with Communist China is no secret. Ever since Pakistan and the People's Republic began their alliance, India has been suspicious. The seizure of both Tibet – whose Buddhist natives are strongly supported by India, where the Dalai Lama and his government are in exile – and 38,000 square miles of Indian territory in 1962 further added to the hostility, as did Pakistan's transfer of a piece of Kashmir to the Communists one year later. Finally, there was Communist China's increasing aid to Pakistan's nuclear weapons development during the 1990's. That, plus the Communists' own nuclear arsenal, forced India to build a nuclear deterrent of its own.

However, the rivalry between Communist China and India go well beyond military battles from the 1960s and nuclear deterrence. The two are economic and diplomatic rivals as well. In fact, in the realm of economics, India does far better in comparison to the People's Republic than is generally known.

Many who support "engagement" point to the "rise" of Communist China as an economic and military power in future years as a reason one cannot be hostile to them. For the most part, "engagement" supporters assume that in its development Communist China will easily outshine all of its neighbors and rivals. Of course, when most think of neighbors and rivals to Communist China, it is usually Japan, South Korea, Taiwan, the Philippines, and possibly Vietnam, Australia, and Russia, that come to mind. Few even contemplate India.

In fact, most economists examining the situation have found that India is likely to roughly match the glorious economic future Communist China is *supposed* to have. One group, the Economist Intelligence Unit, actually put India *ahead* of Communist China as a climate for business and investment.

This shouldn't surprise anyone. India has made great strides in economic and political reform over the last decade – the former due largely to the policies of the BJP, the latter simply due to the new two-party political situation. Compared to Communist China, with its sclerotic, dictatorial regime, India's democratic government and British-based legal system give it some important advantages.

Meanwhile, the supposed record of white-hot growth of which the People's Republic is so proud is already coming under fire from outside analysts, who have noticed that the figures simply do not add up. The fact is the nationwide figures come from compilations of provincial figures, which themselves come from aggregations of county figures. In other words, at both the local and the provincial level, Communist cadres have the opportunity to fudge the figures in their favor. As a result, many are beginning to find that the glowing numbers on growth in the People's Republic are nothing more than the collection of a slew of Enron-like reports from local and provincial Communists. Even Communist China itself was forced to admit to sixty *thousand* statistical errors in its economic calculation.

However, an economy is important for more than reasons dealing with the proper balance for international investment portfolios. It allows a nation to project power, either economically or as a base for military development. Thus, the perception of Communist China as the lead economic power in Asia has colored how many see the political situation on that continent. Just as many underrate India's economic strength, its future geopolitical potential is also underestimated.

Given Communist China's hideous "one child" policy, one can see a future in which India passes the People's Republic in population. Perhaps that's what it will take for some to notice the potential of India. One of the most overused phrases in the history of recent economic and financial parlance has been the reference to Communist China's "one billion customers" as a justification for suffering any indignation, corruption, or financial loss from investment in the People's Republic. India, at present, is rapidly approaching "one billion customers" in its population; in fact it may have already reached it by the time of this printing. Whether this will be enough to garner more attention from Wall Street and other financial sectors remains to be seen. Perhaps it will need to pass Communist China, and become the most populous nation in the world, first. The sooner it happens, the better – not just for India, but for the American people, the cause of world liberty, and even for Wall Street itself.

In the meantime, the Bush Administration, in its actions both before and after September 11, 2001, has made closer relations with the largest democracy on the planet a high priority. This has greatly increased the potential for advances in both the war against terror and Cold War II against Communist China.

In many respects, what India faces and what the United States faces are the same. Both are federal democracies with strong state governments. Terrorist groups and Al Qaeda have targeted both. Both have suffered terribly by terrorist attacks on its soil. Both have earned the wrath of Communist China numerous times. Now, in cooperation, both are advancing joint interests together, in the process providing benefits to themselves and to their mutual allies, such as Israel and Turkey.

Meanwhile, in Pakistan, the military that helped to put the Taliban in power, provided "moral support" – at the very least – to the Kashmir terrorists, and spurred an incursion into India in 1999, has overthrown a democratically elected government, and then given Islamists a taste of power in order to skew the outcome of a subsequent parliamentary election. The Musharraf regime has provided inconsistent help to American efforts against the Taliban – even in the Afghan theatre – while backtracking on pledges to do something about the terrorists, including those with al Qaeda ties, in Kashmir. It has aided the Stalinist regime of North Korea in becoming a nuclear power and ransom the world for its survival, while in exchange improving the ranges of its missiles deployed against India.

Which regime has Communist China chosen as its friend an ally? Pakistan. That alone should tell us all we need to know about where the People's Republic stands in the war on terror.

Communist China's efforts to be seen as a supporter of the United States in the war on terror while providing aid and comfort to our enemies to exploit its position against the United States in Cold War II simultaneously is mirrored in the efforts of Pakistan to be seen as an enemy of al Qaeda and the Taliban in Afghanistan while refusing to deal with them and their fellow terrorists in Kashmir. Both have been able, for the most part, to fool the world on their intentions and policies. However, they have not been able to stop the two nations most likely to resist their efforts – India and the United States – from working together. In this respect, despite numerous successes elsewhere, the People's Republic remains vulnerable in Cold War II.

The intersections of the terrorist war and Cold War II are as prevalent in South Asia as they are in Central Asia, the Middle East, East Asia, and throughout the world. However, in India and Pakistan, the contradictions of Communist China's feigned support in for the fight against terror and its actual indifference to that fight in light of its own interests in Cold War II are quite obvious. Pakistan's duplicity on terrorism and its protection it receives from Communist China are glaring examples of how in order to win the war on terror, the United States must take up the fight in Cold War II as well. A critical component in both the terrorist war and Cold War II is building an alliance to the nation most likely to develop as an equal to the People's Republic: India. Thankfully, the building of that alliance has already begun. The United States must now continue and accelerate it in order to ensure victory in both conflicts.

Chapter 5:
Other Terrorist Issues and the Dangers of Engagement

The preceding chapters have dealt with Communist China's numerous ties to some of the most infamous sponsors of terror and anti-American regimes – Iran, Ba'athist Iraq, North Korea, the Taliban, al Qaeda, and the Kashmir terrorists. These are not the only ties Communist China has to terrorism. In fact, the Communist Chinese model for international diplomacy has led to ties with other sponsors and perpetrators of terror, and could lead to more of them in the future.

Communist China's ties to terror are numerous; some have gone largely unnoticed by many Americans. One recipient of Communist China weapons technology is Libya's Moammar Gadhafi, the same Gadhafi attacked by the United States in 1986 for supporting terrorism, and whose operatives were responsible for the crash of Pan Am Flight 103, over Lockerbie, Scotland, in late 1988.

In 1990, Gadhafi said he wanted to build a missile that could reach, and hit, New York City. Communist China has been quite helpful to Libya in its aims. Starting in 1998, the People's Republic began helping Libya in advancing their indigenous Al-Fatah missile program. In 1999, the China Precision Military Import-Export Company – a Communist-run firm – took over the aid to Libya. The following year, the head of the al-Fatah program visited the University of Aeronautics and Astronautics in Beijing, China's premier training center for missile scientists and technicians. He wasn't the first visitor either; Communist China had already hosted and trained other missile specialists for Gadhafi. All this was for the man who engineered the bombing of Flight 103.

The Lockerbie bombing was far from Gadhafi's only act of terror. In the mid-1980s, Libyan agents bombed a disco in then-West Berlin, killing scores of people. It was this attack that caused the United States to retaliate in 1986. Ever since, except for Lockerbie, Gadhafi has been largely out of the terror business. However, his pursuit of long-range missiles clearly reveals his anti-American has not disappeared. One can expect Gadhafi may even be willing to entertaining re-entering the terrorist business after he achieves his ambition of being able to hit New York with a missile. Communist China is bringing that day closer and closer.

Libya is not the only terrorist sponsor to come from North Africa. Prior to entering Afghanistan, Osama bin Laden was operating his terrorist network from Sudan, where a radical Arab Muslim regime has held power since 1989. It has been fighting ruthless, bloodthirsty civil war against the black Christian and animist tribes in southern Sudan ever since. In the early half of the 1990s, it was also Osama's host.

Sudan has been able to prosecute its brutal civil war, which includes enslaving the black tribes, through oil. One of the major oil investors in Sudan is none other than PetroChina (this same firm also landed pipeline deals in Libya). Communist China has done more than simply help fuel Sudan's brutal regime against its enemies. It has also lent troops to Sudan – one report put the figure at an astronomical 700,000 – and nearly three-dozen fighter jets to help crush the southern rebellion. All this was for a regime that willingly hosted Osama bin Laden as he built al Qaeda until 1995, when he left to set up shop in Afghanistan.

Communist China also has ties with Syria, where the Ba'athist Assad family has led in a reign of terror for over thirty years. Hafez al-Assad, the late leader of Syria, revealed his method of governance early in his tenure when faced with an uprising in the city of Hama: population 10,000: he literally bombed Hama off the map. Other opposition decided it would be better to "vanish" in a more figurative method. Meanwhile, both Hafez and his son Bashar, the current leader of the Ba'athist regime, have made Syria one of the most consistently anti-Israel, nationalistic, expansionist, and terrorist-sponsoring regimes in the Middle East – only Iran and Iraq have been worse.

Syria has been involved in nearly every war with Israel, losing the Golan Heights to the Jewish democracy in 1967. In the 1970s, it helped destabilize Lebanon, whose capital Beirut was once considered the Paris of the Middle East. Lebanon fell into a bloody civil war that decimated the country, and made it a breeding ground for anti-Semitic terrorists. Lebanese terrorists, backed by Iran – whom Syria backed throughout the 1980s – held more than a dozen Westerners hostage during the 1980s. In 1990, the Syrian military moved in, and placed a puppet regime in power, making the only satellite state in the Middle East (not that the people in most of the non-satellite states in that region really have it any better).

Moreover, according to some reports, Syria went so far as to allow Ba'athist Iraq to send its weapons of mass destruction across their joint border – safely in the hands of a fellow Ba'athist state, and out of reach of the United Nations weapons inspectors. When Iraq fell, Syria may have also allowed some of the major players themselves in the old regime to hide in, and escape through, its territory.

During the 1990s, Communist China sent missile parts to Syria after pledging not to do so, and in a very dramatic speech in Syria – with President Bashar al-Assad looking on – a Communist official lambasted Israel as a "colonialist plot aimed at detaching from the Arab nation a part that is dear to it – Palestine." Who let loose with this incendiary rhetoric? He was Hu Jintao, now the President the People's Republic and head of the Chinese Communist Party.

Communist China has also been busy helping Syria with "nonconventional" weapons. As Deputy Under Secretary of Defense Lisa Bronson put it to the United States-China Commission, a commission examining the People's Republic appointed by Congress, "Chinese entities…have supported some nuclear and chemical programs in rogue states," including, according to Bronson, Syria.

Such things would normally convince one to avoid dealing with a regime such as Communist China. Sadly, this is not been the case. American policy regarding the People's Republic at times seems to be conducted in spite of this information, rather than because of it. In fact, Bronson herself noted that the United States trade policy would continue, if only in "the larger national security and foreign policy agenda set by the president, who has said that 'America's next priority to prevent mass terror is to protect against the proliferation of weapons of mass destruction and the means to deliver them.'"

Where Communist China is concerned, however, that larger agenda is disturbingly absent from Administration thinking. Last fall, as the Administration was attempting to build international support for the liberation of Iraq and the demise of the Ba'athist regime, it was pushing to *loosen* technology export controls to Communist China. This as past technology sent to Communist China for "civilian use" was converted to military applications.

In many respects, American policy on Communist China suffers from a serious disconnect. This is due to the fact that many policymakers see Communist China from a purely economic perspective, focusing not on its weapons sales, its saber-rattling against its neighbors, or its unstinting support of Stalinist, terrorist North Korea, but instead on its façade of "reform" and its voracious desire for foreign capital. This has clouded what should be very clear – that Communist China is a danger to America's interests and American security.

The ties to Ba'athist Iraq, Iran, and North Korea would normally be enough to reveal this to all but the most naïve observer. However, the Communist ties to Syria and Libya reveal something more. Ties to Iran and Ba'athist Iraq can at least have some ostensible value beyond anti-Americanism. Each can be a major supplier of petroleum, and both have tremendous strategic value in the Middle East. Syria and Libya have no such bounty of resources to entice outside observers. Sudan, meanwhile, had its major oil find during its civil war.

In fact, their ascension to the world stage was due almost entirely to anti-American leaders and actions. In Syria's case, the Ba'athist regime won it the support of the Soviet Union for years. Libya used acts of terror as its anti-American card. Sudan had hosted Osama bin Laden. If the People's Republic of China were truly concerned about the interests of the United States, arms deals with these regimes would be foolish, at best. That they have taken place and have continued even through the terrorist war, is a sign that Communist China has more the economic interests at heart in its weapons sales to terrorist states throughout the Middle East.

Missile and arms sales like these forced the United States in the 1990s to pursue a missile defense for the protection of the American people against "rogue states," in particular the very states that have been recipients of Communist Chinese and North Korean military deals. One would think that the People's Republic would be hesitant to comment on an American course of action designed to rectify a problem caused in large part by Communist Chinese military sales, if it saw the United States as a friend.

How the Communists actually responded is quite telling. The People's Republic took every chance it had to blast the United States for planning – not building, but *planning* – a missile defense against the regimes the Communists was helping to arm. The People's Republic threatened an arms race. It demanded the United States preserve the Anti-Ballistic Missile Treaty – a treaty that it never signed. It even tried to stiffen Russian resolve to preserve the treaty.

Some would note that Communist China might have been worried that it would be a target of the missile defense itself. This begs the question: why would the Communists consider themselves weakened by an American missile defense, unless they were planning to point missiles at us? If Communist China were our friend, and so deserving of "engagement," it would have no concern for a missile defense. A regime that helps arm "rogue states," is planning to attack the American military if need be to retake Taiwan by force, and is trying to push the United States out of its role as the leading power in the Pacific and around the globe would react, well, just like the People's Republic did react.

None of this has had any impact with the supporters of "engagement." In fact, a number of them are in deliberate denial. During the 2000 debate on Permanent Normal Trade Relations (PNTR), the most dramatic recent battle between the "engagement" backers and those with a more clear-eyed view of Communist China, one lobbyist – former Democratic Congressman Michael Kopetski – provided the best example of this. Kopetski told the *Legal Times* that his plan to sell the deal was "to get members (of Congress) *to shift from thinking about human rights and all those other Asian security issues* and bring them back to the idea that this is the best trade deal ever negotiated (emphasis added)". Normally, ignoring national security is *not* considered to be in any nation's best interests.

Another example came from Congressman Frank Wolf. The Virginia Republican was a leading opponent of PNTR, for those human rights and national security reasons that the supporters of "engagement" would rather we ignore. He noted a certain report – which he did not describe because it was classified – detailing Communist China's threats to American interests and national security. When he recommended it to one of his fellow Congressmen – left unnamed for a very different reason – he received this response: "I'm already committed to vote yes" on PNTR.

In the end, PNTR passed narrowly in the House of Representatives, and overwhelmingly in the Senate. Supporters praised the move, saying that since Communist China would come into the World Trade Organization, it would be forced to "follow the rules" on international issues. Yet the arms sales did not stop, and the threats to Taiwan continued – to say nothing about how the Communists treated their own people. All that seemed to change were the falling of barriers between Communist-run companies and money from Western firms with visions of "a billion customers" in their heads.

Meanwhile, "engagement" has also left the military more unprepared than it should be to face the 21st century. This may seem an odd connection to make, but it is there. In many respects, post-Cold War I thinking on the military has been based on the assumption that there is no major hostile power to challenge the United States. This has been one of the major reasons behind the increasing focus on "rapid reaction" units over the need to maintain a large projection of force in the world. In particular, a staple of American military strength – the ability to fight and win two major wars simultaneously, fell by the wayside in recent years.

This is not to discount the need for rapid reaction forces, which are certainly required today. However, the acknowledgement of the People's Republic as a major hostile power would quickly demolish the fantasy that a large projection of force – the basis for the military of Cold War I is no longer required. American military planners would be more properly balanced in their thinking, building a fighting force capable of both the small, quick deployment and the massive projection required to deter, or as a last resort fight, a major conflict. However, so long as "engagement" continues to predominate, that thinking will largely be missing from policymakers. As such, when the nature of the Communist threat does finally hit home to those on whom the duty of defending our nation depends, they will be in a much more difficult position to do so, and those who set policy will need time – perhaps too much time – to rebuild the military capabilities to best execute the objective of holding off Communist China geopolitically.

At present, our military is still smaller than it was at the end of Cold War I, while the opponent in Cold War II – Communist China – has a *larger* army than the Soviet Union did, and the technological gap between the People's Liberation Army (PLA) and the United States Armed Forces – painfully obvious to the PLA top brass in the 1990s – has been greatly reduced today. This means American military technological superiority, one of its main advantages over opponents in the first Gulf War, Bosnia, Kosovo, and the liberation of Afghanistan, would be of much lesser advantage to the United States in Cold War II.

To be fair, the Communist navy is still practically meaningless beyond coastal waters, but they are leaving no stone unturned in trying to end that disadvantage. Their efforts have mainly consisted of buying and/or reverse engineering Russian naval vessels and weaponry.

In any event, it should be obvious that in order to confront Communist China in Cold War II, we need a larger military – one that can satisfy the "two war" requirement and project enough force throughout the world to give the Communists pause. Of course, the same malady afflicted the United States before World War II and Cold War I, so the matter can be rectified. However, it would certainly be better to rectify it now rather than later, especially given the fact that in Communist China, Cold War II has effectively been going on for nearly a decade and a half. The latest American military budget increase of 11 percent – the largest in 20 years – was still smaller than the Communist military increases of 17 percent in both this *and* last year, and that was just the military spending to which the Communists would admit publicly.

Of course, this would require a quick end to "engagement" as the prevailing American policy towards the People's Republic, in favor of one the recognizes Communist China as a regime whose interests are inimical to ours, and as such must be treated in much the same way the Soviet Union was. Those who support "engagement" would recoil in horror at that notion. Many of them refuse to believe that the People's Republic is hostile at all. Even those who do acknowledge that Communist China has behaved badly in many areas still insist that it can be brought into the community of nations, and behave accordingly.

That the Communists have grown more belligerent – and their ties to terrorist regimes multiplied – as the United States moved closer to them in the 1990s should have shown to the supporters of "engagement" that their expectations have gone unfulfilled, at best. The evidence of the failure of "engagement" is quite apparent from a geopolitical perspective. Continuing "engagement" would continue the failure, and leave American vulnerable to the continuing and growing threat from the People's Republic.

In fact, the supporters of "engagement" actually believe, and have led many other Americans to believe, that Communist China can be *helpful* in the terrorist war. Of course, the Communists have been more than eager to peddle this line at every chance they've had. Right after September 11, 2001, Communist China suddenly decided that an independence movement in what it called Xinjiang – many in the local population prefer it return to its pre-1949 status as a the independent state of East Turkestan – was a network of terrorists sympathizing with al Qaeda, and worthy of earning the Communists world sympathy as a "victim" of terrorism. While the Communists' claims have largely been shown to be spurious at best (as can be seen in the next chapter), they did manage to convince the United States to label the East Turkestan Islamic Movement (ETIM) as a terrorist group. The fact that, according to one report, ETIM had "never carried out operations on Chinese (controlled) soil" did not change the Administration's decision, nor did it change the perception that the United States had swallowed the Communist Chinese line on East Turkestan.

This is not the only time Communist China has tried to don the cloak of fighting terrorism as cover for its geopolitical objectives. Months before September 11, 2001, Communist China created the Shanghai Cooperation Organization (SCO), along with Russia, and four former Soviet republics: Tajikistan, Uzbekistan, Kazakhstan, and Kyrgyzstan. The SCO had as part of its original objective a campaign against "terrorism, separatism and extremism." It was, as the post-September 11, 2001 public relations offensive was, an attempt to, as Willy Wo-Lap Lam of CNN put it, "justify their often brutal campaigns in Xinjiang." Before September 11, 2001, the Communists called them "separatists," but not supporters of Osama bin Laden, but the independence movement was still a useful excuse to forge ties with Central Asia, which had terrorism of a more authentic variety to combat, and Russia, whose problem with Chechnya became dramatically apparent in Moscow last fall.

The long-term objective for the SCO was audacious, a Communist Chinese answer to the North Atlantic Treaty Organization. In the weeks that followed the launch, the Communists hyped the organization, and the ties among the six nations that could come from it, as the beginning of the People's Republic becoming the leading power in Central Asia, and a major power in the world.

Regarding the two major signatories to the SCO, the warming of ties began well before the signing ceremony. Throughout the 1990s, Russia and Communist China moved closer together in many alarming ways. Numerous statements on opposing "hegemony" and a "unipolar" world – both code words for the superpower status of the United States – came out of Beijing and Moscow, to near silence in Washington. That silence applied to both the Clinton and the Bush Administrations. The Communist Chinese unstinting support of the Russian campaign against Chechnya – particularly during the 1994-96 phase in which Russia received unmitigated criticism from nearly every other corner of the globe – brought Moscow and Beijing closer together. Russia won an ally in its insistence that Chechnya was an internal affair, while Communist China won support for its continued crackdown against the Muslim Uighurs in East Turkestan.

Sadly, cooperation between the two also includes military weapons and technology sales. No one buys more military hardware from Russia than Communist China, and no one sells more weaponry *to* the People's Republic than Russia. The deals included deep sea, "blue water" naval vessels, high-tech anti-ship naval missiles, air-radar systems, and a number of categories of jet fighters. The military sales from Moscow to Beijing are now worth billions of dollars. To date, the United States, through successive Administrations, has kept a stunning silence on this arms trade – an especially troubling silence given that one of the prime reasons the Communists are interested in a blue water navy is to greatly improve their chances for a successful invasion of Taiwan.

The growing coziness between Russia and Communist China seemed a solid foundation for the SCO; the Communists even hoped for it to be an answer to the North Atlantic Treaty Organization (NATO). The high hopes for this "Chinese NATO" took a hit on September 11. Within a year of the terrorist attack, three of the founding nations, Uzbekistan, Kyrgyzstan, and Tajikistan, had welcomed American troops onto its soil. Things quickly got worse for the "Chinese NATO." One year after its launch, five of the six nations got together to attempt to plot military cooperation. Uzbekistan, the nation with the most American troops of any ex-Soviet republic, did not even send a representative to the talks, which made no progress in any event.

Even ties that had nothing to do with SCO or the war on terror gave the People's Republic headaches. In January 2002, Communist China signed a border agreement with Kyrgyzstan. As part of the deal, the former Soviet Republic agreed to hand over 90,000 hectares of land to the People's Republic. Opposition to the deal spread like wildfire, in part aided by a government that had stalled on political reforms and had now given the political opposition a nationalist cover for going after the government. The Kyrgyz regime under President Askar Akayev responded by throwing a leading opposition figure – Azimbek Beknazarov, who had come out against the treaty – in prison. The demonstrations intensified, the tension mounted, and by summer five protestors were shot. Akayev dissolved the entire government, released Beknazarov, and was forced to reach out to the opposition to avoid adding fuel the fire. The border agreement itself was ratified, and is far from threatened, but Akayev *et al* are likely to be a lot more skittish about moving closer to Communist China in the future.

More ominously for the People's Republic, Russia began a partial shift toward Washington after September 11, 2001. This drift was duly noted in both Washington and Beijing – although the reactions were obviously quite different. Communist China has a lot invested in Russia, first and foremost its desire for Russian military hardware. The two have contracts that now total over $4 billion in weapons sales. This would, of course, make Russia think twice about cutting back its arms sales to the Communists, but the People's Republic – dependent on Russia to jump-start Communist Chinese ambitions for a more modern military in general and a "blue water" deep sea navy in particular – is still going to be nervous. The People's Republic would be right to worry about *any* movement toward the

United States by its major seller of military hardware, even if the Russian "drift" slowed considerably during the Security Council wrangling on Iraq.

Of course, despite all the talk about a major shift in Russian geopolitical thinking, Russia still agreed to billions in weapons sales to the Communists in 2002, and this was actually an *increase* over its previous arms sales to Communist China. That the United States could continue to ignore this is a sign of a glaring flaw in "engagement" with the People's Republic.

Of course, September 11, 2001 did change Russia's view of the United States, and vice versa. American support for the Northern Alliance, the lead rebel force against the Taliban in Afghanistan, helped to achieve a major objective of Russian Central Asian policy. Meanwhile, Communist China's biggest card – its refusal to criticize Russia about its actions in Chechnya – slowly faded as American criticism of the Chechen campaign was quickly muted. Both the fall of the World Trade Center and the rather foolish 1999 Chechen invasion of Dagestan – a neighboring region in Russia and more than content to stay that way – did quite a bit to silence American criticism. When Chechen terrorists seized a Moscow theatre last October, the tactic of gassing the theatre to incapacitate the terrorists led many to criticize the Russians, particularly when over 100 hostages died. The United States made a point of not being one of the critics of the rescue operation; President Bush even publicly defended Putin – calling him "my friend," – for his handling of the hostage situation.

However – and here, the negative effects of "engaging" Communist China could not possibly be more obvious – despite the Russian move toward the United States, few in Washington have even *considered* asking the Russians to end, or substantially reduce, the weapons pipeline to the

People's Republic, which includes everything from jet fighters to anti-ship missiles at the cutting edge of the military technology curve.

Communist China's ties to the regimes that sponsor terror still have yet to pierce the "engagement" balloon for many American policymakers. However, they are clearly a threat to American interests and our national, to say nothing of personal, security. They also provide enough historical evidence to predict the reaction of the People's Republic to freedom's arrival in Iraq and, hopefully, Iran. Thanks to the policy of "engagement," Communist China presently has the cover it needs to build new anti-American ties to terror sponsors and regimes that have played on both sides.

The "engagement" problem is best symbolized by the policies toward North Korea and Pakistan, as discussed in earlier chapters. In the case of the former, "engagement" leads many to believe that Communist China can "restrain" its Stalinist allies in their nuclear ambitions. The fact that it would have no real interest in doing so has no effect on those who continue to peddle the theory. Regarding the latter, the ties to Communist China are practically ignored, creating a sense of *American* influence that is far greater than the reality. Thus, when Pakistani President Pervez Musharraf shifts *away* from fighting terrorism in Kashmir, the role of the People's Republic is marginalized, despite the fact that part of the disputed region is now Communist Chinese territory thanks to an agreement with Pakistan in the 1960s.

So long as the U.S refuses to see Communist China as the enemy in Cold War II, deafening silence on subjects such as these will likely continue. Russia can still arm the People's Republic, while claiming to be closer to us. Our refusal to resolve this absurd contradiction will certainly come back to haunt us in the future, and not simply because it will enable the Communists to strengthen their military prowess without consequence as they continue to build ties to anti-American and terrorist sponsoring regimes. It will also make it much easier for Communist China to find new regimes to replace Iraq – and possibly Iran – as "checks" against the United States, regimes like the Saudi Arabia, the United Arab Emirates, and Yemen.

In looking for a future anti-American replacement to Iraq (and possibly Iran), Saudi Arabia is the leading favorite. It has several ties to Pakistan, going all the way back to the anti-Soviet mujahedin in Afghanistan. In fact, during the fight against Soviet Communism, the United States largely let Pakistan and Saudi Arabia handle the details of the Afghan resistance. It was a less than perfect arrangement, as became all too painfully obvious on September 11, 2001.

What the United States did not see as it allowed the Saudis and Pakistanis to take the lead roles in Afghanistan was the virulent strain of radical Islam peddled by the Saudi royal family: Wahhabism. This relatively recent brand of Islam (from the eighteenth century) is arguably the most reactionary worldview on the planet. The heavy role of Saudi Arabia allowed Wahhabism to gain a foothold it would not have otherwise had in Central Asia – where Islam has generally been of a moderate variety.

Wahhabism is anything but moderate. Under Saudi law, women are not allowed to drive cars, go anywhere without the male escort, hold property or exercise anything near the rights men do. Not that the men have many rights either, for both sexes, conversion to Christianity is a capital offense. The Saudi royal family is sovereign there – even the name of the country comes from the founder of the House: Ibn Saud. In one of the most dramatic example of the twisted version of Islam known as Wahhabism, women and young girls trapped in a school on fire were forced to perish in the flames because a religion official refused to allow them to come out without their faces covered.

This was the worldview Saudi Arabia brought to Afghanistan via the Taliban – aided by the Pakistani Inter-Service Intelligence (ISI). After the Taliban won control of Afghanistan, it invited al Qaeda – and Osama bin Laden – to be its "guests." Things quickly went downhill for the Afghan people.

Meanwhile, Saudi Arabia and was one of only three regimes to recognize the Taliban as the legitimate government in Afghanistan during the late 1990s, as the rest of the world turned away in disgust to the Russian and Indian-backed Northern Alliance. Saudi Arabia also has numerous questions to answer about al Qaeda. According to numerous reports, including statements entered into court records as part of a lawsuit by survivors of the World Trade Center attacks, Saudi officials had a number of ties to al Qaeda that they have not been willing to discuss, despite Osama bin Laden's very publicly stated goal of overthrowing the Saudi royal family. More ominously, recent reports had the terrorists from September 11, 2001 getting indirect support from a member of the Saudi royal family.

Communist China has paid little attention to Saudi Arabia thus far, but that little attention did include the sale of intercontinental ballistic missiles to the Wahhabist regime. Moreover, with the liberation of Iraq – and the possibility of the revolt against the mullahs in Iran succeeding – the People's Republic will be looking for more allies in its quest to block American "hegemony." Saudi Arabia is just about the perfect candidate for such an overture. Saudi Arabia also has a number of advantages for the Communists that do not apply to their northern neighbors. They have a large supply of oil, without any international restrictions to violate. This is of critical importance to any regime desperately trying to keep its economy at pace with its population growth, let alone a Communist one trying to fulfill its objectives of becoming a world power and the dominant regime in Asia. Part of Communist China's relationships with Iraq and Iran can be found in their petroleum fields. With one or both of them gone, the Saudis become the most likely substitute. Add to this Saudi Arabia's history of religious and political repression, and this has the makings of what, for the United States, would be a very ugly friendship.

Saudi Arabia is also the leading regime in the Arab world. Communist China prides itself as the regime of choice for developing nations to support against the "unipolar" world in which America as the lone superpower. Ties to Saudi Arabia would be far more effective than to either Iraq or Iran in advancing that argument. In part that is because the Saudis' international reputation, while suffering a bit thanks to the uncovered ties to al Qaeda and their well-known support of the Taliban, is far better than that of either Iraq or Iran. This would greatly improve Communist China's efforts to win over other nations in the region.

At present, Communist China's ties to the late Ba'athist regime in Iraq and the mullahs in Iran make this difficult, at best. With at least one of them gone, replaced by a secular American ally that would likely frighten the Wahhabists far more than Saddam does at present, this would become easier. Communist China can also reach Saudi Arabia through Pakistan. Their history of cooperation in Afghanistan can be a "card" – to use the favorite geopolitical lingo of the Communist Chinese – to play.

Finally – and this matters most if the United States continues with its foolhardy policy of "engagement" of Communist China – Saudi Arabia is an ostensible American ally. This serves two purposes at once. First, it provides the Saudis with at least some cover. An America hostile to Communist China – moving to contain it, pressing to isolate it, supporting dissidents to undermine it – would be deeply miffed if Saudi Arabia began shifting toward the People's Republic. An America "engaging" Communist China would be unable – and at first, possibly even unwilling – to react in same manner. Moreover, reaching out to Saudi Arabia would make the end of "engagement" infinitely more difficult, forcing the United States to effectively drop both regimes at once. Even with a friendly government in Iraq, the United States would find breaking with the Saudis difficult. Rather than using the international dynamic to keep the Saudis *away* from Communist China, America would be forced by "engagement" to stay close to the Saudis and the Communists.

The precedent for this future Communist entente with Saudi Arabia already exists today – in Russia. That the former Soviet state is allowed to continue to sell more military hardware to Communist China than anyone else in the world, while still being able to claim closer ties to Washington, and garner benefits for that claim, is a contradiction that could greatly damage the United States in the future. This contradiction will not be lost on the People's Republic – odds are they have taken note of it already. The Saudi royal family will certainly not fail to notice.

In the time lost until "engagement" loses its political viability, an alliance between Saudi Arabia and Communist China would not only make Cold War II more difficult to win, but also put all the gains from the terrorist war at risk. An American foreign policy that considers the People's Republic a hostile power may very well spook Saudi Arabia away from reaching out to the Communists. A policy of "engagement" will be all the encouragement the Saudis need to build a relationship with the People's Republic of China. This would make them less dependent on the United States, and its Wahhabist activities throughout the world infinitely more dangerous than they already are.

Outside of Saudi Arabia and Pakistan, the only other nation to recognize the Taliban was a regime on the southern shore of the Persian Gulf: the United Arab Emirates. It is a regime that has also served as host to a number of al Qaeda operatives, and it was believed to be the transit nation for the money behind the attacks of September 11, 2001. The United Arab Emirates (UAE) has the façade of a modern state, led by a President and an advisory, Cabinet-like structure. In reality, however, the Emirates are a group of sheikdoms governed by families much like the Saudi royals. Michael Ledeen, a Middle Eastern expert, even called Dubai, a major city in the UAE "the Iranian colony."

Yemen is a country that has only recently won American attention, due to al Qaeda's attack on the *U.S.S. Cole* on October 12, 2000. The attention it has been getting since then is far from good. Yemen is an uneasily re-merged state, formed in 1990 when pro-American North Yemen and anti-American, Communist South Yemen reunified. The wounds of the past were reopened during a 1994 civil war, but even before then, the reunified Yemen had been somewhat squeamish about the United States, even opposing the United States-led liberation of Kuwait during the 1991 Gulf War.

Since the attack on the *U.S.S. Cole*, Yemen, like Pakistan, has tried to deal with the reality of al Qaeda on its soil. The most dramatic example of that came last October, when an American Hellfire missile killed six al Qaeda members, including one widely believed to be a plotter in the *Cole* attack. The Yemeni regime appeared more than willing to allow that operation to proceed.

However, also like Pakistan, Yemen has been caught trying to take both sides. Just this past winter, there were reports that Yemen was receiving missiles from the great anti-American armaments merchant: North Korea. This was a clear sign that while Yemen was more than willing to help the United States where al Qaeda was concerned, broader support against terrorism, states that sponsor it, and anti-Americanism in general is far from certain.

In fact, as late as August of 2002, Yemen not only acknowledged it had bought Scud missiles from Stalinist North Korea, but insisted it had the right to do so no matter what the United States thought. It even received a shipment of Scuds from North Korea in December 2002. Although the Spanish navy intercepted the ship making the missile delivery, Yemen demanded the missiles be delivered to them, and inexplicably, the United States, to which Spain gave control of the vessel, complied with that request, and the Scuds made it to Yemen. The Yemeni government said the Scuds were needed for self-defense, without ever mentioning who specifically worried them enough to require the missiles. More ominously, it soon became known that Yemen had promised to stop buying North Korean weaponry as early as July of 2001, a full *seventeen months* before the shipment in question was intercepted. Yemen also denied that the December 2002 Scuds were headed in its direction – until the United States stopped them.

Yemen promised that the Scuds would never go to anyone else – supposedly a key factor in allowing the shipment to be made – but never provided proof of that claim. Moreover, Yemen has had problems maintaining control of its weaponry before – with terrible consequences. According to *Newsweek*, the SA-7 surface to aid missiles fired upon an Israeli airliner late last year were "stolen from a Yemeni government arsenal." This further makes Yemen's promises on the safety of the Scuds ring hollow. Another, more dramatic sign of Yemen's weak credibility came less than two weeks after the Scuds were released. The *New York Post*, citing an Israeli source also quoted in the Israeli newspaper *Ha'aretz*, reported that the Scuds themselves were not meant for Yemen at all, but actually destined for none other than Ba'athist Iraq.

At present, Yemen and Saudi Arabia are ostensible American allies – although neither have been doing a particularly good job of playing the part lately – while it's likely that few Americans have heard of the United Arab Emirates. These nations could become much more important in the future, as the war on terror moves forward. Together, these regimes could build a new axis of states with ties to the People's Republic on one end and terrorists on the other. Without a determined anti-Communist American policy, Communist China can use these nations to rebuild what it lost with Iraq, and may lose soon with Iran. It would also reverse much of what was gained by defeating terrorism in Afghanistan and the northern Middle East.

In fact, the North Korean missile trade with Yemen reveals how the Communists could reach out to the Saudis, the UAE, the Yemenis, and others in the region. Despite the unending gaze of the United States – and the focus on America and its allies on Yemen in the war on terror, due to the attack on the *Cole* – the Stalinists still managed to make a sale to Yemen in *2002*, one which Yemen was willing to defend despite pledges made over a year earlier that the weapons sales from the Stalinist regime were over. They even managed to get the weapons delivered with military action in

Iraq looming, and despite the fact that they were intercepted by Spain. One can imagine what Communist China, with a much better and less deserving reputation in international affairs, would be able to accomplish. Of course, the People's Republic did quite a bit to justify such imaginations – no matter how dark – with its nearly successful shipment of patrol craft armed with missile launchers to Ba'athist Iraq, without any negative consequences.

This does not even address the three nations whose support for terrorism and opposition to America is already well documented: the aforementioned Libya, Syria, or Sudan. At present, all three have been relatively quiet after September 11, 2001. In some cases, they have even been cooperative. In others, however, they are still advancing anti-American interests, with Communist China and its Stalinist ally providing aid through the sale of weapons, missile parts, and military technology. To some extent, they, like Russia, can provide a blueprint for future regimes in balancing the United States, Communist China, and terrorist groups.

This is not a balance that is in America's best interests. A policy of "engagement" with Communist China not only allows the People's Republic more time to marshal its military and geopolitical forces against America, it enables regimes such as these to avoid tough choices about whom they will support when the United States finally does see the Communist regime for what it really is. A tough, anti-Communist policy would go a long way toward convincing regimes such as these that Communist China is the wrong place to look for a friend. It may also encourage in particular the Saudis, the UAE, and Yemen to choose to end terrorist ties and terrorist groups in their nations, rather than seek out Communist China as a possible cover to continue them.

Despite the obvious and necessary focus on the axis of evil, other regimes that currently back terror, either explicitly or vaguely, should – and to be fair, likely already do – have America's attention. Their current and possible future ties to Communist China must be a part of the equation in the diplomatic side of the war on terror. The People's Republic has a number of potential replacements for Iraq, and if need be, Iran. If Communist China is able to forge new ties in the Middle East, the terrorist war will become longer and much more difficult. Continuing the policy of "engagement" would make it all the more difficult to stop these ties from being formed. Ending "engagement" in favor of a policy that recognizes the People's Republic for the enemy it is would make it all the more difficult for the Communists to form those and maintain those ties in the first place.

In fighting the terrorist war, Cold War II is not a distraction. Communist China has brought them together numerous times, in many of its policies, arms deals, and public statements. It is bound to continue to do so in its efforts to find "checks" against the United States. Thanks to these actions, the two wars are intricately connected. America cannot ignore this fact in the fog of "engagement." To win the terrorist war, and assure that Communist diplomatic maneuvering does not force America to lose the gains it has acquired in blood, fighting and winning Cold War II is essential. The possibilities for Communist China in Saudi Arabia, the UAE, and Yemen alone should be enough to shake America from its complacency.

The United States did not ask for the terrorist war, and it did not ask for Cold War II either. It certainly did not ask for them to be so deeply intertwined and connected. However, al Qaeda, Iraq, Iran, *et al*, did ask for the terrorist war, and Communist China is fighting Cold War II as we speak. If we do not win Cold War II, we could easily lose gains made in the war on terror, and find ourselves back at the geopolitical equivalent of square one. The United States cannot afford to make such a mistake.

D.J. McGuire

Chapter 6:
East Turkestan – the Communists' Big Lie on Terrorism

When Osama bin Laden declared war on the United States in 1996, he predicted a "clash of civilizations," in which the Western world, particularly the United States, would find itself at war with all followers of Islam. After September 11, 2001, many predicted just such a "clash of civilizations" was inevitable, citing the praise and celebrations Osama won from Muslim radicals from Palestine to the Philippines. Even after the United States helped to liberate Afghanistan, winning high praise from the Afghans themselves, Osama's demand cum prediction for a Western-Muslim world war seemed likely to many analysts.

Throughout this entire time, however, from the moment the World Trade Center fell and the Pentagon was hit on September 11, 2001, and even through the few dark days of the Afghan conflict – after the American bombing had begun but before the first Taliban-held city fell – one Muslim ethnic group has been uniformly, steadfastly, and whenever possible, loudly pro-American throughout. Sadly, that voice was continuously muffled by the brutal Communist Chinese dictatorship, so much so that few Americans are even aware of this group – one that can arguably claim itself as America's best Muslim friends in the world, and would feel no dishonor in it.

This brutally persecuted, largely unknown, and America-loving people are the Uighurs of the formerly independent East Turkestan. They have suffered for over five decades (the People's Republic of China has even imposed its own name on the region – Xinjiang). Their quest for independence and human rights has gone largely unnoticed in America and the rest of the West, in large part due to a lack of religious fervor that has endeared Tibetan resistance to the outside world. This is not to disparage the devout Buddhist followers of the Dalai Lama; it *does* point out the painful irony that the Uighurs' resistance to radicalized Islam, which normally would establish it as a well-known symbol of how Muslims can adapt to the modern world, is the very thing that has muffled their ability to get the world's attention to their horrible plight. In fact, it even made it easier for Communist China to spread its big lie around the world: that the Uighur resistance to its reign of terror is intimately tied to Osama bin Laden and al Qaeda. While most who know of the situation in East Turkestan find the notion laughable, the People's Republic was able to convince the United States to tag one group – the East Turkestan Islamic Movement (ETIM), which may not have even set foot in the troubled former independent republic – as a terrorist group. This led many to believe that the United States believes the Communist line, and approves of its brutal campaign – and worse, had led many casual observers to accept the Communist line, even after the United States refuted it this past December.

Far from the Osama-loving terrorists in the Communist portrayal, the Uighurs are deeply supportive of the United States. The combination of relentless Communist anti-American propaganda, which has not lightened up nearly as much as many would like to believe, and their traditional lack of radicalism have made the Uighurs fervently pro-American.

This chapter, however, is not here merely to reveal the plight of the Uighurs for the purpose of winning them international sympathy (although it certainly was *one* of those reasons for the chapter and, it is hoped, a likely result of it). This chapter will also dispel a number of myths about both the terrorist war and Communist China's role within it. The insistence of the People's Republic that America, and Americans, can count on it as an ally in the war on terror – and empathize with it as a victim of terror – is based almost entirely on how it describes the situation in East Turkestan. The Communists have relied on muzzling all opposition to its rule in this region, and the world's memory of September 11, 2001, to hide the truth about East Turkestan. The Communists' line has also allowed them to continue its numerous acts of supporting regimes that sponsor terror – their alliance with North Korea, their arms deals with Iran, Ba'athist Iraq, Syria, and Libya, their outreach to the Taliban, and their unstinting support of Pakistan – without anyone challenging them. After all, how could Communist China be considered a regime of suspicion in the war on terror – or, even worse, an outright enemy – if it is suffering from terrorism itself, sponsored by bin Laden, no less?

The truth about East Turkestan exposes the Communist line as bunk, and put the rest of Communist China's actions in a far more honest and suspicious light. If the People's Republic were itself a victim of real terror, that fact could be used as a way to prod them away from its ties to other terrorist regimes. If, as is really happening, Communist China is merely using the war as cover to repress an independent nation it has conquered, then weaning the Communists off their ties to real terrorism is ridiculous to assume, and the anti-Americanism of Communist policies comes much more into focus. In short, the truth about East Turkestan reveals the truth about Communist China and the terrorist war – it is not a fellow victim and ally in the war to protect America from terrorists, but a cynical liar and exploiter of the war against America by using the terrorist attacks as a cover.

In fact, whatever violence has occurred in the region, and even the Communists reports are scattered, come with little evidence of links even to East Turkestan independence groups, let alone Osama bin Laden and al Qaeda. Even the United States calling the ETIM a terrorist group was badly undermined when word got out that ETIM may never have actually reached East Turkestan. Only one East Turkestan group has acknowledged a terrorist act, and it wasn't ETIM. It was the Organization for Turkestan Freedom (OTF), a group based in Turkey that bombed a Beijing bus in 1997, and most found that claim "didn't ring true."

In order to best understand the struggle for freedom in East Turkestan, it is best to look to the past. In many respects, the Uighurs were the first people to be betrayed by the Communists – although the rest of the population under control of the Chinese Communist Party took it on the chin quite quickly thereafter.

For centuries, the Turkic peoples of the region had their own nation, until the Chinese empire conquered in it the 1700s. After a brief stint at independence in the mid-19th century, the Chinese conquered the region again, and renamed it "Sinkiang" in the 1880s (the modern version of that name is "Xinjiang"). The East Turkestan Republic, after a very brief life in 1933, was founded again in 1944, carved out of the then-Republic of China in the midst of World War II.

What happened between 1944 and 1949 is less than perfectly clear. According to one account, East Turkestan largely governed itself, until the Communists drove the Nationalist government of Chiang Kai-shek to Taiwan in 1949. According to another, its self-rule was undermined by the very regime that helped bring it forward, the Soviet Union. In either event, the Communist victory over the Nationalists dramatically changed the political landscape.

Unlike Tibet, then outside the Communist orbit and determined to stay that way, the East Turkestani leadership was open to autonomy within the People's Republic. Several leaders of East Turkestan prepared to visit Beijing (then Peking) to meet with Mao and the Communist leadership. Mao himself had high praise for the Uighur leaders, saying, "Many years of your struggle is one of the component of whole Chinese people's democratic revolutionary movement."

It didn't take long for Mao and his henchmen to decide that some components were more important than others. After most of the East Turkestani leadership died in a plane crash on August 27, 1949, the Communists began taking apart the East Turkestan state. In many respects, East Turkestan became the first victim of Communist repression and betrayal.

During the next forty years, the Uighurs suffering was similar to that of everyone else in areas controlled by the Chinese Communists, with one horrifying addition– nuclear testing. Communist China detonated over forty nuclear weapons in the former independent republic – almost all of them above ground until 1980, the rest underground. Communist China has refused to let anyone they can't control examine the possible loss of life and health due to the repeated nuclear fallout. The closest thing we have to an estimate comes from a number of sources cited by the Eastern Turkestan Union (ETU) in Europe – which put the figure at 210,000 in East Turkestan killed by the nuclear testing. They were not the only victims. The same reports cited by the ETU put the number of cancer sufferers in the former independent state at *1 in 10*. The Communists' own hospital in Urumqi, where the capital of the puppet regime in the "autonomous region," has admitted to thousands of reported cases of cancer annually.

The Communist repression against the Uighurs included the usual crackdown against religious and ethnic freedoms. Communist China only allows five religions, all of which are beholden to the Communists, and Islam is one of these "patriotic" religions. Muslim clerics are not allowed to speak out of turn, or try to move away from Communist propaganda to speak for the people in their mosque. If they do, they risk jail, or worse.

Then, came June 4, 1989, and as with nearly everything else in Communist China, the Tiananmen Square protests utterly changed the fate of East Turkestan and the Uighur people. The fate of what the Communists called the "counter-revolutionary rebellion" in Beijing made it clear to anyone that peaceful resistance to Communism in China would be met with violent force. It also gave Communists throughout the People's Republic the excuse they needed to wipe out dissidents under the guise of eliminating a "counter-revolutionary rebellion."

True to form, in 1990, the local Communist regime banned the construction of all mosques in the region. Soon after, the Communists closed down a mosque just before a religious festival. On April 4, a small protest in the town of Baren – with at most 200 people – called for more religious freedom, and a day later lead a public prayer service of about 2,000. The Communists called the prayer service a "counter-revolutionary rebellion," and sent in the armed police.

The Uighurs, who saw a prayer service being transformed into a Communist mini-massacre, decided to fight back, taking control of the town from the police, and declaring the return of the independent Republic of East

Turkestan. According to the ETU, nine other small towns joined in the new fight for independence.

It didn't last particularly long. Within days the military was called in, with "air cover," i.e., bombers, behind them. Against at most 2,000 freedom fighters, Communist forces were sent in over 200,000 soldiers. The towns were bombed, and the resistance was wiped. According to the ETU, even the Communist-appointed "Governor" of the region was appalled by the carnage.

From that point forward, any political opposition to the Communists in East Turkestan became "splittist," "separatist," and eventually, "terrorist." Thousands of Uighurs were jailed, and a number of them were executed, for their political beliefs. Killing Uighur dissidents is one of the main reasons Communist China has earned the dubious honor of executing more people than the rest of the world *combined*. A mass arrest in early February 1997 in Yining led to a protest on February 5. According to one eyewitness account, the Communists responded with water hoses and bullets, killing hundreds. According to the BBC, the number of protesters arrested was "between 3,000 and 5,000." Twelve of the organizers were executed. The Communists put the number lost at nine and renamed the protests a "riot." One of those arrested, Abduhelil Abdulmejit, died in prison three and a half years later. The Communists said he died of pneumonia, and buried him without allowing anyone, including the Abdulmejit's family, to see his body.

Throughout the remainder of the twentieth century, the crackdown against dissidents intensified dramatically. Over half a million Uighurs fled. In 1999, one of the most respected Uighur women in East Turkestan, Rebiya Kadeer, mailed newspaper articles from the region to her husband, an anti-

Communist activist living in exile in the United States. The Communists had highly praised Kadeer in the past, allowing her to run a "private" business, and using her as a symbol of the modern, "patriotic," Uighur in the People's Republic.

Once they caught wind of her sending out articles, the Communists changed their tune. They jailed her for "leaking state secrets," which outside Communist China is not a normal term for newspaper articles. Later arrests, such as those of university professor Li Shaomin and researcher Gao Zhan, would reveal that "state secrets" – in this case books and magazine articles – effectively means anything that Communist China finds embarrassing. Kadeer's relatives in America, the House of Representatives, and human rights activists all called for her release, specifically citing her health (she suffers from heart disease). It was to no avail; Kadeer remains behind bars in a Communist prison to this very day.

As for the supposed acts of terror in East Turkestan, the most the Communist can point to are the "riots" of 1997, the aforementioned OTF's questionable bus bombing claim, reports of other bus bombings in that year, and the 1990 "battle" of Baren. Outside of that, all that has been reported are random whispers of various attacks, all of which were few and far between, and none of which were tied to a larger terrorist organization. This is not meant to belittle those attacks that did occur, particularly the 1997 bombing, or to excuse them. It *does* cast doubt on the Communist claims of a region-wide terrorist network, doubt shared by many analysts and diplomats both inside and outside East Turkestan.

To be sure, there have been events in the region. In September of 2000, a military truck exploded in Urumqi, killing 73 people and injuring 300 more. Initially, the Communists were silent about what happened, giving the world media time to remind everyone about the "violent" anti-Communist independence movement in the region. A few days after the incident, after the world had been inundated with the Communist propaganda, the People's Republic came forward and admitted it had been a military accident. Two months later, however, the Communists fired three newspaper editors in the region, including Yang Xiaofeng of *Lanzhou Daily*, for violating "news discipline," i.e., reporting and investigating the explosion independently – which leads one to wonder just what the Communists might have said about the incident if they were able to have complete control of the information. This is especially a concern given that Xinhua, the Communist Chinese news agency, had "remained very quiet about the circumstances of the explosion," according to Reporters Without Borders. That, along with the conflicting accounts of the 1990 and 1997 "riots," also makes one wonder about the 1997 bus bombing reports.

Up to this point, the situation in East Turkestan had garnered little, if any, attention from the outside world, and the Communists were more than happy to keep it that way. September 11, 2001 changed that. From almost the moment that World Trade Center fell, Communist China saw a chance to exploit American concern over Islamic terrorism. As the bombs fell on Taliban positions in Afghanistan, the Communists began to play their East Turkestan terrorist "card."

The first thing Communist China did was to dramatically inflate, and make much more sinister, its caricature of Uighur opposition to their rule. What had been local bandits largely under Communist control were magically transformed into menacing terrorists working with Osama bin Laden to destroy the People's Republic and every other nation that didn't support radical Islam.

The Communists also launched more "anti-terrorism" operations, including blowing up mosques and executions or life sentences for dissidents. Meanwhile, the People's Republic loudly demanded that the rest of the world support its crackdown in East Turkestan, no matter how brutal it may be, or how large the gap may be between the Communist claims of links between al Qaeda and East Turkestan and the actual evidence of such a link. In press conference after press conference, and declaration after declaration, Communist China repeatedly attempted to link the crushing of Uighur dissent in East Turkestan to the worldwide campaign against terrorism.

Communist China's hope that the rest of the world to fall in line with praise and support fell flat the first eleven months after September 11, 2001. There were several reasons for this. The most important reason was that the Communists dramatically overplayed their hand in the initial aftermath of that day. Rather than focus on simply the dubious situation in East Turkestan, Communist China tried to extend their quest for anti-terror justification to nearly *every* dissident issue they could find. Suddenly, if the Communists were to be believed, terrorism was commonplace not just in East Turkestan, but also in Tibet and among supporters of Taiwanese independence. Even Falun Gong, the religious movement suffering under a Communist crackdown since the summer of 1999, was slapped with the label "semi-terrorist." This led a number of people to be dubious about the Communists' claims. After all, if they were going to call supporters of Taiwanese independence "terrorists," who wasn't a terrorist in their eyes?

The truth about the crackdown in East Turkestan made things infinitely worse for the Communists. The United States Department of State, Amnesty International (AI), and the United Nations High

Commissioner for Human Rights all ripped the People's Republic for its "strike hard, severe suppression" campaign. The campaign included "thousands" of arrests, and so many hidden executions of political prisoners that AI itself couldn't get an accurate count of dissidents killed by Communist China.

The Communists also attacked the Uighur culture, and its Muslim faith, at every turn. In the summer of 2002, the People's Republic commanded Xinjiang University – named after the Communist term for East Turkestan – to stop teaching the Uighur language. The practice of Islam was banned on its grounds. According to one *Time Asia* report, "University officials forced 10 students secretly fasting during the holy month of Ramadan to march into the cafeteria and eat."

The Communists also used massive economic development projects, and the mass emigration that came with it, as part of its "Sinicization" policy for "Xinjiang." Under a policy with which Tibet watchers are infinitely familiar, the Communists have infused East Turkestan with large construction and other mass development, sent millions of ethnic Han Chinese as laborers and new residents, and directed the overwhelming majority of the economic benefits to the new arrivals. This has created a large and growing Chinese minority wholly dependent upon the Communist Party for its prosperity, while the increasingly embittered Uighur majority not allowed to practice its faith or its culture except under severe restrictions, and deprived of any economic or political advancement in the region they call home, and where they were once their own masters.

However, the most important flaw in the Communist propaganda campaign was the dearth of evidence the Communists put forward to back up their claims of al Qaeda activity and terrorism in East Turkestan. The problem for the Communist Chinese campaign began almost immediately, when the East Turkestan National Congress – one of the most well known East Turkestan human rights and independence groups – harshly condemned the terrorist attacks of September 11, 2001, and restated its goal of East Turkestan as an independent secular democracy. For almost a year, things went downhill from there for the Communists.

After the September 11, 2001 attacks, the Communists were putting specific numbers to their terror claims, but outside sources came up with very different numbers of their own. Since November of 2001, Communist Chinese officials put the number of al Qaeda trained terrorists at 1,000, all tied to bin Laden and a leading force behind the independence movement. Almost immediately after it was spoken, a spokesman for the People's Republic said he didn't really know how many al Qaeda terrorists were in East Turkestan. About a week later, the Communists were at it again, claiming "several hundred" Uighurs were al Qaeda terrorists – and boldly declared they had "hard evidence" to back them up. What was that hard evidence? They did not say. Meanwhile, diplomatic sources found the Communist numbers spurious, at best.

Just how little credibility the Communists had on the subject was revealed at the end of 2001, when reports came out that the United States had a "handful" of Uighurs among its prisoners from the liberation of Afghanistan. The Communists demanded that the United States hand the Uighurs over to them. The United States not only refused to hand them over, but stated the following reason, as reported by Stratfor: "(the United States government) does not recognize Uighur separatists as terrorists." It was a major departure from their handling of most other prisoners from

Afghanistan, and a damning indictment of the Communist effort to convince the world that the Uighurs were bin Ladenites.

As 2002 dawned, Communist China continued to claim that the Uighurs were all supporters of Osama bin Laden. In January of 2002, the People's Republic released a report providing its most detailed charges up to that time of terrorism in East Turkestan, claiming that "terrorists" had killed 162 people, and injured 400 more, in 200 "incidents." The Communists also claimed that Osama met the leader of the East Turkestan Islamic Movement in 1999. It was the first time the Communists mentioned ETIM.

All the while, source outside Communist China were looking at the Communist claims and dismissing them, repeatedly saying that any terrorists in East Turkestan are few and far between, and that almost all of the people arrested, imprisoned, or executed by Communist China were peaceful, political dissidents. Dru Gladney, a specialist on East Turkestan from the University of Hawaii, noted this as well: "When you talk to the Uighurs and the organizations, they always come back and say, 'No, Islam is one issue among many,'" such as "sovereignty and human rights." This would not be expected to come from fervent supporters of Osama bin Laden.

In the summer of 2002, history repeated itself, as East Turkestan supporters were hit once again with the terrorist label for an incident completely unconnected to them. At the end of June, a Communist Chinese diplomat in Kyrgyzstan was shot in the Kyrgyz capital of Bishkek. The consul and his driver died. Initially, Kyrgyz security officials said the incident *might* be related to the anti-Communist Uighur independence movement. From there, Russian media tied the murder to a group called Free Turkestan, of which no one had previously heard (in fairness, they might have meant OTF). The East Turkestan terrorist line on the murder went around the world for three days. Then Kyrgyz officials – who had neither mentioned Free Turkestan nor said for certain that the murder was political in nature – announced that the *driver*, not the diplomat, was the target, and that the murder was over a "criminal dispute." The Kyrgyz Interior Minister himself announced that there had been no political issue behind the killings.

However, in August of 2002, after a year of trying, the People's Republic finally scored its coup – the United States agreed that the East Turkestan Islamic Movement was a terrorist organization. It was quite a diplomatic victory, but became pyrrhic very quickly.

For the most part, the evidence behind the American move appeared to be based on the numerous Communist reports from January. It also seemed to have a lot to do with two other factors completely unrelated to East Turkestan: Communist Chinese weapons proliferation and Iraq. The fact that ETIM label of terrorist came from the United States just as Saddam Hussein's Foreign Minister was making an appearance in Beijing also raised a few eyebrows. For most of 2002, as the United States turned from Afghanistan to Iraq, the Communists were hoping to use their potential veto in United Nations Security Council to wring concessions out of President Bush, and this certainly could have been one of them. Additionally, at roughly the same time the United States announced its position on ETIM, word came out of a new, supposedly tighter, Communist policy on weapons sales. It would soon become apparent that this supposed tightening would go the way of previous pledges to restrict arms sales to terrorists and states that sponsor terrorism, pledges that continue to go unfulfilled to this day.

Whether or not an the implicit *quid pro quo* was involved, the United States began parroting the Communist line on the ETIM within days of the announcement. They even included to the very statistics the Communists used from January. Now, they were all laid at the foot of the mysterious ETIM. The United States also insisted that East Turkestani terrorists were responsible for a planned attack on the American Embassy in Bishkek, Kyrgyzstan, despite the fact that Kyrgyz authorities themselves were less than certain about the claim.

As the first anniversary of September 11, 2001 came and went, the United Nations (UN) agreed to list ETIM as a terrorist organization – at the request of the United States, Communist China, and Kyrgyzstan. The Communists were gleeful, hoping that this could "blunt Western criticism of Chinese efforts to stamp out Xinjiang separatism," as CNN analyst Willy Wo-Lap Lam put it. Of course, they meant *all* separatists, violent or peaceful, and any other dissident they could throw in for good measure. They were soon to be disappointed.

Later that month, Communist China announced that it had "smashed" roughly 40 ETIM bases in East Turkestan. The announcement would have been far more effective in advancing the Communist line on the entire region but for two factors: a complete lack of evidence backing up their assertion, and a stunning report out of *Time Asia* on the ETIM. The magazine's sources revealed ETIM as "an Afghanistan-based group that is thought to be defunct and moreover never carried out operations on Chinese soil." Suddenly, the line on ETIM and its terrorist role in East Turkestan that had won over the Americans looked a lot like more Communist snake oil.

About a week before the word of ETIM's demise hit the press, the Communists put the word out that they would likely avoid vetoing any UN resolution by itself, preferring instead to allow France and Russia to lead opposition to the United States in the Security Council – a fact that was validated when the People's Republic joined in the 15-0 November Security Council vote against Iraq. It is doubtful that the two were related, but the Communists certainly timed it well.

While no correlation can be found with American policy either, it certainly didn't take the United States very long to revert back to its pre-August policy on East Turkestan in general – whatever the statements on ETIM. As then-Communist President Jiang Zemin – fresh from waxing his rivals in a planned Communist leadership reshuffle – came to Crawford, Texas to meet with President Bush at the latter's ranch, he called his country, again, a "victim" of terrorism. President Bush used the summit press conference to tell Jiang, and the rest of the world, "(N)o country should suppress the rights of ethnic minorities under the pretext of fighting terrorism." Among Communist China and East Turkestan watchers, everyone knew exactly what he meant.

Two months later in December of 2002, Lorne Craner, Assistant Secretary of State – and the top United States human rights official – visited East Turkestan and publicly refuted the Communist claims on the Uighurs: "It is our understanding that our decision on ETIM is being presented by some Chinese officials as a licence (British sp) – that the US has bought into the notion that Uighurs are terrorists. We want to dispel that notion."

The dearth of Communist evidence to back up their claims of mass al Qaeda support among the Uighur people was no surprise to those who have examined East Turkestan for quite some time. In order to be fertile ground for Osama bin Laden, an ethnic group must be more than simply Muslim. It must also have a wide following for radical Islam, particularly of the Wahhabism that drove bin Laden himself to start al Qaeda. There must also be a wide and deep anti-Americanism – the lack of which in Afghanistan led to the rapid fall of the Taliban. Without at least one of these characteristics, a Muslim group is not likely to embrace al Qaeda, and many who have examined East Turkestan have found is that the Uighur people have neither of them.

The Communist Chinese campaign began being undermined almost immediately when the East Turkestan National Congress blasted the terrorist attacks of September 11, 2001, and made sure the world was aware that its vision for East Turkestan was an independent, secular democracy. In time, Western media found that this was neither an accident nor a ploy, but a perfectly representative statement of a people that were arguably the most pro-American Muslims on the face of the earth.

The first American media source to peek behind the Communist curtain was the *Washington Post*. What *Post* reporter John Pomfret found was nothing like what the People's Republic advertised. For starters, unlike the halls of Communist Chinese universities and corridors of power, the streets of East Turkestan were heavily pro-American. Pomfret's story hit the press in the middle of October, when the bombing had just started, no major cities had been liberated, and the Taliban was loudly broadcasting reports – later refuted – of civilian massacres. At the time, criticism of the United States throughout the world, but especially in the Muslim world, was quite high. Pomfret visited two of the more religiously minded cities in East Turkestan – where one would expect Muslims to be more critical of the United States – and found that "head scarves patterned after the United

143

States flag are sold in the streets." Whatever anger there was at Communist China – and Pomfret found quite a bit – almost none of it was transferred to the United States. Instead, he found support for the United States throughout the region.

As Pomfret accounts went to print, the Communists destroyed another mosque in the East Turkestan town of Hotan – the third it razed to the ground that year. About 180 local residents protested the destruction – the Communists arrested them all.

Meanwhile, *Asiaweek* threw more cold water on the Communist campaign – again from East Turkestan itself. Ron Gluckman called the Communist rule of East Turkestan "an apartheid-like state." Meanwhile, on reports of terrorism, he cited the aforementioned University of Hawaii analyst Dru Gladney: "Even official Chinese reports list only a few small incidents, very spread out. It really doesn't seem to indicate some terrorist network." Thus Communist China's own reports on the East Turkestan situation undermined its very claims of a terrorist network tied to Osama bin Laden.

The most damning information comes at the end of the piece, regarding the views of the Uighur people. Once again, the Uighurs made clear where they stand, with the United States, not al Qaeda: "A common sentiment expressed isn't that the United States should halt the war. In fact, many wish it would be extended." Gluckman ends with this telling comment from a Uighur student, *"They should go on bombing. We just wish they would bomb China* (Emphasis added)."

In October 2002, the *Washington Times* took its own look at East Turkestan, and found the Uighurs, according to specialists it cited, "among the most liberal and pro-United States Muslims in the world." In the same story, it noted that Human Rights Watch found Communist claims of ties between al Qaeda and the Uighur independence movement "spurious," and that those few Uighurs in Afghanistan came "on an individual basis and had no connection to al Qaeda."

Given that al Qaeda members tend to boast of their affiliation, and that Human Rights Watch later became one of the few human rights organizations to lambaste the Palestinian Authority (PA) for its "unwillingness to…deter the suicide bombings, particularly in 2001, when the PA was most capable of doing so," its observations carry a powerful refutation to Communist China's insistence that al Qaeda terrorists are behind the East Turkestan independence movement.

What the media and others found, in everything from statements by the Uighurs themselves to the Communists' own data on the subject, was clear – the Uighur people are clearly pro-American, and a barren wasteland for al Qaeda. This should not be as surprising as it sounds. One must remember that East Turkestan is a nation suffering under a brutal Communist dictatorship – a dictatorship that has included heavy nationalism as part of its propaganda machine, and numerous anti-American policy decisions as part of Cold War II. The experience of Eastern Europe, which suffered enormously under Soviet dictatorship from 1945 until 1989, is telling. Today, some of our strongest supporters since 1991 – including in the war on terror – come from the former Soviet block in Eastern Europe.

Like the nations of Eastern Europe, the Uighur Muslims have suffered bitterly under Communism. As such, they are much more likely to see the United States as their potential liberator, rather than as their oppressor. The liberation of Afghanistan also pointed to this. The Afghan people did not see the United States in the same way they saw the Soviet army in the 1980s, especially since the United States was the major financial backer of the anti-Soviet *mujahedin*. That ensured, at the very least, a greater willingness on their part to help us against Osama's bitterly hated al Qaeda "guests."

As mentioned above, the Uighur people of East Turkestan were the first victims of Communist betrayal. Before Mao had even begun the mass persecution of his own people, he was undermining the formerly independent East Turkestan, filling its government and party posts with lackeys loyal to him and the Chinese Communist line, and purging any opponents. The "anti-rightist campaign", the "great leap forward," and the bloody Cultural Revolution all had precedents in the Communist co-opting of East Turkestan. Having been betrayed and persecuted by Communist China for decades the Uighurs naturally looked "to the United States to provide moral support in their fight against oppression by Beijing." This appeared to continue even despite the ETIM issue.

Another reason for the strong pro-American feeling of the Uighurs has to do with the people themselves. Like a number of Central Asian ethnic groups, the Uighurs of East Turkestan predominantly follow a much more moderate version of Islam than the Wahhabism of the Saudis. This has made it a less-than-perfect breeding ground for terrorism and terrorist groups. ETIM may actually be the exception that proves the rule. The fact that the only Uighur organization the United States has called a terrorist group was based *outside* East Turkestan, likely never set foot in the place, and is probably out of existence is in and of itself the best indication of terrorism's lack of appeal with the East Turkestani people.

In fact, it may be this very moderation in Islam that has led to the Uighurs' inability, at least in part, to spread the message of their persecution to the rest of the world. In neighboring Tibet, the deep religious reverence for the Dalai Lama has been the uniting force that enabled the Tibetan government in exile to continue its resistance to Communism for over four decades. It has also led to support from throughout the world, from all corners of life and along every inch of the political spectrum: from conservative anti-Communist Republicans to the liberal Hollywood *glitterati*.

The best example of this came just last December, when two ethnic Tibetans from a part of Tibet the Communists transferred into Sichuan province received death sentences for their supposed roles in bomb explosions in Sichuan's provincial capital. Human rights groups challenged the convictions immediately, and the media quickly reported their reaction. The fact that one of the defendants was a well-known student of the Dalai Lama did quite a bit of damage to the Communist propaganda effort.

Given the nature of the Tibetan Buddhism exemplified by the Dalai Lama, most find the reverence and deep faith of the Tibetan people as both comforting and inspiring. The Middle East long ago made many in the world much more nervous about fervent Islamic faith. The moderation of the Uighur people has made it very resistant to the various strains of radical Islam. Unfortunately, given the decentralized traditions of Uighur Islam, the energy that fuels Tibet's cause is not available to East Turkestan. Although the Communists have treated the Uighurs with the same persecution, heavy-handedness, and cynical manipulation they have shelled out to every other faith in the People's Republic, the very thing that has made the Uighurs barren ground for Islamic terrorists, has also made it much more difficult to get out the truth of the brutal Communist crackdown.

Some might wonder why Communist China has spent so much time trying to suppress the independence movement in East Turkestan. There are several reasons. First the Uighurs of East Turkestan are blessed – although "cursed" may seem more appropriate given the events of the past half-century – with living in a nation of vast energy resources. Coal, oil, and natural gas are all over East Turkestan, and Communist China is desperate to exploit those resources to fuel its economy, which must grow at a rate of over seven percent a year just to keep up with population growth. Communist China cannot afford to see those resources in the hands of a Muslim group who would likely be closer to Central Asian nations – some of whom are now American allies – than to Beijing.

There is also an obvious political reason for the campaign of repression by the People's Republic. Just south of East Turkestan is Tibet, the more famous conquered nation under Communist Chinese control. The People's Republic claims that both nations have been under Chinese ruler throughout history. In reality, they were independent until the 18th century. In fact, the very name the Communists give East Turkestan ("Xinjiang," which means "new dominion") betrays the lack of historical validity to the claims of Chinese domination of these nations going back for millennia.

Backing down in East Turkestan would make keeping control of Tibet – which had a recent history of independence that lasted forty years (1911-1951) in comparison to East Turkestan's five (1944-1949) – much more difficult, if not impossible. The Communists may be able to let Tibet go – not that they want to do so – and still hang on to the more anonymous East Turkestan. It is impossible for them to do the reverse.

This viewpoint will not change now that Jiang Zemin has ceded some of his power to Hu Jintao, another false dawn for "engagement" supporters. In fact, it could make the situation worse for both peoples. The Tiananmen Square massacre occurred during Hu's tenure as Tibet party chief (1988-1992). In response, Hu engineered a mini-Tiananmen in his own; the crackdown he unleashed led to a slew of tortures and deaths, and has made a number of Tibet watchers understandably skeptical about his aims. The last thing Hu can be expected to do is undermine the Communists' claims to Tibet, for it would undermine one the very things that brought him to Beijing and on the fast track to power – Hu went from Tibet party head to Deng Xiaoping-anointed Politburo Standing Committee member in 1992. This, in combination with the slew of Central Committee seats for "Xinjiang" party and military officials – all but one of whom are Han Chinese, not Uighur – makes it all but certain that the crackdown against the Uighur people will continue, if not intensify.

This does not even take into account the myriad of other ethnic minorities in the People's Republic. The Communists have to worry about them as well. Although rebellions from ethnic minorities can win the Communists support among ethnic Chinese, Communists will always choose total control over a rebellion that may be exploited here and there. Losing East Turkestan, or Tibet for that matter, could embolden those other minorities to rebel against Communist domination – and should they ever manage to reach out to ethnic Chinese dissidents on a large scale (the Dalai Lama has been more active than most in this regard), the Communists are in real trouble.

The Communists also finds East Turkestan an exceedingly useful place to exert greater control over their ethnic Chinese population. Over the last half-century, the Communists have sent millions of ethnic Chinese into East Turkestan, either for military service, as Communist officials, or to lead and work on economic development projects. This ethnic Chinese migrant population, which rose from less than one million in East Turkestan in 1949 to well over six million today, is largely dependent on Communist China for their prosperity and their livelihood. As such, one would be hard pressed to find *any* ethnic Chinese dissidents in East Turkestan, or any other region where ethnic Chinese are in the minority. Reports of terrorism, even overblown ones, can certainly be counted on to increase the dependence of these ethnic Chinese migrants to the Communist leadership.

The final reason for the Communists' determination to hold onto East Turkestan is its nationalist agenda. Communist China has used nationalism as a crutch to maintain power after the collapse of Deng Xiaoping's partial-reform rationale in 1989. With the bloody crushing of the Tiananmen protests, the Communist Party desperately needed another ideological structure on which to build its *raison d'etre*. Marxism had fallen by the wayside with the death of Chairman Mao in 1976, and the combination of economic development and minor economic reforms died thirteen years later – with thousands of protestors.

That left nationalism as the last refuge for the Communists, and they have exploited it to the hilt. A combination of genuine ill-treatment by some foreign nations, such as the Japanese occupation before and during World War II, and some rather spurious Communist claims of being slighted, such as the Korean War, have given the Communists a very powerful propaganda weapon in its battle to convince its own people that its reign should be continued. While it certainly has not convinced the Chinese people of their supremacy as political rulers – the mass corruption nationwide and complete deprivation of the rural interior painfully belies that notion – it has enabled the Communists to don the garb of national protector.

The nationalist card is critical to the Communists' survival. As such, it is certainly clear that *without* East Turkestan, all bets are off; the Communist nationalist mantra would exposed as a lie, and the number of Chinese people who would wonder if the nationalism was worth the deprivation, brutality, *et al* would reach a critical mass. The Communists are terrified that this might already be happening in regards to Taiwan, over which they have no actual power, and must resort to threats and business deals in a clumsy (and largely unsuccessful) attempt to win over the Taiwanese people. In East Turkestan, where the Communists *do* have the power to quiet dissent – they will certainly continue to pull out every stop.

The recent "reshuffle" during last fall's Communist Party Congress revealed the extent to which Communist China is ready to keep East Turkestan, and silence all opposition forces in the formerly independent nation. For the first time in anyone's memory, the Communist Party Secretary (i.e., the party leader) in "Xinjiang," Wang Lequan, won a seat on the Chinese Communist Party's Central Committee, as did his vice party secretary, Zhou Shengtao. Three Communist generals from the military district that includes East Turkestan also landed Central Committee slots – Li Qianyuan, Liu Dongdong, and Chang Wanquan. The "governor" of "Xinjiang," Ablait Abdureschit – the only native Uighur in the group – was also placed on the Central Committee.

The Communist objective in East Turkestan is clear – not defeating terrorism, but stifling all dissent. Terrorism is simply a convenient excuse, and Islamic terrorism is much more of a convenient one in the aftermath of September 11, 2001. This is not to excuse terrorism, in any way shape or form. East Turkestan independence groups themselves have been more than willing to condemn terrorism. The problem in dealing with East Turkestan is that the actual information on terrorist acts largely comes from one source: Communist China – a source with a history of bending, folding, spindling, and mutilating the truth whenever it suits its purposes.

The Communists have themselves unwittingly provided two very recent examples of their willingness to label any dissenter as a "terrorist." The first is the aforementioned Tibetan bombing trial. The second involves Wang Bingzhang, a Chinese dissident who was exiled in 1979. Wang attempted to meet with labor dissidents in the summer of 2002, and was never seen again until nearly six months later, when Communist China sentenced him to life in prison. Wang's supposed crimes included the usual Communist espionage charge: giving "state secrets" to Taiwan, but this time the People's Republic added more outlandish claims. Communist China claimed Wang had tried to organize a terrorist cell in Thailand and blow up the Communist embassy there. He was even accused of plotting bombings and assassinations of Communist cadres in 1999 – while still in exile in the United States

These and other examples of Communist China's use of colossal falsehoods to silence dissidents have led many to echo this question from the editors of the *Washington Post*: "given its secrecy and media control, how much trust or confidence can there be in the (Communist) regime's descriptions of violent Muslim separatism in its western regions?"

It doesn't help when outside experts in the region, almost unanimously, call the Communist claims and charges untrue. This consensus runs the ideological gamut – from Jesse Helms, who spent thirty years in the United States Senate as one of its most conservative members, to human rights groups such as AI. Even groups such as Human Rights Watch, which criticized Yassir Arafat and the PA on its complicity in allowing suicide bombers to run rampant throughout Israel, the West Bank, and Gaza, are not buying the Communist line on East Turkestan.

Sadly, different people use different standards to describe terrorism. Europeans have usually been less willing to define the PA's al Aqsa brigade – one of the lead suicide bomb squads – as terrorists. The people of Chechnya were largely considered anything but terrorists until the invasion of Dagestan in 1999 revealed a movement far more radicalized than anyone outside of Russia had previously suspected. Communist China was certainly looking forward to such a re-evaluation on East Turkestan. Outside of the ETIM, it has not gotten it, and the efforts to expand it beyond ETIM have fallen flat. The American people, having seen numerous critics throughout the world refuse to agree with them on who is and who isn't a terrorist, have developed a healthy inclination to dismiss those who would challenge assertions of terrorism. What they should know is that even those with common sense definitions of terrorism look at East Turkestan, and the people who actually live there trying to resist the Communist persecution under which they are suffering, and simply do not see terrorism. This includes, at least according to Assistant Secretary of State Craner, the United States government itself.

Ever since September 11, 2001, the Communists have tried, desperately, to make its repression of the Uighur people equivalent to the American war on terror. Armed with enough propaganda, the continuous elimination of dissent, the power of a possible Security Council veto regarding Iraq, and its specious promises to end its weapons sales to terrorist sponsors, Communist China very nearly achieved their goal this past August.

Yet, to quote John Adams, "facts are stubborn things," and the facts have stubbornly obstructed Communist efforts to tar all East Turkestan dissidents as terrorists. Even as the People's Republic attempted to use the ETIM terrorism label to justify its claims of widespread bin Ladenism throughout East Turkestan, the United States has pointedly, if quietly, refused to go along.

This has not reduced the suffering in East Turkestan, however. The religious persecution, execution of political prisoners, and the economic exploitation – of the kind no free market would ever allow – in favor of waves upon waves of ethnic Chinese migrants sent there by the Communists to "Sinicize" the former independent republic continues apace. As America seeks allies, particularly among followers of Islam, in the terrorist war, one of the most pro-American Muslim ethnic groups on the planet is slowly, but viciously and bloodily, ground out of existence.

The people of East Turkestan, whose moderate Islam and pro-Americanism prove the outlandish Communist propaganda about them to be utterly false, deserve better. Few examples of American support for freedom in the Muslim world would be more enlightening then focusing on the plight of the Uighur people. Support of East Turkestan, would do more than simply earn points with followers of Islam. It would buttress an ethnic Muslim group that has been stubbornly resistant to radicalism, and give them hope and support in their fight for freedom against Communist China.

The war on terror gave the Communists the chance to declare itself a "victim" in common cause with the United States. However, the enemies America has fought and continues to fight during the war have proven extremely difficult for the Communists to use as a caricature model for the Uighurs of East Turkestan. As such, the great fig leaf they desired to cover their *real* objectives during the terrorist war has remained out of their reach.

Those who would consider Communist China an "ally" in the war on terrorism would do well to examine, repeatedly, just what Communist China calls terrorism. Mere days after it signed an economic agreement with al Qaeda's benefactors in Afghanistan, the People's Republic was suddenly seeing bin Laden supporters everywhere in East Turkestan. The history of the Uighurs, the history of the Communists, and the actual facts of the ground have shown otherwise. The question the United States must answer is this: will the terrorist war become the moment when America saw through the Communist charade and chose to help bring the Uighur people closer to freedom at the expense of a regime that has repeatedly sold arms and given geopolitical support to states that sponsor terror? Or will the Uighurs become another victim of "engagement"?

The answer to this question will certainly have a dramatic impact in Cold War II. What is less obvious, but just as true, is that it will also have a major impact in the war against terror. Helping the dissidents in East Turkestan will send a signal to moderate Muslims, and strike a blow against the People's Republic at the same time. The Uighurs are a reminder that the war on terror and Cold War II are about the same thing – the fight for freedom and the rule of law against the forces of tyranny and the reign of terror.

D.J. McGuire

Chapter 7:
Why Communist China Supports Our Enemies in the Terrorist War

On September 11, 2001 is a date that no American will ever forget. In contrast, June 4, 1989 is not a date that so dramatically sears the American consciousness. It is, however, a critical date in American history, one far more critical than most Americans realize. It is the date of the Tiananmen Square massacre; the date China changed forever; the date that the Chinese Communist Party dramatically reassessed its geopolitical situation.

To say the result was harmful to American interests would be a tremendous understatement; June 4, 1989 led the Communists to shift away from the first Cold War – between the Soviet Union and the United States – and lay the groundwork for Cold War II – between themselves and the United States. For this reason, the Communists see the war on terror as nothing more than another event in the midst of Cold War II, to be exploited wherever possible. In fact, America's enemies in the terrorist war are stronger today than they would be thanks to Cold War II, and Communist China's determination to win it.

Prior to June 4, 1989, the Chinese Communist Party was in the midst of partial reform of its economy, while at the same time gingerly moving towards political reform under the direction of two Communist Party General Secretaries – Hu Yaobang (1981-87) and his successor Zhao Ziyang (1987-1989). The plan was buttressed by warming ties between the People's Republic and the United States, due to the great suspicion each held for the Soviet Union's ambitions. In 1989, as the Soviets were losing their empire in Eastern Europe, the Chinese people began calling for political reform.

They made their most dramatic statement in the spring of that year. It began as student protest in Beijing against a Communist snub of the late Hu Yaobang, whose advocacy for political reform was a bit too strong for the cadres. By late May, it had grown into a nationwide demonstration for reform and democracy that spread to hundreds of cities and millions of people – over 1 million called for democracy in Tiananmen Square alone. The Communists were faced with the most dramatic challenge to its absolute rule since Mao brought them to power in 1949, and a monumental choice to make.

If it had followed the will of Zhao – Hu's successor as Party boss and, in the normal course of Communist politics, the leader of the People's Republic of China – the Communists would have looked for a peaceful solution. Zhao had been pushing for reform and democracy ever since he took over from Hu Yaobang. If he had the final say, the people's demands would have been heard, and the move to reform might have become irreversible. However, Zhao learned quickly that he did not have the final say at all.

That fell to the "behind-the-scenes" leader, Deng Xiaoping. Deng had taken power in 1978, and began a policy of steady economic development, haphazard political reform, and closer ties to the United States. As the 1980s progressed, Deng allowed others to take the role of Communist General Secretary while he wielded power from the post of Chairman of the Central Military Commission (CMC). This enabled him to replace Hu Yaobang with Zhao Ziyang in 1987. As the protestors descended upon Tiananmen Square and numerous other cities and towns in Communist China, Deng was still the authority in the People's Republic.

With that authority, on June 4, 1989, Deng made a fateful decision. Armed with the support of other "party elders" and then Premier Li Peng, Deng overrode both Zhao and the Politburo Standing Committee, and ordered the military to crush the protesters. Under the direction of Li, who had lobbied Deng heavily to come this decision, the military was sent into streets, and murdered thousands. To this day, no one knows the exact number of protestors who died on June 4, 1989. Thousands were under arrest, and many more fled for Hong Kong or the United States. The Communists forced Zhao to resign and placed him under house arrest; he has almost never been heard in public life since. His top aide Bao Tong was also arrested. Most importantly, political reform – in any way, shape, or form – was dead.

The Communists had preserved their power against the "counterrevolutionary" threat, but as a consequence, they were faced with a major problem at home. The regime's justification to its own people for its continued, unchallenged rule had literally been shot away. While this would normally not concern dictatorial regimes, the Chinese Communist party, like most Chinese, took a far longer view than dictators elsewhere. Authoritarians – dictators who focus on maintaining power and nothing else – are almost always temporary. *Totalitarians* – especially those that have devised an ideological rationale for their continued dominance – have far greater staying power. So long as the reasons for power still exist, a totalitarian regime can, and often did, create enough energy within itself to justify and fuel the brutality required to survive by terrifying the imprisoned population.

Further highlighting the problem was the fact that the Tiananmen protests were inspired and begun by students of Beijing University. To avoid a repeat performance, the Communists had to ensure that young Chinese were properly indoctrinated into the ideology that best suited Communist aims. In 1989, the Communists had gone through two worldviews to justify their place as the rulers of China. From 1949 to 1976, the rationale was Maoism, a bloodthirsty mix of Stalinism and Confucianism, with a strong anarchist dose thrown in during the Cultural Revolution. With Mao's death, and the rise of Deng, the Communists seized upon "reform" and economic development as the new rationale for its continued rule. This had the added advantage of actually improving the standard of living for some Chinese, giving the regime a boost of public support.

The Tiananmen massacre ended the charade of "reform," and as the 1990s progressed, the Communists came to realize that the economy alone was not enough to ensure long-term survival – particularly given the fact that much of it was limited to a handful of cities on the Pacific Coast. Outside of the Communist showpieces of Beijing, Shanghai, Shenzhen, and Hong Kong, the people of Communist China still suffer from mass poverty and deprivation. The overwhelming majority of the Chinese people – roughly 1 billion – live in the highly oppressed, abysmally impoverished rural interior, where the order of the day is massively corrupt local Communist regimes, failed state-run factories, unpaid wages and pensions, and brutal, violent repression of any dissent. Meanwhile, economic "development" outside the Pacific Coast has led to rampant ecological disasters, the forced displacement of millions, and promises of prosperity that have proved specious, at best. The conditions are so terrible it led to 100,000 *protests* –not protestors – in the year 1999 alone.

Another problem with economic development – even in the prosperous cities – is the rampant corruption within the Communist Party. Corrupt Communist officials number in the thousands. Hundreds were sent to jail, fired, or executed for their part in a multi-billion dollar smuggling scandal in the coastal city of Xiamen. It was by far the largest scandal in the history of Communist China – until a larger tax evasion scheme in neighboring Guangdong province was discovered less than a year later. Both scandals cleared the ten billion dollar mark (the Guangdong scheme hit twelve billion). The situation has become so grave that the Communists openly talk of corruption as being as issue that could end the Party's grip on power – a stunning admission from a regime who came to power in the belief that its continued, endless reign was inevitable.

The massive corruption, both among Communist themselves and their friends in supposedly "private" business – private property has no actual legal protection in the People's Republic, and in many cases must pay state-run firms to "rent" business licenses – has led to the embarrassing development of a Communist Party becoming a party representing interests of the wealthy few. The workers and farmers in Communist China have become political orphans in a state made in their name – the only labor union allowed is the one under the control of the very same Communist Party.

The final reason that economic growth could not be the *raison d'etre* for the Communist regime is that people have begun to stop believing the very growth figures upon which the Communists depended, and about which they have boasted for so many years. In fact, some outside economist have said PRC-wide economic growth figures are inflated by anywhere from 1% to 1.5%, at least. The Communists themselves have admitted to over sixty thousands of statistical errors over a period of *less than six months*. Thus, the economic justification for continuing Communist rule is undermined by the very metrics the Communists use, and abuse, to back up their claims.

For all these reasons – corruption, betrayal of labor rights, the plutocraticization of the Communist dictatorship, and lack of faith in the economist statistics – economic development as a justification for the continued rule of the Communist Party has clearly left a lot to be desired. What else could be offered as the reason for Communist rule by the barrel of a gun?

The answer became nationalism. It was an easy choice, for more that just the fact that there was no other option left. As John Lewis Gaddis noted in an analysis of Mao, the Chinese people "(do) not regard (their) country as having a marginal position in the universe." Most, if not all, Chinese readily agreed with the Communist Party that the "Middle Kingdom" is the most important nation on earth. Additionally, the Communists had been shrewd enough to nurse every Chinese grievance with the rest of the world – from the very real atrocities by Japan in World War II to the somewhat spurious assertions of American "imperialism" in the Korean War. As a result, nationalism was easily the most effective rationale for the Communists to use, especially in the universities, which have produced a slew of professors and graduates repeating the propaganda of the Communist Party.

However, although nationalism is certainly an effective weapon, it can also be a dangerous one. At some point, the people begin to wonder what the fuss is all about. As the 1990s began, the Communists realized that in order to preserve its reign, it had to provide tangible signs of growing Chinese power. Chief among them were the "reunification" of Taiwan and establishing the People's Republic as the leading power in Asia, and in the long run, a world superpower. These became the foreign policy goals of the Chinese Communist Party. Such things could not happen with the People's Liberation Army that Communist China had in 1989; that became quite obvious to the Communists as they watched the United States military in action during the 1990s. Communist China responded with an across-the-board military modernization and a massive build up. The People's Republic increased military spending by more than 17% in each of the first two years of the new century – and that's just the military spending the Communists were willing to publicly acknowledge.

The events of June 4, 1989 also increased the influence of the military in Communist politics. Reinforcing this was the change in political hierarchy that had begun under Deng. At the time of the Tiananmen Square massacre, Deng had relinquished all of his official posts in the Communist Party and the government of the People's Republic, except one – the aforementioned title of CMC Chairman . From here, he quietly wielded power and influence. After the massacre, Deng wielded ultimate power from the CMC Chairmanship, but he wasn't nearly as quiet.

Deng's power play made the People's Liberation Army a force of much greater political importance. Therefore, its desire for a more powerful Communist China in international politics would have become a much higher priority even without the cadres resorting to nationalism as a rationale for political survival. Since nationalism forced the Communist Party to move toward a more aggressive foreign policy anyway, the growing power of the military in 1990s Communist China found little opposition. What opposition did come was from the few liberals – called "rightists" in the Communist lexicon – who had survived the post-Tiananmen fallout. Few had any incentive to listen to them.

The 1997 Communist Party Congress put the possibility of any move away from this course, i.e., a move toward real political reform, to rest. During that conference, a surprise petition from the deposed Zhao Ziyang made the rounds. In the petition, Zhao asked for the Congress to adopt political reforms in order to hand over power in the People's Republic to the people themselves. The Communists, led by Jiang, rejected his letter. It was the last time any statement came from Zhao. Although still alive at 83, he is still under house arrest, and is effectively a ghost.

Jiang himself followed the Deng pattern during the Communist Party Congress in 2002. Originally billed as the Congress during which power in Communist China would be transferred from the "Third Generation" (Jiang's) to the "Fourth Generation" (the one supposedly led by Hu Jintao), it became the Congress that all but codified Jiang's continuing control of the People's Republic.

The Chinese Communist Central Committee, "elected" by the Congress, elevated Hu Jintao to the title of General Secretary of the Party. Jiang turned over the post of President of the People's Republic to Hu the following spring. However, Jiang remained Chairman of the CMC, and his faction took a majority of slots on the Politburo Standing Committee. At the very least, Jiang had effectively boxed in Hu. More importantly, Jiang re-emphasized the importance of the military, and the CMC in particular, in Communist Chinese politics (it certainly didn't hurt that Jiang also ensured the military would have a larger role in the Politburo and the Central Committee).

Many expect Hu to take over the CMC Chair from Jiang within a few years, but would Hu try to establish better ties with the United States? Given his history, that's unlikely. In fact, Hu had this to say about the United States during a "private" address to party cadres:

(The United States) strengthened its military deployments in the Asia-Pacific region, strengthened the US-Japan military alliance, strengthened strategic cooperation with India, improved relations with Vietnam, inveigled Pakistan, established a pro-American government in Afghanistan, increased arms sales to Taiwan, and so on. They have extended outposts and placed pressure points on us from the east, south, and west. This makes a great change in our geopolitical environment.

Thus, any expectations that Hu would be more conciliatory toward the United States than Jiang are likely to be dashed. In fact, as Hu consolidates his power base when Jiang does retire, he may actually push for *more* hostile relations with the United States, and as such, *closer* ties with states that sponsor terror. His stinging comments on Israel in 2001 (see Chapter 5) – further reveal a man who is very unlikely move Communist China away from its ties to anti-American terrorist regimes.

Hu's record within Communist China should also give the optimists pause: his reign over Tibet from 1988 to 1992 included a bloody crackdown on opposition groups, including Tibet independence supporters and other followers of the Dalai Lama, and he was the first provincial party boss to "congratulate" Deng, Li, *et al* for the 1989 Tiananmen Square massacre.

While the Communists' nationalist agenda was reinforced by political events at home, it ran to serious problems abroad. In fact, the 1990s presented the Communists with several obstacles to their aims – or to be more accurate, the same obstacle several times over.

The nationalist goals of Communist China were, and still are, these: the absorption of Taiwan under Communist rule, the establishment of the People's Republic as the leading power in Asia and a world superpower, an end to American "hegemony," and the "Sinicization" of the restive western regions of Tibet and "Xinjiang" – better known to the native Uighurs as East Turkestan.

Who was preventing Taiwan's "reunification" with the mainland by selling weapons to Taiwan under the Taiwan Relations Act of 1979? Whose President said they would do "whatever it takes" to prevent Taiwan from being swallowed up by the Communists under "reunification?"

Answer: the United States.

Who had alliances with Japan and South Korea, with major military presences to match? Who repeatedly frustrates Communist Chinese ambitions of being the leading economic and military power in East Asia?

Answer: the United States.

Who was the obstacle to Communist China's quest to establish itself as a rival to American and end American "hegemony?"

Ok, that one's too easy – the United States.

Who continually provided succor, aid, or inspiration to anti-Communist movements from Tibet, East Turkestan, Taiwan, the Falun Gong spiritual movement, and political dissidents from the People's Republic?

Answer: the United States.

After September 11, 2001, who has established a strong military presence in Central Asia, knocking Communist China off its perch as the lead power in a region the People's Republic considers its "backyard"?

Answer: the United States.

What would the Communists have to do to achieve the nationalist goal required to ensure their own survival?

Answer: confront and dislodge the United States.

This realization, it should be noted, was not forced upon the People's Republic by American actions. In fact, as the Communists began implementing their nationalist agenda, the United States elected two of the most pro-Beijing Presidencies in American history. The Administration of George H. W. Bush sent its national security advisor to Beijing less than two months after the Tiananmen Square massacre to pledge America's friendship. The now former President Bush also continued to waive United States trade law that banned such trade benefits to Communist nations by granting Most-Favored-Nation trading status (MFN, now known as Normal Trade Relations) with Communist China, usually over the objections of Congress. While these policies came from the Reagan Administration, and were left largely unchanged, one of the major justifications for those policies – the danger of the Soviet Union to both the United States and the People's Republic, had literally vanished in 1991. Meanwhile, the Tiananmen Square massacre provided a strong justification to *end* these policies, but the now former President Bush never even considered a policy change. He still considered "engagement" the best policy for Communist China as 1992 began. The campaign of that year, coming right after the Soviet Union dissolved in 1991, was an excellent opportunity to discuss the new order, and ask the pertinent question: what to do about Communist China?

Only one candidate came close to discussing this issue: Bill Clinton. It may be difficult to remember now, given both the kaleidoscope of events that was the 1992 campaign and Clinton's policies toward the People's Republic since then, but he was easily the most anti-Communist-China candidate in the 1992 election. He talked of tying MFN trade status with the People's Republic to its human rights record. He railed against "coddling dictators from Baghdad to Beijing." While the sound bite didn't seem to make much sense regarding the former, given the Gulf War of 1991, it was very appropriate to the latter. Clinton even invited two Chinese dissidents to the Democratic National Convention that year. Meanwhile, former President Bush continued to back MFN for Communist China, while third-party challenger Ross Perot was also sanguine about United States policy towards the People's Republic.

Thus, Clinton was in a unique position to build an anti-PRC coalition, and prepare the United States for Cold War II. To say he squandered that opportunity is a huge understatement. After a year of attempting to use MFN as a prod to force the Communists not stop abusing the Chinese people, Clinton dropped the idea in 1994, and reverted to the *status quo ante*. He changed the label of Most Favored Nation to Normal Trade Relations, which, whatever its intentions, belied the trade privileges given the People's Republic, which were by no means normal for a Communist regime. To make matters worse, Clinton not only reverted to the policies of "engagement" with Communist China, he expanded on them, as he and Jiang Zemin declared what Jiang called a "strategic partnership" between the United States and the People's Republic.

DRAGON IN THE DARK
How and Why Communist China Helps Our Enemies in the War on Terror

Clinton quickly reciprocated by publicly rebuking Taiwan's attempts to win more international recognition, doing so on Communist Chinese radio while visiting the People's Republic in 1998. The Clinton Administration even went so far as to call Taiwan an espionage threat to the United States in 2000, a move that stunned many outside intelligence analysts.

Adding insult to injury, the Clinton Administration placed Taiwan's elected President Chen Shui-bian under effective house arrest during his stopover in Los Angeles on his way to Latin America. The Clinton Administration confined Chen to a hotel room while in Los Angeles. The following year, after Clinton had left office, Chen had free reign during similar stopovers in New York City and Houston.

How did Communist China repay the two Administrations for their generosity? It sought out closer ties to America's enemies. It sold arms and military technology to Iran, Syria, and Libya. It maintained its decades-old allegiance to Stalinist North Korea – even after the North tried to withdraw from the Non-Proliferation Treaty and become a nuclear state in the 1990s, then violated the 1994 Agreed Framework and continued its nuclear ambitions. It sold missile parts to Pakistan, was instrumental in helping the regime acquire its own nuclear capability, and even sought economic ties with Pakistan's pre-September 11 ally, the Taliban. It even paid millions to Osama bin Laden, the Taliban's most beloved "guest," for unexploded American cruise missiles in 1998 – the Communists were hoping to reverse engineer the missiles, i.e., figure out how to build the missiles themselves. Meanwhile, al Qaeda had a quick influx of capital for its terrorist operations against the United States.

These weren't the only anti-Americans to whom Communist China reached out its hand in friendship. The People's Republic made a number of overtures to Communist parties in Western nations, attempting to repeat the Soviet policy of building ties to Communists in Western Europe and North America. It began negotiations with Cuba to take over ex-Soviet spy facilities from Maximum Leader Fidel Castro. It courted Venezuela *caudillo* Hugo Chavez, whose radical policies have led to mass protests, some killed by violent Chavez sympathizers. Meanwhile, a Venezuelan defector, Major Juan Diaz Castillo, said Chavez asked him "to organize, coordinate, and execute a covert operation consisting of delivering financial resources, specifically $1 million, to [Afghanistan's] Taliban government, in order for them to assist the al-Qaeda terrorist organization". These examples reveal a regime that is not going to stand aside and let the United States win the war on terror.

In addition, the People's Republic is also looking to challenge the military might of the United States. The recent increases in military spending – which some say still hides how much the Communist Chinese really spend on its People's Liberation Army – are not the only signs of this. Communist China has also focused its military strategy on "asymmetric warfare" and, in particular, weapons designed to counter America's advantage in information technology, a critical aspect to military communications and coordination.

More ominously, Communist China complemented its military build up with the aforementioned major arms purchases from Russia. The former adversary of the People's Republic has become its biggest supplier of military hardware, and the People's Republic is Russia's largest client. Russia does this in part to keep its military-industrial complex from collapsing, while Communist China has decided it's much more efficient to have Russia build them a navy and upgrade its air force than to put in the effort to do it themselves. The arms deals are now measured in billions, and include, as mentioned in Chapter 5, high-tech anti-ship naval missiles and submarines, air-radar systems, and a number of categories of jet fighters. This has dramatically shortened the time Communist China needs to become a major military power.

Finally, Communist China has also directly challenged the United States in the military arena, albeit on a small scale. In late 2000, the People's Republic began challenging American reconnaissance air flights off the coast of the southern mainland, despite the fact that the American military flights were well outside the Communist Chinese water line, and as such in international waters. The Communist Chinese air force began flying its pilots dangerously close to the United States reconnaissance planes. The United States told the People's Republic to cut it out. Watching American planes was one thing; risking a crash simply because you don't like where they fly is something else again.

The People's Republic ignored the American requests and warnings, and on April 1, 2001, the inevitable happened: a Communist pilot flew too close to an American EP-3 surveillance plane, collided into the plane, and crashed somewhere in the South China Sea, and died. The American plane, with a military crew of twenty-four, was forced to make an emergency landing on Hainan Island, just of the mainland.

Communist China immediately "escorted" the plane crew to a hotel, took apart the plane, and demanded the United States apologize before they would let the crew return to the United States. The brazen behavior was both a symptom and a piece of the Communists' nationalist agenda. By endlessly calling itself the sole defender of Chinese interests in a hostile world – and not allowing the truth to be known about how the Hainan collision really happened – the People's Republic had ensured it could not back down, or at least say it could not back down, from a confrontation without the Chinese people beginning to wonder what the rationale for continued Communism in the first place. Additionally, the belligerent attitude was part and parcel of its plan to push the United States out of the area.

The crew was "detained" – no one in the Administration was willing to say "held hostage" – until the United States apologized. After a week of back and forth over "regret," the United States gave something close enough to an apology – and in Chinese it apparently was an apology – to get the crew back to the United States. The plane was sent back in pieces, and Communist China had won a chance to examine American reconnaissance and surveillance equipment first hand.

After the troops came home, Communist China had the audacity to demand one million dollars in compensation for the "guests." The United States sent a check for shipping the plane, roughly $34,000. The Communists angrily rejected it as too low. Meanwhile, the Communists did lose on one point – the flights resumed very quickly.

But didn't September 11 "change everything"? Not for Communist China it didn't. If anything, September 11, 2001 led a number of Communist Chinese generals and "academics" to believe that the United States was weakened. While the rest of the world contemplates the war against terrorism, Communist China probes for opportunities – particularly regarding Taiwan.

The importance of Taiwan to the Chinese Communists cannot be overestimated. Taiwan was a Japanese colony for fifty years, returning to Chinese control after World War II. Before the war, the Chinese Communist Party was battling a civil war with the Nationalist government for control of the Middle Kingdom. The Japanese invasion of the 1930s forced them into an uneasy alliance; the civil war immediately resumed soon after World War II ended.

Within four years, the Nationalists, under Generalissimo Chiang Kai-Shek, were defeated on the mainland. They retreated to Taiwan in 1949. The Communists, upon founding what they called the People's Republic of China on October 1, 1949, claimed Taiwan as theirs, despite never having set foot on the island.

Nationalist China – as Taiwan was usually called back then – and Communist China stared each other down across the Taiwan Straits for years. This continued even as the PRC tilted closer to the United States. In 1979, the United States followed the United Nations' move of eight years earlier and established diplomatic relations with Communist China. Staying with the "one China" policy, the United States broke off relations with Taiwan at the same time, although it pledged to sell Taiwan whatever weapons it needed to defend itself under the Taiwan Relations Act, the Nationalist regime was much more isolated in the world after 1979.

The critical event in modern Chinese/Taiwanese history was the elevation of Lee Teng-hui to the Taiwanese Presidency in 1988. The first President of the Republic of China (Nationalist China's official name) in 60 years not from the Chiang family, and the first born on Taiwan, Lee had two objectives: increase Taiwan's international profile, and reform politics at home. By the time he left office in 2000, he was one of the most important leaders in East Asian history.

He began quickly at home – dissidents were released, opposition parties were legalized, and local elections were held. The most dramatic example of the new era in Taiwanese affairs came in 1994, when Chen Shui-bian, then a human-rights lawyer and political gadfly, was elected mayor of Taipei. The capital city of Taiwan was now in the hands of the opposition, pro-independence Democratic Progressive Party (DPP).

Lee also increased Taiwan's profile abroad, best symbolized by a visit to the United States in 1995. Lee's dramatic call for the world not to forget Taiwan's struggle for survival – the Communists never rescinded their claim to Taiwan – on American soil infuriated the People's Republic. More ominously for the Communists, Lee dramatically put his own position on the line in 1996, offering himself as a candidate for his job for a four-year term in a democratic election. The Communists were faced with the reality of democratic regime on what they called Chinese soil. Every argument against democratization on the mainland – Western politics would never work, Chinese were different, and other nationalist propaganda – were exposed as lies. In a heavy-handed, desperate move to intimidate voters away from Lee, Communist China fired several missiles over the island democracy. It was a classic Communist response, one that revealed both the regime's reliance on thuggish behavior and its complete lack of understanding on the political reality on Taiwan.

The Nationalists had always supported reunification, even after it became clear the Communists were solidifying their control of the mainland. As Taiwan democratized, however, the people soured greatly on reunification. By 1996, Lee himself was putting a condition on reunification: the mainland had to be a democracy before Taiwan would even consider it. Naturally, the Communists were less than happy with that. Reunification was supposed to justify Communist rule in China, not end it.

So off the missiles flew, to scare Taiwanese voters away from Lee. It didn't work – on Election Day 1996, Lee won over half of the vote, an increase from his pre-election support according to polls. The second place finisher in Taiwan was Peng Ming-min, candidate of the overtly pro-independence DPP. Two candidates supporting unconditional reunification – the New Party – never made any headway. The Taiwanese voters refused to be intimidated, and in the process made a damning indictment of Communist China.

Lee's elected term was filled with turmoil. His Nationalists split in two over his anti-Communist stance, and even the faction that stayed with him was suspicious of him. By 2000, there were three major parties – the Nationalists, the ex-Nationalist People First Party, and the DPP – each of which ran its own candidate. Chen Shui-bian ran again on the DPP banner, and the Communists made very clear they preferred anyone but him. The Communist-run press ripped the former Taipei mayor – he had lost his 1998 re-election bid – and quickly established Chen as the anti-Communist candidate, so much so that rumors abounded that the Communist-hating Lee was secretly pulling for his former rival to win.

Communist Premier Zhu Rongji personally warned Taiwan against voting for the DPP nominee, all but threatening they would not be allowed to vote again. The thinly veiled threat, coming from the man portrayed as the leading "reformer" in Communist China, galvanized the anti-Communist vote behind Chen. He won the election, becoming the first leader of the Republic of China not to come from the Nationalist Party. Within two years, Lee himself left the Nationalists in favor of the more anti-Communists Taiwan Solidarity Union.

One might be wondering, what on earth does this have to do with the war on terror? From the Communist Chinese perspective, it has everything to do with it. In fact, Communist China sees the terrorist war as one of many means to its end – Taiwan under Communist control, instead of a democratic symbol to the mainland of what might have been, and can still be. Taiwan is the refutation of everything the Communist Party has been trying to tell the people on the mainland for decades. While it was a Nationalist dictatorship, the battle was between elites. Lee Teng-hui brought the Taiwanese people, and freedom, into the discussion. As Communist China became more repressive and militaristic, Taiwan became freer.

Additionally, there is the fact that the Communists still consider Taiwan to be theirs, and have spent decades telling that to the Chinese people. This makes Taiwan a double threat. Not only is it a "democracy on Chinese soil," it is one that rejects and refutes the nationalist card that Communist China has chosen to play after June 4, 1989. It would be difficult, at best, for the Communists to claim they are a major power, even regionally, without "resolution" of the Taiwan issue – and for the PRC, the only resolution is absorption. Taiwan's continuing resistance also gives hope to the resistance in Tibet and East Turkestan, compounding the Communists' problems.

Naturally the Communists responded with an intimidation campaign against Taiwan, deploying missiles targeted at the island democracy at the rate of over 75 a year. It now has well over 450 missiles aimed at Taiwan already. This has reduced the time Taiwan has before it loses its long-held military advantage in the cross-straits balance of power. In fact, some analysts have projected that the balance of military power between Communist China and Taiwan will tip in favor of the former by 2005.

Taiwan is the first, second, and third priority of Communist foreign policy, and since Taiwan's main supporter is the United States, that makes it a threat as well. America's support for Asian democracies is also threatening – Communist China needs to have its influence continue to grow in order to appease the nationalist impulses it has cultivated. For now, however, Taiwan is the critical issue, and the United States is the biggest obstacle to short-term triumph and long-term survival.

The Communist obsession with Taiwan has led many to believe that without it, the People's Republic would act like a "normal" country. Nothing can be further from the truth. While Communist China would certainly be thrilled to absorb the island democracy, the Communists would still have to deal with the demands of the Chinese people. Moreover, "reunification" – either through conquest or intimidation – would leave the Communists with resistance from millions of Taiwanese. The nationalist message will have to be intensified to justify Communist rule. That will require the People's Republic to eclipse Japan as the most prominent power in East Asia, as well as the United States and India in Central Asia. Communist China cannot achieve ether objective without a confrontation with the United States.

From a purely geographic standpoint, Japan's early 20th century domination of Asia is completely senseless. Japan is a grouping of islands with far fewer resources than the Chinese mainland. However, due to its determination to keep foreign influence as low as possible, Japan was able to maintain a stronger state than Imperial China, and to invade Nationalist

China during the 1930s. The horrors suffered by the people of the mainland are well known, and the Communists have used them repeatedly to stoke nationalistic, anti-Japanese sentiment. Despite this, Japan remained the lead power in Asia during Cold War I – thanks in large part to American backing and democratization. Communist China, suffering through the anti-rightist campaign (which killed unnumbered millions), Great Leap Forward (which killed even more unnumbered millions), and the Cultural Revolution (which killed unnumbered *tens* of millions), has taken decades to recover from the wounds inflicted by its own leaders.

Of course, while Communist China is more than willing to allow some criticism of Chairman Mao, it's mainly been crimes against other Communists that have earned the founder the wrath of his successors. His horrifying actions against his own people – and the consequences thereof – get little mention. The Communists have instead chosen the Japanese crimes of World War II and the foreign influences pre-war era as the culprits of the weakness of the People's Republic. Even Taiwan, which Japan seized in 1895 and did not return to China until forced to do so at the end of World War II, could be squeezed into the all-foreigners-are-enemies theory.

Of course, Japan is not prepared to simply fade into second-class status, and the United States still considers Japan its most important ally in Asia. Thus we become the regional obstacle as well as the Taiwan obstacle.

The nationalism of Communist China extends to the southeastern frontier as well. Up to six nations have some claim to islands in the South China Sea, including the disputed Spratly archipelago. The Philippines, Vietnam, Taiwan, Malaysia, and Brunei all lay claim to at least of piece of the Spratlys. Communist China, however, claims m the entire South China Sea, including the Spratlys, for itself. It is the only regime to establish its claim with outposts – a source of serious diplomatic discord with the nations in Southeast Asia. Communist China even fought a brief skirmish with Vietnam over the fate of the islands.

Central Asia is a new arena of competition for the Communists. During the liberation of Afghanistan, the United States won an agreement with Uzbekistan for troop deployments in former Soviet bases left behind when the U.S.S.R. dissolved in 1991. For Communist China, the presence of American troops in its "backyard" is particularly galling. For years, Communist China tried to build closer ties with the Central Asian republics – as the former Soviet dominions are called. Their efforts culminated in the founding of the Shanghai Cooperation Organization in the summer of 2001, and were nearly destroyed less than a year later. Such does not endear the Communists – particularly the military, to the United States of America. Communist China also has one other large obstacle to increasing influence over Central and South Asia – India. As mentioned earlier, the Sino-Indian conflict, both hot and cold, has been one of the few consistencies in this region over the last 50 years.

When Communist China threw in with Pakistan, India moved closer to the United States, especially after the Communists 1962 border war grab. To this day, the Communists claim more territory in northeast India belongs to them. When the United States and Communist China began to drift toward each other in the 1970s, India drifted towards the Soviets. When the Soviet Union collapsed, India kept close ties with Russia, but gradually began to realize that Pakistan by itself was not as dangerous as its large Communist neighbor. By the late 1990s, the Indian people elected a government that saw the People's Republic, not Pakistan, as its biggest threat. Last summer's joint Indian-American military exercise was, for India, as much about Communist China as about the war on terror.

India is also host to the Tibetan government-in-exile, which highlights another great threat to Communist China's nationalist agenda. Tibet has been nothing short of a public relations disaster for Communist China. Democracies throughout the world have large constituencies focusing on the Dalai Lama's followers and their brutal treatment by the Communists. In fact, the entire western region becomes a problem for the People's Republic, although the situation in East Turkestan is very different. There only the United States inspires the Uighur anti-Communist movement, even with the aforementioned ETIM controversy. This puts the focus of Communist angst squarely on the United States, again.

In each of the three major geopolitical objectives for Communist China – the absorption of Taiwan, the expansion of Communist power in Asia, and the suppression of Tibetans and Uighurs – the United States stands in the way. This could lead some to assume that the best thing for the United States is to get out of the Communists' way. This should be scrupulously avoided for several reasons.

First, consider what this might mean for Taiwan, Japan, Korea, and Central Asia. The fall of democracy in the Taiwan – easily the most open political system in East Asia – would deal a crushing blow to American prestige, and be a chilling betrayal of 23 million Taiwanese. While Japan and South Korea have been reaching out to the People's Republic, neither would choose to be part of a region dominated by its Communist neighbor. The Central Asian republics are literally caught between Russia and Communist China. An American withdrawal from the region will likely lead to a return to the *status quo ante* – authoritarian regimes moving closer to Beijing, while Moscow would have yet another reason to stay close to the People's Republic: to maintain its influence with the former Soviet republics. This would be received with great alarm in India, which had been moving closer to the United States ever since its nuclearization in 1998. An American pullback would leave the world's largest democracy geopolitically weaker and more isolated.

Moreover, just as Taiwan would not leave the Communists satiated, there is no guarantee that allowing the People's Republic to become the largest power in Asia would do anything to quell their ambitions. In fact, it may feed them. As Communist China flexes its muscles against its neighbors, its own people will become poorer, angrier, and maybe more willing to act. This is the trap nationalism sets for all tyrants who use it – the battle can never end. Additionally, as the most prominent democracy in the world, the United States would still be an inspiration for pro-democracy, anti-Communist activists throughout the People's Republic, and thus, it would still be a threat.

Already, the Communist rhetoric and policies are beginning to reveal global ambitions. It has claimed "superpower" status in one of its numerous overtures to Taiwan (the Taiwanese people were not impressed). Of course, the Communist Chinese may have dropped the Stalinism of Mao Zedong, but the rationale for continued Communist control has forced them to act with Stalinist global lust for power, albeit with more subtlety. Rather than fix their internal problems or allow their own people the right to determine how they are governed, the Communists have found – and must continue to find – outside influences to exploit as enemies in justification of its rule. In every major area, the top outside influence is none other than the United States of America.

For these reasons, the Communist ties to anti-American terrorists and terrorist states are not accidents. They are part of a deliberate policy to find allies to challenge American "hegemony" throughout the world. As American Presidents and Congresses discussed "engagement" and "managing" China, the Communists sold weapons to our enemies, made economic deals with terrorist-sponsoring nations, and floated code words like "multi-polar" and "anti-containment" to hide their plans to build a world-wide anti-American alliance.

These plans will not end with the fall of the Ba'athists in Iraq, or even should the mullahs in Iran pass from the scene. Any Middle East regime whose ties to terror have strained relations with the United States (Saudi Arabia, the United Arab Emirates, and Yemen to cite aforementioned examples) could substitute for the axis of evil members. The Saudis will be particularly valuable as they are a plentiful source of petroleum. While Saudi Arabia purports to be an American ally, reports of Saudi ties to terrorism are plentiful. They were an open ally and theological role model for the Afghan Taliban. Most importantly for the Communists, they have a history of cooperation with Pakistan. This makes them the most ideal target for a Communist charm offensive. The result could be a dramatic setback for the war on terror.

Since September 11, 2001, few have focused on the People's Republic, but the Communists have not lost their focus on the United States. They are still reaching out to America's enemies, including supporters of terrorism. They established links with the now-fallen Taliban, and tried to sell weapons to Saddam Hussein, even as the United States prepared to liberate Iraq from his Ba'athist tyranny. They also helped Saddam integrate his air-defense system. The mullahs of Iran were able to take years off their quest for weapons of mass destruction, and missiles to deliver them, due to Communist help. Beijing also helped Pakistan acquire and build its nuclear capability, and thus its ability to deter India from aggressive action against Kashmir terrorists. Finally, it has allowed its client state of North Korea to become both the world's leading ballistic missile merchant, and a become a nuclear-armed regime.

These are not actions of friends in the war on terror. They are actions of a regime that sees the terrorist war as just another part of the bigger conflict to them: the new cold war against the one power that can thwart its ambitions and threaten its long-term survival – the United States of America.

Chapter 8:
Cold War II – How to Win It and Win the Terrorist War

As the United States continues to fight the war against terrorism, Communist China continues to fight its undeclared, but very real, cold war against the United States. Can America handle the terrorist war and Cold War II at the same time? Yes, we can. In fact, victory in Cold War II can ensure a faster, and more lasting, victory in the terrorist war.

Victory in Cold War II and the terrorist war will come when American policy makers realize that the two are linked in several areas, and that both our enemies act for the same reason – fear of the United States and the liberty under which it governs itself. Both the terrorists and the Communists know they cannot measure up to American freedom. In order to defeat them, the United States must do the following:

- Ensure the American military is strong enough to project power in defense of American interests, and resist Communist China's acts of aggression around the world
- Make emphatically clear that a central American interest, in both the war on terror and Cold War II, is the advancement and triumph of liberty
- In that vein, work to build democratic regimes in the nations liberated from the sponsors of terror
- Do what we can to support those who resist and oppose terrorist regimes from the inside their home nations, in

particular the Iranian revolt against the mullahs in that country, and also anti-terrorists in Libya and Syria
- Endorse the liberation of Stalinist North Korea and subsequent reunification of the Korean peninsula under a democratic government
- Build and strengthen ties to new anti-Communist, anti-terrorist allies, in particular India
- Link any and all warming between the United States and Russia to the end of Russia's arms sales to Communist China
- Maintain and strengthen ties to current anti-Communist allies, such as Taiwan, South Korea and Japan
- Push for the liberation of the ethnic victims of Communism – the Tibetans and Uighurs being the most prominent examples, both to pressure the Communists and, in the case of the Muslim Uighurs, to prove beyond any possible doubt that the war against terror is not a war against Islam
- Push for the liberation of all other victims of Communism – especially the Chinese people themselves, who have suffered more at the hands of Communism than any other people on the face of the earth

These policies will not only lead to victory in Cold War II, but also ensure a more speedy victory in the war on terror, and a firmer foundation for a post-war, terror-free world.

First and foremost, we need to be prepared with a strong military to ensure peace through strength when possible and peace through force when necessary. The need for a strong military became painfully evident after September 11, 2001. Without the strength we already have, victory in Afghanistan and Iraq would not have been conceivable, let alone possible.

However, the level of military strength has fallen dramatically since the first cold war, on the assumption that the United States was past the days when it would have to face a major international power with allies across the globe to threaten American interests. That was a very erroneous assumption, as Communist China's ties to terrorism have made clear. While, the American military does still need the aspects of a small, quick force, the challenge of Communist China also requires a military that is capable of holding it off. This will require a greater increase in military strength, especially in light of Communist China's recent dramatic military increases, and in particular its focus on cyber-warfare against the United States. To win Cold War II, the current focus on the ability to win conflicts quickly with a rapid reaction force will have to be balanced with the recognized need to deal with a major hostile power with allies and influences around the globe. It will likely mean the end of whatever remains of the "peace dividend" of the 1990s, but such is the cost of the world's lone free superpower in Cold War II.

The necessary complement to this – for both the war on terror and Cold War II – is the advancement and defense of liberty. American policy must be about more than the world chess game or arms balances in order to succeed. It must emphasize that in defeating and ending the regimes that aid terrorism, including Communist China, America is also freeing the long-suffering peoples imprisoned by those regimes. Not only will this energize the American people for Cold War II – to say nothing of maintaining its determination for the terrorist war – it will also enlist the silent, repressed peoples of these regimes on our side, making victory in both much easier. During the 1980s, the desire for liberty among the Eastern European people, combined with the fact that the United States eagerly supported their efforts where it could, and condemn their tyrants where it couldn't, led to the peaceful revolutions of 1989.

Our enemies in the terrorist war and Cold War II hold more in common than just anti-Americanism – they encompass the most brutally repressive regimes on the planet. What's more, September 11, 2001 has shown us just how far the enemies of liberty will go to destroy us. Make no mistake: it is American liberty – not American policies – that led to those terrorist attacks. At the time, the United States was making absolutely no efforts to end the Taliban rule over Afghanistan. It was not talking of removing Saddam Hussein from power in Iraq, or even tightening the sanctions against his regime. American policy on Iran was still based on hopes of reaching out to the mullahs. Yet the Taliban's "guests" killed nearly 3,000; Saddam still cheered the murders of that day, and the Iranian mullahs continued their anti-American, terrorist policies. It was not because of what we did; it was because of who we are.

The United States has brought down numerous governments simply by existing – beginning with our first international ally King Louis XVI of France. The American ideal of freedom – the "shining city on the hill" – is a threat to every dictator on the face of the earth. World War II and Cold War I revealed what an active America on the world stage can do – half of Europe and half of Asia was liberated in four years of war, the other half of Europe was liberated four and a half-decades later.

Even in Yugoslavia, less than two years after the American air force flattened Belgrade, a dissident movement clandestinely backed by United States advisors and the International Republican Institute inspired the people to overthrew Communist Slobodan Milosevic. One can be certain that Communist China, whose actions on the world stage very much resemble Milosevic's attempts to use nationalism to stay in power more than anyone else's, took note of this. The terrorists and their sponsors also took note. While the goals of the People's Republic and the terrorists may differ – their chief obstacle, the United States, is the same. American liberty is the one political ideal that can overwhelm Islamism, Communism, and Ba'athism – and they all know it.

The people of Taiwan have grown more assertive in their independence as they have grown democratic. A democratic China could make its case on reunification much more easily than the People's Republic can. At present, nearly every major Taiwanese politician – even those who support reunification in principle – refuse to support a Taiwan under Communist control. Thus the Communists are undermining the very nationalist objectives they used to justify their own reign. The same could be said for its desire as a major world power. The rise of a China that is democratic would worry Japan and the United States a lot less than the Communist version. Evidence of that can be seen in Japan itself – whose very democracy made its development as an economic power a major foreign policy *goal* of the United States less than a decade after World War II ended.

For the terrorists, pan-Arabism or radical Islamism is the goal. While democracy and *sharia* are largely incompatible, forced virtue of Islamic law is far less desirable than the virtue of a free society. One need look no further than Iran – where the Islamic government not only utterly failed to halt the spread of drugs and prostitution, but has likely encouraged it through its harsh, depressing rule – to find the merit in this argument. The fate of Afghanistan can also attest to this.

As for Ba'athism, the history of Iraq and Syria make clear that there has been little more damaging to the Arabian people than the totalitarian regimes that Ba'athism has given them. Syria's efforts to become a regional power have led to a loss of the Golan Heights in 1967. Iraq, meanwhile, fought two debilitating wars – one draw with Iran, one partial loss to the United States – lost control of nearly a third of its territory, and sank into economic malaise before the Ba'athist regime was put out of its people's misery. Far from uniting the Arab peoples behind him, Saddam failed even to unite his own country. This is hardly what one would call an impressive record of achievement.

Without the moral argument of liberty, all of the policies and objectives mentioned below are nothing more than moving geopolitical game pieces. While American interests would be served, the rest of the world might start to wonder, what's in it for us? Meanwhile, neither the Communists nor the terrorists – who need no primer on what the promise of freedom can do to tyrannies large and small – will fail to let up on us simply because we are not so willing to spread the gospel of freedom. Even without the issue of liberty, Communist China has several reasons to oppose the United States, and thus incentives to give aid to anti-American, terrorist sponsoring states.

In our efforts to expand liberty throughout the world, we need to show we are ready to provide it to the nations whose anti-American regimes have been defeated and destroyed by the United States military and indigenous anti-totalitarian forces. The first examples of this, of course, are Afghanistan and Iraq.

The invitation the Communists sent to the Taliban's number two, months after they were driven from power in Afghanistan, is more than enough evidence that the People's Republic is still looking to the Wahhabist terrorist group as a "check" against the United States.

It also makes clear that the United States cannot turn its back on Afghanistan. Democratization of Afghanistan cannot be discounted. The defeated nations of World War II became the allies of whoever occupied them, but the allies of the United States supported us as much for our willingness to give the governments of those nations back to the people as anything else. In Japan, hatred of America in the 1940s became near-complete admiration in the 1950s, due almost entirely to the determination of one man – General Douglas MacArthur – to bring democracy to the country, based on Japanese cultural norms. Afghanistan can be the same way.

Some will wonder if such an effort is needed, given the vast unpopularity of the Taliban in Afghanistan. While the Afghans may hate the Taliban, the Communists do not. Even without the Taliban, an Afghanistan friendly to Communist China could pose problems for the United States, particularly if it resurrects the Beijing-Kabul-Islamabad-Kashmir alliance.

Iraq can also be an example of American willingness to bring freedom to those whose dictatorial regimes forced us to oppose them. Iraq's liberation cannot come simply with a military victory. In order to ensure Iraq is never again a potential "check" on United States power, a democratic government must take Saddam's place. The continuing attacks by Ba'athist remnants and would be bin Ladenites against American troops there makes the need for democracy and the rule of law in Iraq *more* important. A democratic Iraq would be able to chart its own future, and become a symbol to the rest of the region, especially to its neighbors in Iran, thus possibly hastening the day the mullahs are forced from power there. Moreover, a democratic government would show the Iraqi people that their future lies with the United States, not with Communist China. The loss of that anti-American "check" will be a big blow to the objectives of the People's Republic, and a great advancement both for America and for world liberty.

While Iraq has received most of the world's recent attention, one of the biggest sponsors of terror is right next to it, Iran. However, Iran also has a burgeoning democracy movement – drawing its support mainly from young Iranians – that has repeatedly taken to the streets in recent years. This movement, despite little outside attention, has continued to grow, and even won the support of far-sighted clerics in Iran who understand the failure the Islamic Republic has become. In order to survive, the mullahs rely on support from outside the country, and rabid anti-American nationalism. That has pushed it in one direction – to the People's Republic.

Communist China has a history of arms deals with Iran, including missile parts and "nonconventional" materials (weapons of mass destruction, of course). It was no accident that Jiang Zemin used Iran as the place from where he ripped the American military presence in Central Asia; it highlighted the two regimes' common interest in working together against the United States.

This, of course, makes it all the more imperative to support, loudly, the dissident movement in Iran. It has often made clear it does not share the mullah's hatred of America. Supporting the dissidents in Iran – and with more than just with words – can do more than just end one of the nastiest terrorist sponsors in the Middle East. It would also knock out a major Communist friend in the region. Additionally, it would quickly solve the problem of access to the land-locked Afghanistan, should either the battle against al Qaeda there require a lightning strike from outside the country or the post-Taliban government in Kabul require help quickly. It would also mean Afghanistan would have a friendly neighbor that does not have a group of rabid al Qaeda supporters just over the border. Pakistan, whose northwest border with Afghanistan has legions of Osama bin Laden admirers, cannot make that claim.

President Bush has made some effort here, publicly announcing his support for the dissidents in July of 2002. More can and must be done, however. Consistent support for the dissidents can go a long way. Fifty years ago, the CIA helped upend an elected government in Iran that had grown largely unpopular. Today, Iran is ruled by a regime that is almost universally hated, and that has *itself* thwarted the will of the people through its arcane Islamic power structure. The so-called Islamic Republic is ripe for the fall. The United States should take advantage of this to help the Iranian people free themselves, remove a leading sponsor of terrorism and anti-American regime, and give Afghanistan a stable and friendly neighbor, all at the same time.

This is not the only place in the Middle East where Cold War II and the war on terror come together. Three other regimes have a history of sponsoring acts of terror while fostering ties with Communist China. While Libya, Sudan, and Syria have been quiet lately, their anti-Americanism can best be described as in remission. Libya has been a beneficiary of Communist Chinese expertise in missile technology, while the radical

Islamic regime of Sudan relies on the People's Republic as a major investor in its petroleum industry, and thus a major funding source for its war against the non-Muslim southern rebellion. Sudan was also Osama bin Laden's headquarters prior to his move to Afghanistan in the mid-1990s. Syria's sponsorship of terror is so deep that some groups actually have offices in the Syrian capital of Damascus.

Sudan's southern rebellion – supported a diverse group in the United States that includes liberal African-American politicians and evangelical conservatives – has tremendous potential. The rebels could greatly weaken, if not remove, a prominent African ally for Communist China. They can also go a long way to restricting, and possibly erasing, one of the most bloodthirsty regimes in the Islamic world.

In Libya, meanwhile, the United States must do more to find and support resistance to Moammar Gadhafi. That it has not centered around a person or a movement means less than it may seem – the Iranian resistance has thrived in part *because* of its leaderless appearance, which has made it almost impossible to contain, let alone eliminate. It would show the Libyan people – to say nothing about the victims of Pan American Flight 103 – that we have not forgotten them. It would also remove one more client for the Communist Chinese military and anti-American "check."

Syria has its own Ba'athist dictatorship. Its current leader, Bashar al-Assad, inherited his position from his father, best known for wiping the 20,000-strong city of Hama off the map. He and his late father Hafaz have incubated and supported numerous terrorists and terrorist groups. Supporting dissidents in Syria would put it on the defensive, distracting it from spreading terrorism in the region. The end of Ba'athism in Syria would be a tremendous victory in the terrorist war – almost equal to Iraq –

and it would also free its puppet state of Lebanon. It would also remove a huge threat to Israel on several levels. Finally it would be the end of a regime with a history of economic deals with Communist China and arms deals with North Korea.

These actions would certainly be expected in a total war against terrorism – one that involves political as well as military actions against those who would destroy America. In addition to working against all long-term anti-American threats, it would force the People's Republic to make a choice. It can either continue to support these regimes, making clear their interests are not those of the United States during the terrorist war, or it would be forced to cut the regimes loose. Either would lead to a dramatic step forward in the terrorist war, either through complete victory against the sponsors of terror or the flushing out of Communist China as the their major benefactor, making isolation of the Communists much more of a certainty. Either way, the forces of anti-Americanism would be greatly weakened.

Iran, of course, is one of the "axis of evil" regimes labeled by President Bush. Its neighbor, Iraq, also made the list before its liberation. While Communist China has several ties to all these members of the axis of evil, its most extensive ties are to the third member, Stalinist North Korea. Meanwhile, the North's ties to terrorist states, and its long-running nuclear weapons program, make it one of the most dangerous terrorist sponsors on the planet.

Any policy that allows for the existence of the Stalinist regime has only three options on the issue of its nuclear weapons – a "surgical strike," indefinite partial containment, or an eventual slew of concessions. None of these can guarantee that the Stalinist regime will end its quest for nuclear weapons, and for one simple reason – the regime would still be in place. In fact, the first two options were already been tried on Ba'athist Iraq. Neither the surgical strike of 1981, nor the attempt at containment that began ten years later has succeeded. As for the last of the three, it was tried with North Korea itself in 1994. There is no reason to suspect any option would succeed with North Korea, particularly given its record of violating every agreement it has signed, and Communist China's refusal to stop its satellite's arms sales to terrorist states.

If the United States truly wishes to face the North Korean threat for what it really is, the most logical policy is not with the goal of coddling the regime or pressuring it to come to terms of an agreement. The correct policy is one with the goal of ending the regime and freeing the people trapped by its tyranny. This policy need not require military action, although it should never be ruled out. It must include a determination to end the North Korean regime, and the nightmare of the people trapped under it.

In establishing the goal as liberation, the United States would end the dichotomy between the Stalinist regime and its fellow members of the axis of evil. It would also reestablish the United States as the strongest advocate for freedom in East Asia. It would make clear, one and for all, that terrorists and states that sponsor terrorism have no place in the 21st century. Finally, it would also put Communist China on notice that its "client state" is not a card to play against the United States and its allies, but a battleground in Cold War II, one on which the Communists will be forced onto the defensive.

One addition to the policy supporting the liberation of Stalinist North Korea would make it far more popular in democratic South Korea – supporting the post-liberation, democratic reunification of the Korean peninsula. The dramatic effects of supporting regime change as a means to a democratic, anti-Communist, reunification of the Korean peninsula cannot be underestimated. American troops nearly united Korea under a free government in 1951, until Mao Zedong sent in over 1 million Communist Chinese to drive the advance back to the rough equivalent of the 38th parallel. Though an armistice was signed, the war never officially ended. Thus, the United States could easily shift its policy to one in support of a reunified, non-Communist, democratic Korea.

A policy of reunification via liberation would accomplish many things. First and foremost, it would bring coherence to United States policy. American policy regarding North Korea has been a hodgepodge of overtures and condemnation. We have treated the regime as partner on non-proliferation (the 1994 nuclear power deal) and pariah. By making it clear that we support, and will strive to achieve, a Korea that is free, democratic, and whole, America can reshape the discussion on both sides of the peninsula, and let the world know the Stalinist regime is deserving of absolutely no legitimacy whatsoever.

A policy of post-liberation reunification would also take into account the longing of the people of South Korea to see their nation whole again. The Korean War did more than divide a nation; it separated numerous relatives who only now have been able to even speak to each other again in brief "reunions." The United States should make clear where blame for this lies – with the Stalinist North Koreans and their Communist Chinese allies and patrons.

This policy would reunite the people of South Korea behind the United States. Most Koreans are thankful that the United States has protected them from the Stalinists to the north, but many younger Koreans have no memory of the Korean War. The current Administration policy, such as it is, seems to many in South Korea as particularly harsh. One likely reason is the fact that for all its tough words, the Administration has never publicly supported the liberation of northern Korea, at one point even when given the opportunity to do so.

An American policy that explicitly supports liberation and reunification as the ultimate goals will go a long way toward bringing the people of South Korea closer to the United States. It would remind the people of South Korea that America's hostility to the Stalinist regime does *not* extend to the 22 million people trapped by Kim Jong-il *et al* in the North. It would provide a real opportunity for a major objective of South Korea – reunification – while at the same time pushing a major goal of the United States – the end of the dangerous regime of Stalinist North Korea.

A policy that establishes the goal of the liberation of northern Korea can be accomplished either through military action or by the combination of isolation and the support of dissidents either directly or through South Korea and Japan. The policy goal need not be dependent upon risks of resources or American and allied lives from military action – depending on the probable casualties from the Stalinist assault on Seoul and United States-South Korean military forces – or inaction – depending upon the likelihood of the Stalinists arsenal, nuclear weapons included, being sold to terrorists and/or the states that sponsor them.

Finally, a liberation policy would bring more attention to the horrible plight of the people trapped in North Korea – for whom more attention is desperately needed. The despicable treatment of the North Korean people by the Stalinist regime is, for now, a running subtext of the crisis. It should at least have equal billing, and by itself would be enough justification to support the end of Stalinism. Much like Communist China, the Stalinists' international brazenness is based on its need to preserve its totalitarian "state." For all of the reasons above, that "state" must end.

Pursuant to this policy, any cooperation with the North must cease, and that means keeping the "nullified" 1994 Agreed Framework dead. The North's history of flouting the agreement prior to "nullifying" it, and the fact that the accord would actually bring the North closer to becoming a nuclear weapons state even if it were to adhere to it, is reason enough not to resurrect it. Why build two nuclear power plants for a regime so determined to nuclearize itself that it continued its ambitions for nuclear weapons in violation of the very agreement that won it the plants in the first place? Add this to its history of selling weapons to terrorist states, which continues to this day without the Stalinists even hinting it is prepared to stop, and there is no reason to provide assistance of *any* kind to North Korea.

The reality is that the Stalinists of North Korea are determined to acquire nuclear weapons, and that Communist China is more than willing to let the North arm terrorists. Do we really want North Korea to survive long enough to convince Communist China that the time is right to arm terrorist sponsors – Iran, Libya, Sudan, Syria, etc. – or terrorists themselves with nuclear devices to use against American "hegemony"?

North Korea is one of the very few repressive nations in the world without any prominent dissident movement fighting the regime from within. This has to change immediately. Support for reunification via liberation would be much stronger throughout the world if they could see North Koreans themselves working for their own liberation. It certainly won't be easy – the Stalinists run the most repressive state on Earth – but America has managed to keep alive dissident movements before – Poland and Yugoslavia being the best-known examples. North Korea also has a near monopoly on internal information, a monopoly that is now being challenged. The United States should join and support these efforts as well. These are critical first steps to a liberated North Korea, and a unified, democratic Korean peninsula.

This would give the United States something it has not had in a long time – a comprehensive policy on North Korea with the goal of ending its tyranny, uniting the Korean Peninsula in freedom, and putting out of business one of the most prolific weapons distributors to terrorist states. It would also force Communist China to exert geopolitical energy and capital to defend its satellite, instead of using it to divide the Asian democracies from each other, and the United States.

North Korea is the intersection point for Cold War II and the war on terror. A policy that makes it clear that it is not a regime to be tolerated will reverberate throughout the world, including, most importantly, in the halls of power in Beijing. The Stalinist regime in North Korea is both the Communist "client state" and the lead supplier of states that sponsor terrorism. Ending this regime would remove a major source of weaponry for Iran, Syria, and others. It would send the rest of the world an important message: we will still use every means possible to oppose you no matter what you try in order to continue your brutal regime and ties to terrorism – even if you manage to acquire nuclear weapons.

The efforts by Communist China to engage and aid terrorist states have enabled it to have numerous "checks" on American power during the 1990s and the early part of this decade. It has also, however, ensured that the *victims* of those terrorist states would become more likely to look askance on the increasing power of the People's Republic. This is the first place to look for allies in Cold War II. Working with them now, we can build an anti-Communist coalition to thwart the nationalistic objectives of the People's Republic, and hasten the day when the Chinese people are finally free.

One such ally in the terrorist war is ready and willing to join America in both the war on terror and Cold War II; in fact the current terrorist war and the undeclared cold war are one and the same to this nation, the lynchpin of the strategy, the nation whose interests most dramatically intersect with American interests in both conflicts, the largest and most recently nuclearized democracy – India.

India is in the unique position of affecting several aspects of both the terrorist war and Cold War II at once, and in every instance, its interests dovetail with those of the United States. First of all, India is surpassed only to the United States, Israel, and perhaps the Philippines as a victim of radical Islamic terrorism. The December 13 Parliament attack galvanized the nation, and drove home the need to defeat al Qaeda. While Pakistan dithered at first after September 11, 2001, India offered the United States whatever it required in terms of troop deployments and use of military facilities. It supported the anti-Taliban Northern Alliance long before the liberation of Afghanistan began, and helped to ensure good relations between the United States and the dominant force in the current interim Afghan government.

India's support for the war on terror is without condition, something painfully lacking in Pakistan. For all its help against the Taliban after September 11, Pakistan helped build the anti-American terrorist sponsors prior to that date. Pakistan has also refused to acknowledge that the "freedom fighters" in Kashmir are, in fact, terrorists. India knows better, and so everyone else.

As part of its campaign against al Qaeda and Islamic terrorist, India has established working alliances with both Israel and Turkey for anti-terror cooperation. Not only does this provide an excellent opportunity to further combine Indian and American efforts, it gives us the opportunity to bring these two long-time United States allies to the forefront of the anti-Communist China alliance. This is especially important regarding Israel, which has become a large arms supplier of Communist China – in part due to the "engagement" policy of the United States in the 1990s.

Since 1998, the Indian government has listed Communist China as its leading security threat. It also is host to the Tibetan government-in-exile, as well as large expatriate Tibetan Buddhist community that longs to return to its homeland, when it is free of Communist aggression. Thus it would be ready and willing to join any American coalition against the People's Republic. In fact, it would most likely see the situation as the United States joining *their* anti-Communist efforts.

In many respects, the United States is already moving closer to India. Continuing the strengthening of these ties is essential. Equally essential is basing this friendship on a joint opposition to the People's Republic. This would bring together the world's most powerful democracy with its largest, in opposition to the largest tyranny on the planet. The fact that India may soon pass Communist China in population is even more reason for optimism in a future anti-Communist United States-India alliance.

In the latter half of the first Cold War, as the People's Republic shifted its outlook and moved closer to Washington, India's opposition to Communist China and its ally Pakistan was so strong it leaned away from the United States and towards the Soviet Union. While the Soviet Union has vanished, the relationship with Russia is still strong. This provides a possibility for what may be one of the best ways outside the People's Republic to thwart the Communist aims – end the Russian arms trade with the Communist military.

Russia is the largest military supplier to the Communists. This includes arms deals totaling four billion dollars last year alone. Russia does this for a slew of reasons, while the Communist Chinese do it largely for convenience. This has, for now, made Communist China's nationalist aims, especially where Taiwan is concerned, dependent upon the Russian arms flow. Without a functioning "blue water" navy, Communist China's plans for projecting its power, and threatening Taiwan with an invasion, don't have a leg to stand on. The Russian arms trade is, for now, solving that problem.

However, Russia has been partially shifting to the United States during the terrorist war, especially after its long-time ally in Afghanistan, the Northern Alliance, triumphed with the help of American forces. This is a trend that must be encouraged and intensified, but only in exchange for an end to the Russian-Communist China arms trade. The arms deals may be good for Russia's economy, but it's a disaster for the cause of freedom, and given the ties of the People's Republic to Iran and Ba'athist Iraq, its not very good for the terrorist war either.

A Russia willing to continue building and advancing the Communist Chinese military is no friend of the United States. However, if Russia is willing to shut down the Communist arms bazaar, the United States can, and should offer friendship and aid – either through at least some move toward the forgiveness of Soviet-era debt or by restarting the stalled plans for the purchase of surplus Russian uranium (both of these policies would be beneficial in their own right). Meanwhile, Russia's ties to India, including keeping the Northern Alliance alive during the 1990s, and Communist China's patronage of Pakistan's missile and nuclear programs should give Russia added incentive to end its arms deals with the People's Republic.

Ending the arms trade between Russia and Communist China cannot be underestimated. This would dramatically alter the balance of power in East Asia by halting Communist China's rush toward superpower status, and give Taiwan the time it desperately needs to continue to stay ahead of the Communists militarily. It might also give the Communists pause about its own brisk arms trade with terrorist states.

Another source for allies in Cold War II is East Asia. Of course, the most important nations are already allied to us – Japan, South Korea, and Taiwan. How South Korea can be included in the new anti-Communist alliance can be seen in the reunification via liberation policy has already been described. Japan and Taiwan can also be useful as allies against Communist China and its North Korean satellite.

Up until very recently, Japan was considered one of the less hostile democracies toward Communist China and North Korea. The rise of the People's Republic, coupled with the North Korean kidnapping trauma, has pushed Japan toward a more hawkish stance. There is a large anti-Communist constituency in Japan, which can be harnessed against the People's Republic. One of its leading spokesmen has been Shintaro Ishihara, the current Governor of Tokyo. Americans may remember him as the boldly nationalist author of *The Japan That Can Say "No"* in 1987. However, in the fifteen years since he has become the leading anti-Communist in Japanese politics, even to the point of calling his country's relations with Communist China a "cold war…much more dangerous than the previous cold war." Although the Japanese establishment tends to look down on him, he is widely popular in his country. As for the possibility of Japanese economic aid to North Korea – proposed as part of diplomatic "normalization" between Tokyo and Pyongyang – Ishihara responded as thusly, "If Japan will pay money to North Korea, it would mean stabbing our [U.S.] ally in the back, because a country once called part of the 'axis of evil' has not changed at all." Ishihara was also the official who first made public Japanese evidence of the Stalinists' aid to Ba'athist Iraq's Scud missile development.

Regarding Communist China, while Japan can be helpful, the best anti-Communist ally is easily Taiwan. Taiwan's very survival as a democracy depends on the United States protecting them, and on Communism's eventual fall. As long as the People's Republic survives, it will never feel secure with a vibrant democracy just across the Taiwan Strait. As such, Taiwan can, sadly, never truly be secure. Taiwan's democracy is, however, an inspiration to the dissident movements within Communist China – everyone from Falun Gong and non-Communist Christians to the China Democracy Party and other political dissidents. It is a continuing embarrassment to the Communists.

If the people of Taiwan are willing, they could serve as a political beachhead for the dissident movement in Communist China. As a stable, prosperous democracy, they would expose Communist propaganda railing against "Western style" democracy as a specious. There is a growing independence movement in the island democracy; this may at first seem contrary to the goal of undermining Communism. It does not have to be. While dissidents within Communist China would much prefer to see Taiwan remain within "one China," an independent Taiwan would shatter the myth of Communism as the vehicle for the nationalist agenda upon which it has based its survival. This could lead to a steep decline in the Communists' respectability, and put the regime itself at risk.

This is what disturbs the Communists the most about Taiwan – no matter which way it goes, it's still a threat. If Taiwan decides to support the democratic and other dissident movements within the mainland, it can provide a link for anti-Communist Chinese of all stripes to a friendly government outside the Communists' control. If the Taiwanese people choose independence, the entire post-Tiananmen justification for Communist rule would break down. Either way, a Taiwan outside Communist China's clutches is an imminent danger to Communist rule on the mainland.

In April of 2001, President Bush told the world that he would do "whatever it takes" to defend Taiwan from a Communist military attack. That was an excellent first step, but more is needed. Communist China's current military build-up can be used to either attack or intimidate the island democracy. The United States needs to make clear, without any ambiguity, that the status of Taiwan will be decided by the people of Taiwan, and *only* the people of Taiwan, without any pressure or threats from the Communist mainland.

This is the most dramatic reason why a strong American military is required. Communist China has, for the most part, already considered American support for Taiwan to be a given. As such, they have already begun preparing for attacks against the *American* military in numerous exercises for the People's Liberation Army. The United States must be prepared to fulfill its promise to do "whatever it takes."

Of course, the people of Taiwan are more than willing to defend themselves. Year after year, Taiwan has asked to buy a slew of advanced weaponry to improve its self-defense capabilities, reducing to the United States either the loss of life to stave off a Communist attack or the chance of Taiwan's defeat should it be left on its own – a scenario much less likely after the President's statement last year. Allowing Taiwan to defend itself is not only absolutely critical to thwarting Communist ambitions in Asia; it reduces the risk to American soldiers and sailors in the process. For numerous reasons, all of them tied to "engaging" the Communists, the United States has actually declined a number of the arms requests; these senseless denials must end.

Outside of Taiwan, Japan, and South Korea, the greatest potential for American alliances against Communism comes from Australia and the Philippines. Both are already American allies in the war on terrorism, and the Philippines have had several confrontations with the People's Republic on the Spratlys, an island chain in the South China Sea claimed by both Manila and Beijing. Australia is a little more complicated. While its support for the United States in the terrorist war has been without stint, its record with Communist China is less than stellar, due largely to economic and commercial interests. To be fair to the Aussies, the policy of the United States toward Communist China has also been heavily influenced by the same types of commercial interests. Once the United States is prepared to drop its "engagement" with the People's Republic, one can expect Australia to do the same, and join the United States in the anti-Communist camp. An ally as strong as Australia is unlikely to abandon us over natural gas contracts.

With these policies, and the willingness to back them up with force if needed, the United States can go a long way toward both defeating the war on terror *and* building a geopolitical coalition to isolate Communist China. This will be critical not only in shoring up our new friends in the war on terror – Afghanistan, Iraq, and hopefully a free Iran – but also convince our old friends – namely Saudi Arabia – that responding to Communist attempts at courtship is a bad idea. "Engagement," with the People's Republic, on the other hand, will lead the Saudis and others to believe they can have one foot in America's camp, and another in Communist China's. This is not something we want them to believe.

Despite their importance, however, isolation and containment are not enough for victory in Cold War II, or even the terrorist war. Cold War II also has a moral dimension, and we must help those willing to join us in that moral discussion. The United States must be prepared to take the discussion to within Communist China itself – highlighting its human rights abuses, labor rights abuses, and crackdowns on dissidents of every stripe. One of the first places to look is one that has largely escaped media attention: East Turkestan.

Few followers of Islam have suffered under worse persecution that the Uighur people of East Turkestan. After a brief independence during the 1940s, the Uighurs saw their religion, their culture, and their way of life come under the crushing blows of a massive Communist crackdown, mass induced and forced migration of Han Chinese by the People's Republic, and economic development steered almost entirely to the local Communist Party and the new Han arrivals. The result has been a region cut in two, the new, seemingly modern Han "Xinjiang," and the impoverished, persecuted East Turkestan.

Support for the people of East Turkestan, up to and including recognition of an independent republic there, would dramatically destroy every accusation of anti-Muslim prejudice thrown at the United States regarding the war on terror. It would also support an ethnic group whose suffering at Communist hands has made it the most pro-American Muslim group on Earth. It would encourage the moderate Islam that is typical of the Uighur people, and be a stark reminder to Muslims everywhere that an anti-American *jihad* is not the path to freedom and independence.

During the Afghanistan resistance against the puppet regime imposed by the Soviet Union, America had an opportunity to cultivate a non-radical Muslim-majority nation. In ensuring resistance to Communism, the United States did quite well. When it came to building a democratic, anti-radical successor state, the United States blew it, deferring to Pakistan and Saudi Arabia during the *mujahedin* of the 1980s, and leaving the nation entirely in their hands during the 1990s. By supporting the East Turkestan independence movement now, we can avoid repeating those mistakes. We can also ensure that those in the East Turkestani independence movement who do succumb to the terrorist impulse are marginalized, and removed, quickly. This would go a long way toward reassuring our new allies in Central Asia that they have nothing to fear from an independent East Turkestan.

This anti-terrorism benefit can extend to other areas of the terrorist war. The more we support the East Turkestani people, the more political capital we have for actions against Muslim-based terrorists. Actions in favor of the moderate, pro-American Uighur resistance to Communist China would make the case that our actions are not against Muslims but against terrorists practically beyond reproach.

Such action would also put the Communists on the defensive – exposing yet another arena of brutal human rights violations and the destruction of a culture from a conquered land. Tibet's travails are known the world over, but the people of East Turkestan have suffered just as horribly, at least. Making their case to the world is just as much of a moral imperative, as well beneficial strategically for the reasons described above. It is the greatest blow we can strike in both the terrorist war and Cold War II simultaneously.

Finally, supporting the East Turkestani cause would once and for all pull the anti-terrorist veneer off Communist China's actions, both domestically and internationally. The Communists have used September 11 to justify its Falun Gong crackdown, its saber-rattling against Taiwan, its arrests of dissidents, and its Tibet brutality. East Turkestan has been the key, the supposed justification and cover for its terrible abuses of its own people, its threats against Taiwan, its destruction of Tibet, and the war on terror. Remove that justification, and the actions of the People's Republic are exposed for what they are – the brutal crushing of dissent by a ruthless, self-absorbed regime exploiting the fears felt by the rest of the world to justify actions that have no real justification.

The American position on human rights in East Turkestan – minus the terrorist designation of the East Turkestan Islamic Movement (ETIM) – is quite good, and was reinforced nicely with the strong words of Lorne Craner. Building upon that policy to one of full support for East Turkestan independence is thus not as difficult as it may seem, and the benefits from such a policy would aid both the war on terror and Cold War II.

None of this is meant to minimize the suffering of the people of Tibet; support for them is also critical both to apply pressure on the People's

Republic and to move closer to India, the host of Tibet's government in exile. In fact, stronger support for Tibet will also add to the American-backed anti-Communist coalition a highly unlikely, but very important, element: the Western European left. Driven by its admiration for the Dalai Lama, the European left is host to some of the continent's leading critics of Communist China. While the possibility of the group as a whole throwing in behind the United States is improbable, the United States can certainly find a 21st century version of the "non-Communist left" that provided some of the most salient – and in Europe, the most politically effective – opposition to the Soviets.

Support for East Turkestan and Tibet can be found in Eastern Europe as well – not surprising given its history of Communist suffering. Estonia has hosted a Uighur conference on East Turkestan, and Poland has been supportive of the Tibetan cause ever since it was liberated from Soviet Communism.

By far, however, internal resistance to the Communists from the Chinese people will be the most critical form of anti-Communism within the area the Party controls. Tens of millions of Chinese demanded change in 1989, only to get the barrel of a gun in response. Communist China has done whatever it can to ensure the "intellectuals" in the Potemkin cities (Shenzhen, Beijing, Shanghai, and Hong Kong) are in its pocket, but many still resist. While Zhao Ziyang – the Communist Party chief placed under house arrest for backing the Tiananmen protests – has been quiet, his loyal aide, Bao Tong, has become a leading spokesman for reform and democracy.

Bao has also noticed a trend within Communist China that can be of tremendous use – the complete abandonment of the Chinese worker and farmer in a state built supposedly in their name. The average farmer in Communist China can barely survive, thanks to illegal taxes imposed by local corrupt Communists. Meanwhile, factory laborers have seen promises of wages and pensions go by the wayside. It has led to a slew of labor actions, including tens of thousands protesting in Lioyang and Heliongjiang provinces last year.

As mentioned earlier, the corruption within Communist China is rapidly growing to the stuff of legend. Billions of dollars in embezzled money and unpaid taxes and customs duties are rapidly becoming normal – Xiamen's short-lived reign as the largest scandal in Communist history, for example, and the Guangdong tax evasion scheme that replaced it. Most within the Communist Party acknowledge that this is the one issue – outside of a lack of success in the nationalist agenda – that could bring down the Communist regime at the hands of an enraged populace.

The rural hinterlands in particular are seething with rage. Protests against the Communists in the rural interior totaled over 100,000 in 1999 alone, and several other independent labor actions, including the formation of anti-Communist labor unions, have occurred, all in reaction to a Communist Party that has become, in Bao's words, "the party of the rich." This is a first for any Communist Party: a sign of its strength in its ability to adapt, but also a sign of its weaknesses in the fury it has unleashed among those it has betrayed.

Those who would discount the power of the hinterland protests should remember that the leading force for change in the Soviet Union, and the man who stood down the coup plotters in 1991, was not Mikhail Gorbachev. The putchists easily outmaneuvered the educated son of an *apparatchik* from Moscow. What they did not anticipate, and could not combat, was the surge in opposition driven and symbolized by the fiery construction worker from Sverdlovsk (now Yekaterinaburg), Boris Yeltsin. In much the same way, the anti-Milosevic protests in Yugoslavia, while certainly impressive, seemed unlikely to depose Europe's last Communist tyranny – until miners from Cacak and other blue-collar workers from industrial cities joined the fray. While outsiders may discount the strength of the resistance in the hinterlands, and what it can do, the Chinese Communist Party, which took power in large part from its strength and support in the rural mainland, is not so foolish. The United States shouldn't be so foolish either.

These policies – supporting dissidents within the People's Republic, supporting the liberation of North Korea and Middle Eastern sponsors of terror, building and strengthening alliances with India, Japan, South Korea, and Taiwan, building democratic governments in Afghanistan and Iraq, and having a military large enough to back up America's interests and the interests of liberty – would bring closer the day that the Chinese people will be able to rise up and take their country back. They would also prevent possible future intermediaries between Communist China and terrorist groups – Saudi Arabia, the United Arab Emirates, and Yemen – from either continuing their terrorist ties *or* reaching out to Communist China. Finally, they will ensure that winning the war on terror will not lead to losing the peace due to geopolitical maneuvering.

An anti-Communist China policy is not a diversion from the war on terror; it is a vital counterpart to it. The war on terror and Cold War II share several connections. Fighting one inevitably leads to becoming entangled in the other, whether America likes it or not. Vigorously fighting both will make winning them far easier.

Terror as a policy aim was practically invented by. The Soviet Union was a leading supporter of Syria – one of the biggest terrorist sponsors in recent history. Both the U.S.S.R. and the Communist China counted North Korea as an ally, and the People's Republic still does. Communist China has found willing military customers in Ba'athist Iraq, Iran, and Libya. It saw Saddam Hussein and Osama bin Laden as a "some kind of check" on American power, in the case of the latter to the point of paying him millions of dollars for unexploded American cruise missiles. It even invited Taliban leaders to Beijing for talks after American Special Forces joined with the Northern Alliance to expel the group from power in Afghanistan. These are not the actions of an ally; they are the actions of an enemy.

The United States must recognize Communist China for what it really is, not what it wants us to believe it is or will be. Unless Cold War II is won, the war on terror will last far longer – if it ever ends – and take many more American lives, including the possible losses of entire cities to nuclear weapons from North Korea, care of Communist-backed terrorists. The greatest obstacle to American liberty and security lies not in Baghdad, Tikrit, Kabul, Kandahar, Tehran, Damascus, or even Pyongyang. It is the Communist dictatorship in Beijing. It must be brought down.

Chapter 9:
Conclusion – What the Future Holds

The forces we face in the war on terror and Cold War II have joined together because they are both enemies of the American idea of liberty and its practical application in our democracy-based republic. The need to defeat the terrorists and their immediate sponsors has been apparent since September 11, 2001. However, without the end of Communism, victory against terrorism, if it comes at all, would accomplish much less than we expect, while the resulting peace will be more short-lived than many realize.

Victory in the terrorist war, by itself, will remove numerous regimes that could become very dangerous both by themselves and as Communist allies. However, it would still leave Communist China to find new anti-American allies, as well as customers for a wide range of arms, including biological, chemical, and possibly nuclear weapons. The policy of "engagement" will simply allow the People's Republic to continue developing its military power and economic clout, making the inevitable conflict with the United States all the nastier.

Many would disagree with this assessment of the future, and would cite, among other things, the change with the passing of the torch from Jiang Zemin to Hu Jintao. Assuming this actually happens – Hu is not expected to take over the Central Military Commission in a couple of years, and in modern Communist China, only with control of the Central Military Commission can a Communist cadre, even the ostensible leader of the party, truly solidify his control over the People's Republic – this change in leadership means a lot less to the United States than is immediately apparent. For starters, the growth of the military in Communist Chinese politics has made it a voice that leaders in the party would resist at their peril. Jiang himself won over the military with big budgets (especially in his last few years as General Secretary), major modernization, and a greater emphasis on nationalism abroad.

Would Hu change course? His history in the party is not comforting. Hu was the party boss in Tibet during the Tiananmen Square massacre, and he reacted like any good Communist chief in Tibet would – he cracked down on dissent. He was also the first regional party boss to congratulate the cadres in Beijing for the Tiananmen Square massacre. He has shown no willingness to moderate the party line on foreign policy, either. In fact, the one of the very few things he has said on foreign policy could be a terrible harbinger for both Cold War II and the terrorist war. No one should forget that while visiting the Ba'athist dictator Bashar al-Assad in Syria, Hu called Israel a "colonialist plot aimed at detaching from the Arab nation a part that is dear to it – Palestine." The line was similar to rants from Saddam Hussein's Iraq, Iran, and Syria, and is actually the closest embodiment of ideological Ba'athism to be heard from a non-Arab official. That it comes from the man taking the reigns of Communist China is, to put it mildly, not a good sign.

This only makes the need for a tough, determined, anti-Communist policy for Cold War II even *more* imperative. Taking diplomatic, economic, and geopolitical action now against the Communists will leave them much weaker and as such, much less able to find nations willing to sign on as a "check" on United States power. It will also leave the Chinese people in a much better position to liberate themselves from the Communists.

An anti-Communist policy would, despite its near-complete absence from the current political discourse, be far more popular with the American people than "engagement." The American people are already deeply suspicious of Communist China and its objectives. One of the crown jewels of "engagement" – Permanent Normal Trade Relations (nee Most Favored Nation status) with Communist China – had always been opposed by a majority of Americans, despite being passed by both houses of Congress two years ago. Even today, in the midst of the supposedly unconnected war on terror, a majority of Americans consider the continued rise of Communist China to be a major issue for American foreign policy. The common sense anti-Communism of the American people has never died; it is simply looking for someone to act upon it.

As the evidence of Communist China's ties to terrorist states becomes public knowledge, it is all but certain that the American people will look for leaders ready to fight Cold War II – leaders who are out there in *both* major parties: from liberals such as House Minority Leader Nancy Pelosi to conservatives such as Congressmen J.D. Hayworth and Dana Rohrbacher. The question is more likely to be when this will happen, rather than if it will happen.

The sooner it happens, the better. Even the most hawkish Communist general would admit that the People's Republic will be in a much better position against the United States in the future – roughly fifteen to twenty-five years from now – than in the present. The balance of military power between Taiwan and Communist China is another matter: that may tip in favor of the People's Republic by 2005, and internal Communists political issues may push whomever is the leader of Communist China – Jiang or Hu – to act against the island democracy.

In order to prevent this, America must be prepared to defend Taiwan, and to let the world – especially the People's Republic – know it. President Bush started well with his insistence that the United States would do "whatever it takes" to keep Taiwan free. Now he only needs to put substance and policy details behind his inspiring words.

Within Communist China, most see the People's Republic acquiring a role of equality or near-equality with the United States in military and geopolitical power as occurring sometime between 2020 and 2030. The question is this: will the United States take the time to focus solely on the terrorist war, ignoring Cold War II? Or will they recognize it as an opportunity to press for the freedom of the Chinese and along the way remove the supply of weapons to anti-American states?

Many who support "engagement" say that Communist China is destined to become a democracy in the future. That is likely true. However, it would have also been true in 1900 to say Germany would be a democracy in the future. By 1990, Germany was indeed a democratic American ally, but few Americans would say it was a painless transition for Germany, the United States, or anyone else in the world. The Chinese people will indeed be free, but *how* and *when* they win that freedom is just as critical for the United States as *if* they win that freedom.

If the United States keeps in place the "engagement" *status quo*, it will be faced with a Communist China that is greatly more powerful a generation from now than it is today. Taiwan, if it still survives, will be a much more vulnerable democracy that may be forced into "Finlandization," i.e., parroting the foreign policy of its more powerful Communist neighbor. Europe may be less inclined to support us in the inevitable clash, forcing us to rely on our new allies in Eastern Europe, India, and Japan, while constantly having to keep a wary eye on Russia – whose continued arms sales to the Communists will ensure it has a foot in both camps, and that could be a very optimistic assessment of Russia's future position in the world under "engagement."

Meanwhile, "engagement" with Communist China would also give it the cover it needs to build new anti-American ties to terror sponsors and regimes that have played on both sides, such as Saudi Arabia. Its ties to Pakistan, its former support for the Afghan Taliban, and its vast supply of oil make it the prime candidate for warmer ties to the People's Republic, which could make American interests much harder to advance in both Cold War II, and the war of terror. The United Arab Emirates and Yemen also have potential for the Communists in this regard.

Finally, North Korea will continue to develop their nuclear arsenal, or even worse, give terrorists and their sponsors throughout the world nuclear weapons capability. Do we really want nuclear weapons in the possession of the Iranian mullahs, Syria's Ba'athists, Hezbollah, Hamas, the al Aqsa brigades, or even al Qaeda itself, who would be more than willing to use them in America's cities?

In short, "engagement" would likely make the terrorist war much more difficult – if not impossible – to win, and could very well cost America at least one major city to a nuclear holocaust in the process. Even should American be able to win the terrorist war, Cold War II would likely come to dominate world politics for the remainder of the century, and the peace the American people are expecting after the terrorist war would be delayed for generations.

In order to avoid this future, the United States will have to drop its "engagement" fallacy, and recognize that Cold War II is real. However, the

United States need not be alone in this war. In particular, Japan, Taiwan, South Korea, and India will be with us, if we are resolute in our convictions, and willing to back them up with support of anti-Communists and anti-terrorists and, if need be, military force. Meanwhile, those who might consider Communist China a useful ally would think again if the United States is vigorously engaged in Cold War II, and the evidence of Communist Chinese ties to terrorists and terrorist states is forced into the public glare. An America willing to fight and win Cold War II would greatly reduce the cooperation, either directly or through intermediaries, between Communist China and terrorist groups. As a result, America would face terrorist forces that are less powerful and resourceful then they otherwise would be, and a Communist China with fewer "checks" to employ against American interests in Asia and throughout the world.

Additionally, the people trapped inside Communist China, seeing that the United States is serious about helping them in their fight for freedom, would become more helpful to us. This is not as difficult, or as outlandish, as it sounds. Resistance to tyranny can come in several forms, and if we are prepared to support all of them, they will certainly increase. Communism in Poland faced a worker-inspired movement, while in Czechoslovakia the intellectuals took the lead. The Soviet Union faced both at the same time, plus a slew of nationalities fighting to reclaim their identity. It should be noted that the Communists' worry about the Tiananmen Square protest reached its height when it became clear that rural farmers and workers had joined the student demonstrators. Add the Tibetan and East Turkestani peoples, Hong Kong activists, the internal political dissidents, underground churches, and Falun Gong, and the possibilities are limitless. All of these groups can become our front lines in Cold War II.

DRAGON IN THE DARK
How and Why Communist China Helps Our Enemies in the War on Terror

Isolated from the rest of the world, forced to expend resources they would rather use elsewhere preserving their choke-holds on Tibet and East Turkestan, faced with a confident Taiwan backed by a world-wide democratic coalition, deprived of any outside friends or any real benefits to show the increasingly frustrated Chinese people, and battling energized dissident communities in matters of faith, economics, and politics, Communist China will fall; America will be secure, and the people of China will at last be free.

In 2003, this may sound far-fetched. However, anyone who predicted the Soviet Union's collapse in December 1979 would seem equally overoptimistic. The only one who even considered the possibilities was a fellow named Ronald Reagan. Not only was he optimistic enough to believe, but hardheaded enough to implement the policies needed to bring it about. A dozen years later, the Soviet Union was dead; its satellite states were free; and the world was infinitely safer.

History will note this century as defined by two dates: September 11, 2001 and June 4, 1989. The former reintroduced to the United States and its elected leaders to the dangers from without; the latter reintroduced to Communist China the dangers from within. Both have reacted to these dates differently, but the Communists have brought those dates together with its continuing support of terrorist sponsoring states, either directly or through its North Korean satellite. By recognizing the importance of these dates to each other, their victims – the American and Chinese peoples – can act against the terrorists and Chinese Communists who made those days tragically memorable. America can be free from terrorism, and China will be free from Communism. The terrorist war and Cold War II can both end in triumph, and together, the people of the United States and of China can bring all the peoples of the world that much closer to banishing both tyranny and its bastard child terrorism from the face of the earth.

The war against terror is a war to preserve freedom. Our terrorist enemies oppose us because they fear what freedom can do. Cold War II exists for the same reason, but unlike the terrorists, Communist China has managed to convince many Americans that its war against the United States does not exist. However, not only is Cold War II real, it is very deeply intertwined in the war on terror. In order to advance its interests with groups that "represent some kind of check" against the United States, the People's Republic of China has reached out to Saddam Hussein's Iraq, Mullah Omar's Taliban, radical Islamic Iran, Stalinist North Korea, Syria, Libya, Sudan, and even Osama bin Laden and al Qaeda, all the while exploiting the very terrorists acts committed by these nations and groups as cover for its brutal crackdown against its internal dissidents and opponents, from Uighur Muslims in East Turkestan and Buddhists in Tibet to pro-democracy supporters throughout Communist China. In order to move closer to a world where terrorism is a thing of the past, and freedom is ascendant, the United States must do more than to simply defeat the sponsors of terror in Afghanistan and the axis of evil. A lasting victory in the terrorist war will only come with victory in Cold War II, and the end of Communism in China.

Works Cited

Ackerman, Peter and DuVall, Jack, *A Force More Powerful: A Century of Nonviolent Conflict*, excerpted by WETA, "Nonviolent Power", *Bringing Down a Dictator*, PBS, http://www.pbs.org/weta/dictator/otpor/nonviolence.html

Agence France Presse, "Dalai Lama, in Poland, still open to talk with Beijing", May 10, 2000, reprinted by World Tibet Network News, http://www.tibet.ca/wtnarchive/2000/5/10_1.html

Amnesty International, *1998 Annual Report on the PRC*, cited in "Eastern Turkestan FAQ", International Taklamakan Human Rights Association, http://www.taklamakan.org/uighur-l/et_faq_p1.html#d3_b

Amnesty International, cited by United Kingdom Foreign and Commonwealth Office, *Saddam Hussein*, p. 14

Anti-PNTR press conference with Gary Bauer and Rep. Frank Wolf, May 22, 2002, (Press release by Bauer's Campaign for Working Families: http://www.cwfpac.com/press_releases_05_22.htm)

Applebaum, "Solidarity, Iranian Style", *Washington Post*, December 18, 2002, http://www.washingtonpost.com/ac2/wp-dyn?pagename=article&node=&contentId=A4376-2002Dec17&notFound=true

Arraf, Jane, "China denies role in Iraq," CNN, February 21, 2001, http://edition.cnn.com/2001/WORLD/asiapcf/east/02/21/china.iraq.02/index.html

Associated Press, "Iraq: Who's In, Who's Out?", reprinted in CBS News, October 13, 2002, http://www.cbsnews.com/stories/2002/10/15/attack/main525593.shtml

Baldauf, Scott, "Al Qaeda regroups for attack", *Christian Science Monitor*, reprinted in *Washington Times*, August 10, 2002, http://www.washtimes.com/world/20020810-4317405.htm

Barrett, R. Morris, "Congress Prepares To Vote On China Trade", CNN, June 23, 1997, Page 1-2, http://asia.cnn.com/ALLPOLITICS/1997/06/23/china/index.html, and http://asia.cnn.com/ALLPOLITICS/1997/06/23/china/index2.html

Barry, John and Thomas, Evan, "China: The Conflict To Come", *Newsweek*, April 23, 2001, reprinted by Taiwan Security Research, http://taiwansecurity.org/News/2001/Newsweek-042301.htm

Bedi, Rahul and Rashid, Ahmed "US demands use of Pakistani air space", *Daily Telegraph* (UK), September 15, 2001, http://www.telegraph.co.uk/news/main.jhtml?xml=/news/2001/09/15/watt315.xml

Bennett, Brian, "How Serious is the Campaign?", *Time Asia*, October 9, 2000, http://www.time.com/time/asia/magazine/2000/1009/chn_corruption_sb1.html

Berke, Ronnie and Koppel, Andrea, "Official: China won't stand in way of U.N. resolution on Taliban", CNN, December 5, 2000, http://www.cnn.com/2000/US/12/05/un.afghanistan/index.html

Bindra, Satinder, "India debates response to Kashmir raid", CNN, May 17, 2002, http://asia.cnn.com/2002/WORLD/asiapcf/south/05/16/india.us.games/index.html

Black, Ian and Borger, Julian, "Rumsfeld accuses Syria of sheltering Ba'athists", *The Guardian*, April 10, 2003, http://politics.guardian.co.uk/foreignaffairs/story/0,11538,933638,00.html

Bohn, Kevin, "FBI: Jailed man tried to call terrorist paymaster", CNN, March 21, 2002, http://www.cnn.com/2002/WORLD/meast/03/21/inv.attacks.uae.calls/index.html

Brooke, James, "Defectors From North Korea Tell of Prison Baby Killings", *The New York Times*, June 10, 2002, http://www.nytimes.com/2002/06/10/international/asia/10KORE.html

Buckley, William F., Jr., "Afloat in Paradoxes", *National Review Online*, November 19, 2002, http://www.nationalreview.com/buckley/buckley111902.asp

Limbacher, Carl and Newsmax Staff, "China Still Meeting With Taliban," Newsmax, September 9, 2002, http://www.Newsmax/showinside.shtml?a=2002/9/9/155340

Chandrasekaran, Rajiv and Lakshmi, Rama, "New Delhi Lays Blame on Pakistani Group", *Washington Post*, December 29, 2001, http://www.washingtonpost.com/wp-dyn/articles/A36985-2001Dec28.html

Chen Jian, *China's Road to the Korean War: The making of the Sino-American Confrontation*, Columbia University Press, New York, 1994, p. 22, as cited by John Lewis Gaddis, *We Now Know: Rethinking Cold War History*", Clarendon Press, Oxford, 1997, p. 64

Chiang, Antonio, "Let History Be the Judge", *Time Asia*, March 27, 2000, http://www.time.com/time/asia/magazine/2000/0327/taiwan.viewpoint.chiang.html

Cho, Joohee and Goodman, Peter S., "Anti-United States Sentiment Deepens in S. Korea", *Washington Post*, January 9, 2003, http://www.washingtonpost.com/wp-dyn/articles/A30309-2003Jan8.html

Cho, and Pan, Phillip P., "N. Koreans Seized at Consulate Freed by China, Arrive in Seoul," *Washington Post*, May 23, 2002, http://www.washingtonpost.com/wp-dyn/articles/A59629-2002May22.html

Chu, Henry, "RESPONSE TO TERROR; China Says Radicals Led Attacks and Colluded With Bin Laden; Asia: Report blames Muslims in restive Xinjiang for 162 deaths," *Los Angeles Times*, January 22, 2002, http://www.latimes.com/news/nationworld/world/la-000005651jan22.story?coll=la%2Dheadlines%2Dworld

Chung, Chien-peng, "China's 'War on Terror': September 11 and Uighur Separatism", The Mail Archive, July 16, 2002, http://www.mail-archive.com/uighur-l@taklamakan.org/msg03176.html, and Tim Healy and Hsieh, David, "No Comfort for Criminals", *Asiaweek*, March 21, 1997, http://www.asiaweek.com/asiaweek/97/0321/nat5.html

Clarke, Michael, "Analysis: Terror group evolution", BBC, September 1, 2002, http://news.bbc.co.uk/2/hi/in_depth/world/2002/september_11_one_year_on/2217177.stm

Cohen, Ariel, "Fighting to the Last Palestinian", *National Review Online*, April 10, 2002, http://www.nationalreview.com/comment/comment-cohen041002.asp

Cohen, "The Nativity Sin", *National Review Online*, April 24, 2002, http://www.nationalreview.com/comment/comment-cohen042402.asp

Constable, Pamela, "Missile Defense Plan Is Uniting United States, India", *Washington Post*, May 20, 2001, http://www.washingtonpost.com/ac2/wp-dyn?pagename=article&node=&contentId=A50483-2001May19&notFound=true

Cossa, Ralph A., "And the Winner Is...Lee Teng-hui", Center for Strategic & International Studies, December 3, 2001, http://www.csis.org/pacfor/pac0148A.htm

Cronin, Audrey Kurth, "What war on terrorism?", *Washington Times*, July 30, 2002, http://www.washtimes.com/op-ed/20020730-21496846.htm

Dan, Uri, "'Yemen' Scuds Baghdad-Bound", *New York Post*, December 27, 2002, http://www.nypost.com/news/worldnews/65620.htm

Derbyshire, John, "Neutral on the Olympics", *National Review Online*, June 26, 2001 http://www.nationalreview.com/derbyshire/derbyshire062601.shtml

DeYoung, Karen, "Bush Seeks Power to Lift Arms Curbs", *Washington Post*, September 24, 2001, http://www.washingtonpost.com/wp-dyn/articles/A14035-2001Sep23.html

DeYoung and Peter Slevin, Peter, "N. Korea Admits Having Secret Nuclear Arms", *Washington Post*, October 16, 2002, http://www.washingtonpost.com/wp-dyn/articles/A37481-2002Oct16.html

Easen, Nick, "Aksai Chin: China's disputed slice of Kashmir", CNN, May 24, 2002, http://edition.cnn.com/2002/WORLD/asiapcf/east/05/24/aksai.chin/

Editorial, "A Pass on Preemption", *Washington Post*, December 12, 2002, http://www.washingtonpost.com/wp-dyn/articles/A42995-2002Dec11.html

Editorial, "China Under Cover", *Washington Post*, September 2, 2002, http://www.washingtonpost.com/wp-dyn/articles/A24663-2002Sep1.html

Editorial, "China's Rules", *Washington Post*, April 26, 2000, http://www.washingtonpost.com/wp-srv/WPlate/2000-04/26/008l-042600-idx.html

Editorial, "Pakistan's Putsch", *The New Republic*, November 1, 1999, http://www.tnr.com/current/editorial110199.html

Editorial, "The year of the defector", *Washington Times*, May 15, 2002, http://www.washtimes.com/op-ed/20020515-67485788.htm

Edwards, John O., "China's Military Planners Took Credit for 9/11", Newsmax, September 25, 2002, http://www.Newsmax/archives/articles/2002/9/24/143618.shtml

Excerpt of Lee Soon Ok's testimony to the Senate Judiciary Committee, *The Guardian* (UK), July 19, 2002, http://www.guardian.co.uk/korea/article/0,2763,757729,00.html

Eyewitness account of Parhat Niyaz, cited in "The Gulja Uprising (February 1997)", Citizens Against Communist Chinese Propaganda, http://www.geocities.com/CapitolHill/1730/yining_97.html#eye1

Farah, Joseph, "China moves on Africa", World Net Daily, August 29, 2000, http://w114.wnd.com/news/article.asp?ARTICLE_ID=15036

Finn, Peter, "Secret Tape Suggests China-Bin Laden Link," *Washington Post*, October 20, 2001, http://www.washingtonpost.com/wp-dyn/articles/A23933-2001Oct19.html

FlorCuz, Jaime, "N. Korea creates 'special economic zone'", September 25, 2002, http://asia.cnn.com/2002/WORLD/asiapcf/east/09/23/nkorea.economic/index.html

Forney, Matthew, "China's New Terrorists", *Time Asia*, September 23, 2002, http://www.time.com/time/asia/magazine/article/0,13673,501020923-351276,00.html

Forney, "One Nation—Divided", *Time Asia*, March 25, 2002, http://www.time.com/time/asia/magazine/article/0,13673,501020325-218371,00.html

Fung, Kelvin, "Back to the Future", *Asiaweek*, October 22, 1999, http://www.asiaweek.com/asiaweek/magazine/99/1022/pakistan.timeline.html

Gaddis, John Lewis, *We Know Now: Rethinking Cold War History*, Clarendon Press, Oxford, 1997, pp. 70-84

Gannon, Kathy, "Afghan warlord to aid al Qaeda", Associated Press, printed in the *Washington Times*, December 26, 2002, http://www.washtimes.com/world/20021226-15353155.htm

Gellman, Brian, "United States Suspects Al Qaeda Got Nerve Agent From Iraqis", *Washington Post*, December 12, 2002, http://www.washingtonpost.com/wp-dyn/articles/A42876-2002Dec11.html

Gellman, Brian, interview with CNN, "Reporter: VX tip comes from a credible source", CNN, December 13, 2002, http://asia.cnn.com/2002/US/12/12/cnna.gellman/index.html

Geostrategy-Direct, "China, Pakistan sign secret pacts", reprinted by World Net Daily, March 21, 2002, http://www.wnd.com/news/printer-friendly.asp?ARTICLE_ID=26907

Gertz, William (Bill), "Allied warplanes expand counterattacks", *Washington Times*, September 17, 2002, http://www.washtimes.com/national/20020917-29771086.htm

Gertz, "China aids Pakistani, 'rogue' missile programs, CIA says", *Washington Times*, February 27, 2001, http://www.washtimes.com/national/default-200122723245.htm

Gertz, "China ships North Korea ingredient for nuclear arms", *Washington Times*, December 17, 2002, http://www.washtimes.com/national/20021217-407202.htm

Gertz, "China steps up air-defense work on Iran's border fears", *Washington Times*, October 18, 2001, http://www.washtimes.com/national/20011018-829249.htm

Gertz, "China supports foreign leftists", *Washington Times*, May 10, 2001, http://www.washtimes.com/national/20010510-83886228.htm

Gertz, "Chinese firm hit with United States sanctions", *Washington Times*, May 23, 2003, http://www.washtimes.com/national/20030523-123039-1385r.htm

Gertz, "Chinese general told threat against United States unacceptable", *Washington Times*, December 11, 2002, http://www.washtimes.com/national/20021211-27417625.htm

Gertz, "CIA uncovers missile moves by China", *Washington Times*, September 8, 2001, cited by Newsmax, September 10, 2001, http://www.Newsmax/archives/articles/2001/9/8/130115.shtml

Gertz, "Exporting weapons draws United States sanctions", *Washington Times*, May 20, 2002, http://www.washtimes.com/national/20020520-3664095.htm

Gertz, "N. Korea delivers semi-submersible gunships to Iran", *Washington Times*, December 16, 2002, http://www.washtimes.com/national/20021216-39526000.htm

Gertz, "N. Korea gunboat shipment helps Iran expand military", *Washington Times*, March 20, 2002, http://www.washingtontimes.com/national/20020320-7218676.htm

Gertz, "N. Korea missile threat increases", *Washington Times*, November 1, 2002, http://www.washtimes.com/national/20021101-11616336.htm

Gertz, "N. Korea ships fuel, missiles to Yemen", *Washington Times*, December 2, 2002, http://www.washtimes.com/national/20021202-71029594.htm

Gertz, "North Korea can build nukes right now", *Washington Times*, November 22, 2002, http://www.washtimes.com/national/20021122-85983350.htm

Gertz, "Pakistan sends supplies to Taliban", *Washington Times*, November 1, 2001, http://www.washingtontimes.com/national/20011031-23126172.htm

Gertz, "Pentagon says China refitting missiles to hit Okinawa", *Washington Times*, July 31, 2003, http://www.washtimes.com/national/20030730-105115-8410r.htm

Gertz, "Reno calls Taiwan an intelligence threat", *Washington Times*, May 24, 2000, http://washingtontimes.com/national/default-2000524233846.htm

Gertz, "Rumsfeld targets Saddam, but not other 'axis' regimes", *Washington Times*, July 31, 2002, http://www.washtimes.com/national/20020731-94716048.htm

Gertz, "Taliban leader cites help by China", *Washington Times*, October 31, 2001, http://www.washtimes.com/national/20011031-81895451.htm

Gertz, "United States confirms weapons-sales sanctions", *Washington Times*, July 20, 2002, http://www.washtimes.com/national/20020720-83976356.htm

Gertz, "United States nabs cache of portable missiles", *Washington Times*, June 1, 2002, http://www.washtimes.com/national/20020601-74768506.htm

Ghattas, Kim, "Lebanon nervous over Hezbollah link", BBC, October 13, 2001, http://news.bbc.co.uk/2/hi/middle_east/1597652.stm

Gluckman, Ron, "Strangers in their Own Land", *Asiaweek*, December 7, 2001, http://www.asiaweek.com/asiaweek/magazine/dateline/0,8782,186269,00.html

Goldberg, Jeffrey "The Great Terror", *The New Yorker*, March 25, 2002, http://www.newyorker.com/fact/content/?020325fa_FACT1

Goldberg, Jonah, "Same Old", *National ReviewOnline*, October 1, 2002, http://www.nationalreview.com/goldberg/goldberg100102.asp

Goldman, T. R., "China Trade Crash Looms", *Legal Times*, February 7, 2000, p. 1

Goldstein, Steven M., "After 53 years, United States still involved in China's civil war", CNN: Taiwan Decides 2000, Undated, http://asia.cnn.com/SPECIALS/2000/taiwan.election/stories/goldstein.dc.view/

Goodenough, Patrick, "Babies Killed In North Korean Prison Camps, Observers Say", Cybercast News, June 12, 2002, http://www.cnsnews.com/ViewForeignBureaus.asp?Page=\ForeignBureaus\archive\200206\FOR20020612b.html

Goodenough, "China Ready For Enhanced Security Cooperation With US – Jiang", Cybercast News, October 24, 2002, http://www.cnsnews.com/ViewForeignBureaus.asp?Page=\ForeignBureaus\archive\200210\FOR20021024f.html

Goodenough, "China Repeats Opposition To Missile Defense; Russian Reaction Low-Key", Cybercast News, December 4, 2001, http://www.cnsnews.com/ViewForeignBureaus.asp?Page=\ForeignBureaus\archive\200112\FOR20011204g.html

Goodenough, "Clinton: We Drew Up Plans To Destroy N. Korean Nuclear Reactor", Cybercast News, December 16, 2002, http://www.cnsnews.com/ViewForeignBureaus.asp?Page=\ForeignBureaus\archive\200212\FOR20021216b.html

Goodenough, "Desperate North Korean Defectors Seek New Life In South", Cybercast News, June 12, 2002, http://www.cnsnews.com/ViewForeignBureaus.asp?Page=\ForeignBureaus\archive\200206\FOR20020612a.html

Goodenough, "Japan-China Row Over Korean Defectors Simmers", Nay 13, 2002, http://www.cnsnews.com/ViewForeignBureaus.asp?Page=\ForeignBureaus\archive\200205\FOR20020513a.html

Goodenough, "Muslim Separatists in China Labeled Terrorists", Cybercast News, August 27, 2002, http://www.cnsnews.com/ViewForeignBureaus.asp?Page=\ForeignBureaus\archive\200208\FOR20020827a.html

Goodenough, "North Korea Reacts to 'Nuclear Lunatics' in White House", Cybercast News, March 14, 2002, http://www.cnsnews.com/ViewForeignBureaus.asp?Page=\ForeignBureaus\archive\200203\FOR20020314a.html

Goodenough, "US Halts Oil Shipments To North Korea Over Nuclear Program", Cybercast News, November 15, 2002, http://www.cnsnews.com/ViewForeignBureaus.asp?Page=\ForeignBureaus\archive\200211\FOR20021115a.html

Grammaticus, Damian, "North Korea steps up economic reform", BBC, September 23, 2002, http://news.bbc.co.uk/2/hi/business/2275707.stm

Grammaticas, "Singapore tops Hong Kong for business", BBC, April 24, 2002, http://news.bbc.co.uk/hi/english/business/newsid_1948000/1948605.stm

Hattori, Ted, "Official sees strain on ties with United States", *Washington Times*, October 15, 2002, http://www.washtimes.com/world/20021015-76824624.htm

Healy, Tim and Hsieh, David, "Mao Now", *Asiaweek*, September 6, 1996, http://www.asiaweek.com/asiaweek/96/0906/cs1.html

Helms, Jesse, "Beware China's ties to the Taliban", *Washington Times*, October 14, 2001, http://www.washtimes.com/commentary/20011014-85295120.htm and "China 'outstrips world' on executions"

Hiscock, Geoff, "Australia wins huge China LNG deal", CNN, August 8, 2002, http://asia.cnn.com/2002/BUSINESS/asia/08/08/aust.chinalng.biz/index.html

Ijaz, Mansoor, "The Clinton Intel Record", *National Review Online*, April 28, 2003, http://www.nationalreview.com/nr_comment/nr_comment042903.asp

Interview with former Prime Minister Benjamin Netanyahu, "Israel's Netanyahu 'absolutely' supports attack on Iraq", CNN, September 12, 2002, http://asia.cnn.com/2002/US/09/12/netanyahu.cnna/index.html

Interview with Northern Alliance spokesperson Haron Amin, "Amin: Northern Alliance will support United States", CNN, September 23, 2001, http://asia.cnn.com/2001/WORLD/asiapcf/central/09/22/amin.afghanistan.access.cnna/index.html

Kagan, Robert and Kristol, William, "A National Humiliation", *Weekly Standard*, April 16/23, 2001, reprinted by Project for the New American Century, http://www.newamericancentury.org/china-20010416.pdf

Kessler, Glenn, "N. Korea Says It Has Nuclear Arms", *Washington Post*, April 25, 2003, http://www.washingtonpost.com/wp-dyn/articles/A32198-2003Apr24.html"

Kessler, "Pakistan's N. Korea Deals Stir Scrutiny", *Washington Post*, November 13, 2002, http://www.washingtonpost.com/ac2/wp-dyn/A45961-2002Nov12.html

Kessler, "Sources Say Iran Lays Groundwork for Nuclear Bombs", *Washington Post*, December 19, 2002, http://www.washingtonpost.com/wp-dyn/articles/A8865-2002Dec18.html

Kessler and Ricks, Thomas E., "United States Frees Ship With North Korean Missiles", *Washington Post*, December 12, 2002, http://www.washingtonpost.com/wp-dyn/articles/A42786-2002Dec11.html

Khan, Kamran and Moore, Molly, "Pakistani Leaders Agree On Measures to Assist United States", *Washington Post*, September 15, 2001, http://www.washingtonpost.com/wp-dyn/articles/A32037-2001Sep14.html

Khan and Ricks, "United States Military Begins Shift From Bases In Pakistan", *Washington Post*, January 11, 2002, http://www.washingtonpost.com/wp-dyn/articles/A28620-2002Jan10.html

Kincaid, Cliff, "N. Korea Tortures Christians, Diverts Food Aid, Doctor Claims", Cybercast News, March 4, 2002, http://www.cnsnews.com/ForeignBureaus/archive/200203/FOR20020304i.html

King, John, "Walker charged with murder conspiracy", CNN, January 16, 2002, http://asia.cnn.com/2002/LAW/01/15/ret.walker.charges/index.html

Koppel, Andrea, "China privately admits helping Iraq", CNN, March 8, 2001, http://asia.cnn.com/2001/WORLD/asiapcf/east/03/07/china.admit/index.html

Kralev, Nicholas, "North Korea admits having nuclear arms", *Washington Times*, April 25, 2003, http://www.washtimes.com/world/20030425-908763.htm

Kralev, "Officials mixed on renewing dialogue with Korea", *Washington Times*, May 24, 2002, http://www.washtimes.com/world/20020524-27079402.htm

Kralev, "Ship seizure sets off diplomatic tiff with United States", *Washington Times*, December 13, 2002, http://www.washtimes.com/world/20021213-26094936.htm

Kurlantzick, Joshua, "Asia Minor", *The New Republic*, December 16, 2002, http://www.tnr.com/doc.mhtml?i=20021216&s=kurlantzick121602

Kurlantzick, "Xinjiang 'terror' crackdown called ploy to foil ethnic group", *Washington Times*, October 23, 2002, http://www.washtimes.com/world/20021023-17842266.htm

Lam, William Wo-Lap (Willy), "800,000 hit in China graft crackdown", CNN, October 15, 2002, http://asia.cnn.com/2002/WORLD/asiapcf/east/10/15/china.graft/index.html

Lam, "A question of faith", CNN, July 10, 2002, http://asia.cnn.com/2002/WORLD/asiapcf/east/07/09/willy.column/index.html

Lam, "Analysis: Behind the scenes in Beijing's corridors of power", CNN, April 12, 2001, http://asia.cnn.com/2001/WORLD/asiapcf/east/04/11/china.plane.wlam/index.html

Lam, "APEC: Jiang's last hurrah?", CNN, October 16, 2001, http://asia.cnn.com/2001/WORLD/asiapcf/10/16/willy.column/index.html

Lam, "Beijing moves to discredit Falun Gong", CNN, July 11, 20002, http://asia.cnn.com/2002/WORLD/asiapcf/east/07/10/china.falungong/index.html

Lam, "Beijing nervous after Japan-N. Korean talks", CNN, September 18, 2002, http://asia.cnn.com/2002/WORLD/asiapcf/east/09/17/china.koizumi/

Lam, "Beijing plays for gains on Iraq showdown", CNN, September 10, 2002, http://asia.cnn.com/2002/WORLD/asiapcf/east/09/10/willy.column/index.html"

Lam, "Beijing raises 5-pointer Afghan solution", CNN November 13, 2001, http://asia.cnn.com/2001/WORLD/asiapcf/east/11/12/china.tjxun/index.html

Lam, "Beijing takes preventative steps", CNN, November 14, 2001, http://asia.cnn.com/2001/WORLD/asiapcf/east/11/13/china.turks/index.html

Lam, "Beijing's diplomatic bridge-building", CNN, October 1, 2002, http://asia.cnn.com/2002/WORLD/asiapcf/east/10/01/willy.column/index.html

Lam, "'Beijing's NATO' hits stumbling block", CNN, May 16, 2002, http://asia.cnn.com/2002/WORLD/asiapcf/east/05/15/china.sco/index.html

Lam, "Bitter harvest may await China's leaders", CNN, January 24, 2001, http://asia.cnn.com/2001/WORLD/asiapcf/01/22/willy.column/index.html

Lam, "Bush in China: Friendly but no breakthrough", CNN, February 22, 2002, http://www.cnn.com/2002/WORLD/asiapcf/east/02/22/china.talks/index.html

Lam, "China a 'global player' in terror war", CNN, October 27, 2002, http://edition.cnn.com/2002/WORLD/asiapcf/east/10/27/china.jiang/index.html

Lam, "China corruption linked to triads", CNN, March 11, 2002, http://asia.cnn.com/2002/WORLD/asiapcf/east/03/10/china.npclaw/index.html

Lam, "China deals United States blow on Iraq", CNN, August 28, 2002, http://asia.cnn.com/2002/WORLD/asiapcf/east/08/27/china.iraq/index.html

Lam, "China draws closer to United States after terror strike", CNN, September 19, 2001, http://asia.cnn.com/2001/WORLD/asiapcf/east/09/19/willy.us.china/index.html

Lam, "China expands anti-terror campaign", CNN, November 18, 2002, http://asia.cnn.com/2002/WORLD/asiapcf/east/11/17/china.xinjiang/index.html

Lam, "China forecasts record budget deficit", CNN, March 4, 2002, http://asia.cnn.com/2002/WORLD/asiapcf/east/03/03/china.npcpla/

Lam, "China keeps watch on United States policy shifts", CNN, October 3, 2002, http://asia.cnn.com/2001/WORLD/asiapcf/east/10/02/willy.column/index.html

Lam, "China launches 'suppression' campaign in Xinjiang", CNN, October 26, 2002, http://asia.cnn.com/2001/WORLD/asiapcf/east/10/25/china.willylam/

Lam, "China opposes United States presence in Central Asia", CNN, April 22, 2002, http://asia.cnn.com/2002/WORLD/asiapcf/east/04/22/china.iran/index.html

Lam, "China opposes United States presence in Central Asia", CNN, April 22, 2002, http://asia.cnn.com/2002/WORLD/asiapcf/east/04/22/china.iran/

Lam, "China raises defense budget", CNN, March 6, 2001, http://www.cnn.com/2001/WORLD/asiapcf/east/03/05/china.congress.budget/

Lam, "China seeks stability among Uighurs", CNN, September 5, 2002, http://asia.cnn.com/2002/WORLD/asiapcf/east/09/03/china.xinjiang/index.html

Lam, "China sends condolences to United States", CNN, September 12, 2001, http://asia.cnn.com/2001/WORLD/asiapcf/east/09/11/china.us.reax/

Lam, "China smashes terror bases", CNN, September 13, 2002, http://asia.cnn.com/2002/WORLD/asiapcf/east/09/13/china.turkestan/index.html

Lam, "China welcomes separatists' terror tag", CNN, September 12, 2001, http://asia.cnn.com/2002/WORLD/asiapcf/east/09/12/china.xinjiang/

Lam, "China: Iraq strikes signal new United States 'aggressiveness'", CNN, February 19, 2001, http://asia.cnn.com/2001/WORLD/asiapcf/east/02/19/china.iraq.reax/index.html

Lam, "China's leaders battle for place in history", CNN, September 17, 2002, http://asia.cnn.com/2002/WORLD/asiapcf/east/09/17/willy.column/index.html

Lam, "China's media slams United States 'arrogance' on Iraq," CNN, February 4, 2003, http://edition.cnn.com/2003/WORLD/asiapcf/east/02/03/willy.column/index.html

Lam, "Combating American hegemony", CNN, June 20, 2001, http://www.cnn.com/2001/WORLD/asiapcf/east/06/19/china.russia.willy/index.html

Lam, "Is China losing its moral high ground?", CNN, December 18, 2001, http://asia.cnn.com/2001/WORLD/asiapcf/east/12/17/china.willydiplo/index.html

Lam, "Jiang faces reform attacks from within", CNN, August 28, 2002, http://asia.cnn.com/2002/WORLD/asiapcf/east/08/28/china.zhao/index.html

Lam, "Jiang seeks to build anti-terror front", CNN, October 1, 2001, http://asia.cnn.com/2001/WORLD/asiapcf/east/10/01/gen.china.terror/index.html

Lam, "Jockeying begins for China's top job", CNN, January 19, 2001, http://asia.cnn.com/2001/ASIANOW/east/01/18/willy.lam/index.html

Lam, "Kyrgystan murder raises Beijing concerns", CNN, July 3, 2002, http://asia.cnn.com/2002/WORLD/asiapcf/east/07/02/china.uighurs/index.html

Lam, "Military pledges allegiance to Jiang", CNN, November 20, 2002, http://asia.cnn.com/2002/WORLD/asiapcf/east/11/19/china.gun/index.html

Lam, "Pakistan to court China", CNN, December 19, 2001, http://asia.cnn.com/2001/WORLD/asiapcf/east/12/18/china.prcpak/index.html

Lam, "PLA wary of United States moves into Central Asia", October 4, 2001, http://asia.cnn.com/2001/WORLD/asiapcf/east/10/04/china.terror.willy/index.html

Lam, "Russian stance troubles China", CNN, May 21, 2002, http://asia.cnn.com/2002/WORLD/asiapcf/east/05/21/willy.column/index.html

Lam, "Shanghai 6 vow to fight 'three vices'", CNN, January 7, 2002, http://www.cnn.com/2002/WORLD/asiapcf/east/01/07/china.sco/index.html

Lam, "Smoke clears over China's United States strategy", CNN, September 26, 2001, http://asia.cnn.com/2001/WORLD/asiapcf/east/09/25/willy.column/index.html

Lau, Emily, "Letter to Hong Kong - June 4th Massacre", Broadcast on RTHK Radio 3, June 10, 2001, http://www.emilylau.org.hk/Emily_E/multimedia/_audio_doc/l2hk_010610.htm

Lawson, Alastair, "Year of upheaval for Pakistan", BBC, December 26, 1999 http://news.bbc.co.uk/2/hi/south_asia/573948.stm

Ledeen, Michael, "Iran on the Brink", *National Review Online,* April 29, 2002, http://www.nationalreview.com/ledeen/ledeen042902.asp

Ledeen, "Scud Surrender", *National Review Online,* December 13, 2002, http://www.nationalreview.com/ledeen/ledeen121302.asp

Ledeen, "The Heart of Darkness", *National Review Online,* December 12, 2002, http://www.nationalreview.com/ledeen/ledeen121202.asp

Ledeen, "The Real War", *National Review Online,* December 11, 2002, http://www.nationalreview.com/ledeen/ledeen121102.asp

Ledeen, "Timing Is Everything", *National Review Online,* April 22, 2003, http://www.nationalreview.com/ledeen/ledeen042203.asp

Lee Teng-hui, "Always in My Heart", The Spencer T. and Ann W. Olin Lecture delivered at Cornell University Alumni Reunion, Cornell University, http://www.news.cornell.edu/campus/Lee/Lee_Speech.html

Liang, Qiao and Xiangsui, Wang, *Unrestricted Warfare*, cited by Newsmax, http://www.newsmaxstore.com/nms/showdetl.cfm?&DID=6&Product_ID=889&CATID=13&GroupID=58

Lodhi, Aasiya, "Turbulent year for India", BBC, December 25, 1999, http://news.bbc.co.uk/2/hi/south_asia/573592.stm

Loeb, Vernon and Ricks, Thomas E., "White House Courts Coalition", *Washington Post*, November 28, 2002, http://www.washingtonpost.com/wp-dyn/articles/A48453-2002Nov27.html

Lowry, Richard, "Be Afraid, Very Afraid", *National Review Online,* March 14, 2002, http://www.nationalreview.com/lowry/lowry031402.shtml

Lowry, "Our SOBs", *National Review Online*, October 1, 2001, http://www.nationalreview.com/lowry/lowry100101.shtml

Lynch, Colum, "Chinese Firm Probed On Links With Iraq", *Washington Post*, March 17, 2001, http://www.washingtonpost.com/wp-dyn/articles/A17882-2001Mar17.html

Lynch, "U.N. Orders Iraq to Disarm", *Washington Post*, November 9, 2002, http://www.washingtonpost.com/ac2/wp-dyn?pagename=article&node=&contentId=A30317-2002Nov8&notFound=true

Malhotra, T.C., "India, United States To Reactivate Defense Ties", Cybercast News, July 20, 2001, http://www.cnsnews.com/ViewForeignBureaus.asp?Page=\ForeignBureaus\archive\200107\For20010720g.html

Malhotra, "US To Resume Arms Sales To India", Cybercast News, January 31, 2002, http://www.cnsnews.com/ViewForeignBureaus.asp?Page=\ForeignBureaus\archive\200201\FOR20020131c.html

Marquand, Robert, "Doctor remains thorn in North Korea's side", *Christian Science Monitor*, reprinted in *Washington Times*, December 6, 2002, http://www.washtimes.com/world/20021206-53444593.htm

Martin, Paul, "Hezbollah calls for global attacks", *Washington Times*, December 4, 2002, http://www.washtimes.com/world/20021204-29720774.htm

McCarthy, Terry, "Profile of a President", *Time Asia*, March 27, 2000, http://www.time.com/time/asia/magazine/2000/0327/taiwan.chenprofile.html

McElroy, Damien, "Beijing produces videos glorifying terrorist attacks on 'arrogant' US", *London Sunday Telegraph,* November 4, 2001, http://www.portal.telegraph.co.uk/news/main.jhtml;$sessionid$431SABQA AB2BBQFIQMFCFGGAVCBQYIV0?xml=/news/2001/11/04/wchin04.xml &sSheet=/news/2001/11/04/ixhome.html

McGreal, Chris, "Suicide attacks 'are war crimes'", *The Guardian* (UK), November 1, 2002, http://www.guardian.co.uk/israel/Story/0,2763,823677,00.html

McMillan, Alex Frew, "China growth myths dispelled", CNN, October 30, 2002, http://asia.cnn.com/2002/BUSINESS/asia/10/29/hk.bnpchina/index.html

McWethy, John, "Bush Cancels Iraqi Strike", ABC News.com, http://more.abcnews.go.com/sections/wnt/dailynews/iraq_mission_aborted0 20819.html

Morahan, Lawrence, "EP-3 Incident Strains United States-China Relations", Cybercast News, July 5, 2001, http://www.cnsnews.com/ViewPentagon.asp?Page=\Pentagon\archive\2001 07\PEN20010705a.html

Morahan, "US Strengthens Military Ties With India", Cybercast News, January 17, 2002, http://www.cnsnews.com/ViewPentagon.asp?Page=\Pentagon\archive\2002 01\PEN20020117b.html

Mowbray, Joel, "North Korea's terrifying exports," *Washington Times*, December 19, 2002, http://www.washtimes.com/op-ed/20021219-93696790.htm

Mufson, Steven, and Pan, Philip P., "United States May Waive China Sanctions", *Washington Post*, October 17, 2001, http://www.washingtonpost.com/wp-dyn/articles/A5384-2001Oct16.html

Mufson, Steven, "United States to Pay China $34,567 for Costs Of Downed Plane", *Washington Post*, August 10, 2001, http://www.washingtonpost.com/wp-dyn/articles/A57188-2001Aug10.html

Nemets, Alexandr, "A Conversation With Friends, Part I", December 16, 2002, http://www.Newsmax/archives/articles/2002/12/16/142651.shtml

Nemets, "A Conversation With Friends, Part II", December 21, 2002, http://www.Newsmax/archives/articles/2002/12/16/142651.shtml

Nordlinger, Jay, "Impromptus", *National Review Online*, May 24, 2002, http://www.nationalreview.com/impromptus/impromptus052402.asp

Nordlinger, "Perfect speech, perfect hypocrisy, perfect awarding, and more", *National Review Online*, October 10, 2002, http://www.nationalreview.com/impromptus/impromptus101002.asp

Oakley, Robin, "Can Libya come in from the cold", CNN, January 31, 2001, http://asia.cnn.com/2001/WORLD/europe/01/31/lockerbie.oakley.diplomacy/index.html

Oakley, "Prague summit to transform NATO", CNN, November 20, 2002, http://www.cnn.com/2002/WORLD/europe/11/19/nato.oakley.analysis/

Osorio, Ivan G., "Chavez Bombshell?", *National Review Online*, January 8, 2003, http://www.nationalreview.com/comment/comment-osorio010803.asp

Pan, Phillip P., "Beijing Says No Evidence Found Of Chinese Role at Iraqi Sites", *Washington Post,* March 7, 2001, http://washingtonpost.com/wp-dyn/articles/A30731-2001Mar6.html

Pan and Pomfret, John, "Bin Laden's Chinese Connection", *Washington Post,* November 10, 2001, http://www.washingtonpost.com/wp-dyn/articles/A5009-2001Nov9.html

Pan, "Separatist Group In China Added To Terrorist List", *Washington Post,* August 27, 2002, http://www.washingtonpost.com/wp-dyn/articles/A64814-2002Aug26.html

Pan, "United States Warns of Plot by Group in W. China", *Washington Post,* August 29, 2002, http://www.washingtonpost.com/wp-dyn/articles/A8875-2002Aug28.html

Peterson, Scott, "After Milosevic exit, time to clean house in Yugoslavia", *Christian Science Monitor,* October 10, 2000, http://csmweb2.emcweb.com/durable/2000/10/10/fp7s1-csm.shtml

Pincus, Walter, "China Training Libyans, Official Says", *Washington Post,* April 14, 2000, http://www.washingtonpost.com/ac2/wp-dyn?pagename=article&node=&contentId=A11430-2000Apr13&notFound=true

Pomfret, John, "Beijing Police, S. Korean Diplomats Scuffle", *Washington Post,* June 14, 2002, http://www.washingtonpost.com/wp-dyn/articles/A48010-2002Jun13.html

Pomfret, "China Censors Anti-United States Reaction", *Washington Post,* September 15, 2001, http://www.washingtonpost.com/wp-dyn/articles/A34491-2001Sep14.html, and United Press International, Unnamed Author, "China signed deal with Taliban on attack day",

Washington Times, September 14, 2001, http://www.washtimes.com/world/20010914-94404684.htm

Pomfret, "China to Buy 8 More Russian Submarines", *Washington Post*, June 25, 2002, http://www.washingtonpost.com/wp-dyn/articles/A38496-2002Jun24.html

Pomfret, "Chinese Capitalists Gain New Legitimacy", September 29, 2002, http://www.washingtonpost.com/wp-dyn/articles/A17207-2002Sep28.html

Pomfret, "Muslim Chinese Fear for Rights", *Washington Post*, October 13, 2001, http://www.washingtonpost.com/wp-dyn/articles/A52343-2001Oct12.html

Pomfret, "Thousands Of Workers Protest in Chinese City", *Washington Post*, March 20, 2002, http://www.washingtonpost.com/wp-dyn/articles/A52370-2002Mar19.html

Powell, Colin, Address to the United Nations Security Council, transcript by CBC, "Powell's address to the UN," February 5, 2003, http://cbc.ca/news/iraq/documents/powell_un030205.html

Prager, Karsten, "China: Waking Up to the Next Superpower", *Time Asia*, March 25, 1996, http://www.time.com/time/magazine/archive/1996/dom/960325/china.html

PTI, "China cautions Israel against selling AWACS to India", reprinted in the *Times of India*, December 27, 2001, http://timesofindia.indiatimes.com/cms.dll/xml/comp/articleshow?art_ID=1415189086

Rahe, Paul A., "Bureaucrats vs. Warriors", *National Review Online*, October 29, 2001, http://www.nationalreview.com/comment/comment-rahe102901.shtml

Rahman, Shaikh Azizur, "Officials cite al Qaeda presence in Kashmir", *Washington Times*, September 27, 2002, http://www.washtimes.com/world/20020927-6357043.htm

Reeves, Phil, "Woman beheaded after being warned to wear the burqa", *The Independent*, December 23, 2002, http://news.independent.co.uk/world/asia_china/story.jsp?story=363459

Reporters Sans Frontieres (Reporters Without Borders), "Protest Letter", November 29, 2002, http://www.rsf.org/rsf/uk/html/asie/cplp/lp/291100.html

Reuters, "China expects big 'haul' of Xiamen graft executions", reprinted by CNN, September 21, 2000, http://asia.cnn.com/2000/ASIANOW/east/09/20/crime.china.death.reut/

Reuters, "TIMELINE: North Korea's nuclear history", CNN, December 23, 2002, http://asia.cnn.com/2002/WORLD/asiapcf/east/12/22/nkorea.nuclear.timeline.reut/

Rouzi, Sidik, "Free My Wife From Prison", Open Letter to President Bush printed in the *Washington Post*, February 16, 2002, http://www.washingtonpost.com/wp-dyn/articles/A18978-2002Feb15.html

Rubin, Michael, "Iran's Myth of Moderation", *National Review Online*, March 18, 2002, http://www.nationalreview.com/comment/comment-rubin031802.shtml

Rubin, "The US Can Collapse the Taliban", *Middle East Intelligence Bulletin*, September 2001, http://www.meib.org/articles/0109_me1.htm

Rubin, "Weakest Link", *The New Republic*, September 20, 2001 (internet post date), http://www.tnr.com/100101/rubin100101.html

Salam, Reihan, "Guide to the Iraq Debate: World Not So Weary", *The New Republic*, November 26, 2002, http://www.tnr.com/iraq.mhtml#china

Sands, David R., "North Korea's nuclear program 'troubling'", *Washington Times*, October 18, 2002, http://www.washtimes.com/world/20021018-345423.htm

Schuman, Michael, "The Hermit Kingdom's Bizarre SAR", *Time Asia*, October 7, 2002, http://www.time.com/time/asia/magazine/article/0,13673,501021007-356131,00.html

Schwartz, Stephen, "Seeking Moderation", *National Review Online*, October 25, 2001, http://www.nationalreview.com/comment/comment-schwartz102501.shtml

Seitz, Barr, "United States Has Small Role in S. Asia", ABC News, May 29, 1998, http://abcnews.go.com/sections/world/DailyNews/america980529.html

Sen, Ayanjit, "New leader for Indian Kashmir", BBC, October 26, 2002, http://news.bbc.co.uk/2/hi/south_asia/2364327.stm

Sieff, Martin, "Pyongyang is unable to turn on the lights", UPI, reprinted in the *Washington Times*, January 7, 2002, http://www.washtimes.com/world/20030108-57237536.htm

Sipress, Alan, "United States Seeks to Lift Sanctions on India", *Washington Post*, August 12, 2001, http://www.washingtonpost.com/ac2/wp-dyn?pagename=article&node=&contentId=A64632-2001Aug11&notFound=true

Smith, Charles R., "Jiang Zemin Is Not Santa Claus", Newsmax, October 25, 2002, http://www.Newsmax/archives/articles/2002/10/24/190700.shtml

Smith, "Sudan gets Chinese jets", World Net Daily, September 13, 2000, http://w114.wnd.com/news/article.asp?ARTICLE_ID=20622

Steinberg, Gerald M., "Blowback Alert," *National Review Online*, March 4, 2003, http://www.nationalreview.com/comment/comment-steinberg030403.asp

Struck, Doug, "An Abducted Daughter's Legacy?", *Washington Post*, October 4, 2002, http://www.washingtonpost.com/wp-dyn/articles/A40946-2002Oct3.html

Struck, "German Doctor Breaks Rules to Aid N. Koreans", *Washington Post*, May 5, 2002, http://www.washingtonpost.com/ac2/wp-dyn?pagename=article&node=&contentId=A33770-2002May4&notFound=true

Struck, "N. Korea Hints at Missile Test", *Washington Post*, November 6, 2002, http://www.washingtonpost.com/ac2/wp-dyn?pagename=article&node=&contentId=A10432-2002Nov5&notFound=true

Struck, "N. Korea Quiets Buzz On Nuclear Assertion", *Washington Post*, November 19, 2002, http://www.washingtonpost.com/wp-dyn/articles/A7851-2002Nov18.html

Struck, "N. Korea Reactor Project on Course", *Washington Post*, March 30, 2002, http://www.washingtonpost.com/wp-dyn/articles/A37976-2002Mar29.html

Struck, "N. Korea's Secret Mission", *Washington Post*, October 13, 2002, http://www.washingtonpost.com/ac2/wp-dyn?pagename=article&node=&contentId=A18308-2002Oct12&notFound=true

Struck, "N. Korean Refugee Advocates Turn to U.N.", *Washington Post*, November 28, 2002, http://www.washingtonpost.com/wp-dyn/articles/A48348-2002Nov27.html

Tindsall, Simon, "Witness reveals horror of North Korean gulag", *The Guardian* (UK), July 19, 2002, http://www.guardian.co.uk/korea/article/0,2763,757783,00.html

Transcript of *CNN Newsroom*, aired December 18, 2001, 4:30 PM Eastern Standard Time, http://asia.cnn.com/TRANSCRIPTS/0112/18/nr.00.html

Transcript of *CNN Newsroom*, aired December 18, 2001, http://asia.cnn.com/TRANSCRIPTS/0112/18/nr.00.html

Tsang, Daniel C., "Interview with Ngo Vinh Long", Critical Asian Studies 34, no. 3 (September 2002), p. 464 (edited), http://csf.colorado.edu/bcas/main-cas/tsang.htm (unedited)

United Kingdom Foreign and Commonwealth Office, *Saddam Hussein: crimes and human rights abuses*, p. 21

United Press International, "Attacks ally India, Turkey, Israel", reprinted in *Washington Times*, January 16, 2002, http://www.washingtontimes.com/world/20020116-15935464.htm

United States Consulate, "Transcript: Clinton/Jiang 10/29 Joint Press Conference", October 29, 1997 http://www.usconsulate.org.hk/uscn/jiang97/1029g.htm

Unnamed Author, "Anti-Jiang protests by the Thames", BBC, October 20, 1999, http://news.bbc.co.uk/2/hi/uk_news/politics/480338.stm

Unnamed Author, "Attack heralds China-US thaw", BBC, September 21, 2001, http://news.bbc.co.uk/hi/english/world/asia-pacific/newsid_1556000/1556032.stm

Unnamed Author, "Attacks aftermath: Russia repositions", BBC, September 13, 2001, http://news.bbc.co.uk/2/hi/europe/1543132.stm

Unnamed Author, "Australia slammed over Tibet policy", BBC, June 6, 2002, http://news.bbc.co.uk/2/hi/asia-pacific/2029266.stm

Unnamed Author, "Beijing delivered missile technology to Libya, United States says", *Washington Times*, April 13, 2000, http://www.washingtontimes.com/national/default-20000413231544.htm

Unnamed Author, "Beijing urges caution with North Korea", CNN, October 18, 2002, http://asia.cnn.com/2002/WORLD/asiapcf/east/10/17/china.korea/index.html

Unnamed Author, "Book suggests Chinese leaders were split over Tiananmen crackdown", CNN, January 6, 2001, http://asia.cnn.com/2001/ASIANOW/east/01/06/tiananmen.papers/index.html

Unnamed Author, "Breakaway party launches in Taiwan", BBC, August 12, 2001, http://news.bbc.co.uk/2/hi/asia-pacific/1487455.stm

Unnamed Author, "Brief History of the Uyghurs", Eastern Turkestan Union In Europe, http://www.geocities.com/CapitolHill/1730/buh.html

Unnamed Author, "Bush turns up pressure on Arafat", CNN, January 12, 2002, http://asia.cnn.com/2002/WORLD/meast/01/10/mideast.wrap/index.html

Unnamed Author, "Bush vows 'whatever it takes' to defend Taiwan", CNN, April 26, 2002, http://asia.cnn.com/2001/ALLPOLITICS/04/25/bush.taiwan.03/

Unnamed Author, "China 'cracks down on Muslims'", BBC, March 22, 2002, http://news.bbc.co.uk/2/hi/asia-pacific/1887335.stm

Unnamed Author, "China 'outstrips world' on executions", BBC, July 6, 2001, http://news.bbc.co.uk/2/hi/asia-pacific/1425570.stm

Unnamed Author, "China and Iran move closer", BBC, April 20, 2002, http://news.bbc.co.uk/2/hi/middle_east/1941030.stm

Unnamed Author, "China anger over spy plane offer", BBC, August 11, 2001, http://news.bbc.co.uk/2/hi/asia-pacific/1486105.stm

Unnamed Author, "China cautious on Iraq action", CNN, September 14, 2002, http://asia.cnn.com/2002/WORLD/asiapcf/east/09/14/china.iraq/index.html

Unnamed Author, "China clamps down on separatists", BBC, October 10, 2001, http://news.bbc.co.uk/hi/english/world/asia-pacific/newsid_1591000/1591040.stm

Unnamed Author, "China concerned at Japanese 'force'", BBC, December 24, 2001, http://news.bbc.co.uk/2/hi/asia-pacific/1726709.stm

Unnamed Author, "China confirms tycoon's arrest", BBC, October 8, 2002, http://news.bbc.co.uk/2/hi/asia-pacific/2305089.stm

Unnamed Author, "China consul killed in Kyrgyzstan", BBC, June 30, 2002, http://news.bbc.co.uk/2/hi/asia-pacific/2075957.stm

Unnamed Author, "China disputes Phillippines claim over Spratlys", BBC, March 17, 2002, http://news.bbc.co.uk/2/hi/asia-pacific/1226370.stm

Unnamed Author, "China Gives Death Sentences To 2 Tibetans", *Washington Post*, December 6, 2002, http://www.washingtonpost.com/wp-dyn/articles/A16449-2002Dec5.html

Unnamed Author, "China links Islamic separatists to terrorism", CNN, November 15, 2001, http://asia.cnn.com/2001/WORLD/asiapcf/east/11/15/china.uighurs/index.html

Unnamed Author, "China links separatists to bin Laden", CNN, January 21, 2002, http://asia.cnn.com/2002/WORLD/asiapcf/east/01/21/gen.china.xinjaing/index.html, and Philip P. Pan,

Unnamed Author, "China Links Bin Laden to Separatists", *Washington Post*, January 22, 2002, http://www.washingtonpost.com/wp-dyn/articles/A16055-2002Jan21.html

Unnamed Author, "China pushes for Iraq diplomacy", CNN, October 3, 2002, http://asia.cnn.com/2002/WORLD/asiapcf/east/10/03/china.iraq/index.html

Unnamed Author, "China Puts 700,000 Troops on Alert in Sudan", Newsmax, August 27, 2000, http://www.Newsmax/articles/?a=2000/8/26/204458

Unnamed Author, "China slammed over N. Korean refugees", CNN, November 20, 2002, http://asia.cnn.com/2002/WORLD/asiapcf/east/11/19/korea.asylum/index.html

Unnamed Author, "China suspected in port deal", *Washington Times*, May 31, 2001, http://www.washtimes.com/world/20010531-50444965.htm

Unnamed Author, "China tightens missile export rules", BBC, August 26, 2002, http://news.bbc.co.uk/2/hi/world/asia-pacific/2216361.stm

Unnamed Author, "China trade fight under way on Capitol Hill", CNN, May 17, 2000 http://www.cnn.com/2000/ALLPOLITICS/stories/05/17/pntr.advance/index.html

Unnamed Author, "China tries to contain scope of looming conflict", CNN, September 14, 2001, http://asia.cnn.com/2001/WORLD/asiapcf/east/09/13/china.pakistan/index.html

Unnamed Author, "China tycoon controversy deepens", CNN, October 9, 2002, http://asia.cnn.com/2002/WORLD/asiapcf/east/10/09/china.tycoon/index.html

Unnamed Author, "China ups pressure on Taiwan", BBC, March 15, 2000, http://news.bbc.co.uk/2/hi/asia-pacific/678155.stm,

Unnamed Author, "China urges stronger ties with Venezuela", BBC, May 25, 2001, http://news.bbc.co.uk/2/hi/asia-pacific/1349795.stm

Unnamed Author, "China warning to future refugees", CNN, March 19, 2002, http://asia.cnn.com/2002/WORLD/asiapcf/east/03/19/nkorea.asylum/index.html

Unnamed Author, "China warns of possible arms race", CNN, May 2, 2001, http://edition.cnn.com/2001/WORLD/asiapcf/east/05/02/china.arms/

Unnamed Author, "China, Taiwan, United States show off military", CNN, August 22, 2001, http://asia.cnn.com/2001/WORLD/asiapcf/east/08/22/china.taiwan.military/index.html

Unnamed Author, "China's fearful Muslim minority", BBC, January 8, 2002, http://news.bbc.co.uk/2/hi/asia-pacific/1748801.stm

Unnamed Author, "China's Hu denounces Israel's 'arrogant use of force,'" Lateline News, January 11, 2001, http://news.1chinastar.com/ll/english/1038710.shtml

Unnamed Author, "Chinese firms help Taliban put phone system in Kabul", *Washington Times*, September 28, 2001, http://www.washtimes.com/national/20010928-343125.htm

Unnamed Author, "Chinese gov't: Urumqi explosion an accident," Lateline News, September 13, 2000, http://latelinenews.com/ll/english/88226.shtml

Unnamed Author, "Chinese official completes sentence for supporting Tiananmen Square protesters", CNN, May 27, 1996, http://asia.cnn.com/WORLD/9605/27/china.bao/

Unnamed Author, *Chosun Ilbo*, cited by Goodenough, "North Korean Nuclear Crisis Deepens", Cybercast News, December 12, 2002, http://www.cnsnews.com/ViewForeignBureaus.asp?Page=\ForeignBureaus\archive\200212\FOR20021212f.html

Unnamed Author, "CIA outlines N. Korean weapons plan", CNN, February 1, 2002, http://asia.cnn.com/2002/US/02/01/cia.nkorea/

Unnamed Author, "Clinton 'threatened' N Korea over nuclear arms", BBC, December 16, 2002, http://news.bbc.co.uk/2/hi/asia-pacific/2578497.stm

Unnamed Author, "Clinton Defends China Satellite Waiver", CNN All Politics, May 22, 2002, http://asia.cnn.com/ALLPOLITICS/1998/05/22/china.money/index.html

Unnamed Author, "Clinton fields calls on Chinese radio talk show", CNN, June 30, 1998, http://asia.cnn.com/WORLD/asiapcf/9806/30/china.update.01/

Unnamed Author, "'Code of conduct' for disputed islands", BBC, November 4, 2002, http://news.bbc.co.uk/2/hi/asia-pacific/2399425.stm

Unnamed Author, "Country profile: Iraq", BBC, October 17, 2002, http://news.bbc.co.uk/2/hi/middle_east/country_profiles/791014.stm

Unnamed Author, "Country profile: Lebanon", BBC, November 2, 2002, http://news.bbc.co.uk/2/hi/middle_east/country_profiles/791071.stm

Unnamed Author, "Country profile: South Korea", BBC, December 20, 2002, http://news.bbc.co.uk/2/hi/asia-pacific/country_profiles/1123668.stm

Unnamed Author, "Country profile: Sudan", BBC, November 2, 2002, http://news.bbc.co.uk/2/hi/middle_east/country_profiles/820864.stm

Unnamed Author, "Country profile: United Arab Emirates", BBC, November 2, 2002, http://news.bbc.co.uk/2/hi/middle_east/country_profiles/737620.stm

Unnamed Author, "Dalai Lama to privatise Tibetan business", BBC, July 15, 2002, http://news.bbc.co.uk/2/hi/business/2129176.stm

Unnamed Author, "Death sentence for Tibetan 'bombers'", BBC, December 5, 2002, http://news.bbc.co.uk/2/hi/asia-pacific/2545123.stm

Unnamed Author, "Defector says Pakistan had nuclear 'first strike' plan", CNN, July 1, 1998, http://edition.cnn.com/WORLD/asiapcf/9807/01/pakistan.defector/

Unnamed Author, "Democracy sprouts in Taiwan", CNN, March 21, 1996, http://www-cgi.cnn.com/WORLD/9603/taiwan_elex/21/index.html

Unnamed Author, "Deng Xiaoping", CNN, June 2, 1999, http://asia.cnn.com/WORLD/asiapcf/9906/02/tiananmen/deng.profile/

Unnamed Author, "Doubts cast over N. Korea nuke claim", CNN, November 18, 2002, http://edition.cnn.com/2002/WORLD/asiapcf/east/11/18/nkorea.nukes/index.html

Unnamed Author, "Eastern Turkestan FAQ", International Taklamakan Human Rights Association, http://www.taklamakan.org/uighur-l/et_faq_p1.html#d1

Unnamed Author, "Eastern Turkestan Republic-1944", International Taklamakan Human Rights Association, http://www.taklamakan.org/uighur-l/archive/etr.html

Unnamed Author, "Episode 5: Korea", *Cold War*, CNN, http://edition.cnn.com/SPECIALS/cold.war/episodes/05/script.html

Unnamed Author, "Estonia Holds Conference on Violations of Uighur Human Rights by China," Baltic News Service, reprinted by the Uyghur American Association, http://www.uyghuramerican.org/recentevents/bbcno1300.html,

Unnamed Author, "Exiled Afghan warlord leaves Iran", CNN, February 27, 2002, http://asia.cnn.com/2002/WORLD/meast/02/27/iran.warlord/index.html

Unnamed Author, "Ex-Saudi intelligence chief defends princess", CNN, November 27, 2002, http://www.cnn.com/2002/US/11/26/saudi.money.trail/index.html

Unnamed Author, "Fernandes fixates on Chinese threat to India," May 7, 1998, BBC, http://news.bbc.co.uk/2/hi/south_asia/89267.stm

Unnamed Author, "Fernandes: Popular but controversial minister", March 15, 2001, http://news.bbc.co.uk/2/hi/south_asia/1223625.stm

Unnamed Author, "Fierce attack on China's ruling elite", BBC, August 29, 2002, http://news.bbc.co.uk/2/hi/asia-pacific/2223016.stm

Unnamed Author, "Fresh China protests", BBC, January 14, 2000, http://news.bbc.co.uk/2/hi/uk_news/politics/603413.stm

Unnamed Author, "Fresh human rights fears on China", CNN, October 13, 2001, http://asia.cnn.com/2001/WORLD/asiapcf/east/10/12/china.rights/index.html

Unnamed Author, "Hardline alliance in Pakistan province", BBC, November 30, 2002, http://news.bbc.co.uk/2/hi/south_asia/2531265.stm

Unnamed Author, "Health worries for alleged United States Army deserter", CNN, December 3, 2002, http://asia.cnn.com/2002/WORLD/asiapcf/east/12/03/nkorea.us.defector/index.html

Unnamed Author, "Heartbreak over Japanese missing", BBC, October 28, 2002, http://news.bbc.co.uk/2/hi/asia-pacific/2263822.stm

Unnamed Author, "Hope for Vietnam China sea dispute", BBC, September 26, 2000, http://news.bbc.co.uk/2/hi/asia-pacific/943082.stm

Unnamed Author, "India and China talks borders", CNN, June 28, 2001, http://asia.cnn.com/2001/WORLD/asiapcf/south/06/28/india.china.border/index.html

Unnamed Author, "India and Russia united over terrorism", BBC, November 6, 1998, http://news.bbc.co.uk/2/hi/europe/1641805.stm

Unnamed Author, "India and Russia's common past", BBC, December 4, 2002, http://news.bbc.co.uk/2/hi/south_asia/2542431.stm

Unnamed Author, "India condemns militant 'conspiracy'", BBC, August 1, 2002, http://news.bbc.co.uk/2/hi/south_asia/2164698.stm

Unnamed Author, "India conducts underground nuclear tests", CNN, May 11, 2002, http://asia.cnn.com/WORLD/asiapcf/9805/11/india.nuclear/index.html

Unnamed Author, "India recalls parliament attack", BBC, December 13, 2002, http://news.bbc.co.uk/2/hi/south_asia/2572091.stm

Unnamed Author, "India says intruders pushed out of Kashmir", CNN, July 26, 1999, http://asia.cnn.com/WORLD/asiapcf/9907/26/kashmir.01/index.html

Unnamed Author, "Iran in the 20th Century", CNN, January 31, 1999, http://asia.cnn.com/WORLD/meast/9901/31/iran.timeline/index.html

Unnamed Author, "Iran: United States allegations are 'outdated and inaccurate'", CNN February 14, 2002, http://asia.cnn.com/2002/WORLD/meast/02/13/iran.afghanistan/index.html

Unnamed Author, "Iran-contra affair", encyclopedia.com, http://www.encyclopedia.com/html/i/irancont.asp

Unnamed Author, "Islamist laws for Pakistan province", BBC, November 29, 2002, http://news.bbc.co.uk/2/hi/south_asia/2526797.stm

Unnamed Author, "Japan 'finds missiles' on mystery boat", BBC, June 26, 2002, http://news.bbc.co.uk/hi/english/world/asia-pacific/newsid_2066000/2066918.stm

Unnamed Author, "Japan pressured over Taiwan visit", BBC, April 16, 2001, http://news.bbc.co.uk/2/hi/asia-pacific/1279937.stm

Unnamed Author, "Japanese anger over North Korean kidnaps", BBC, November 18, 2002, http://news.bbc.co.uk/2/hi/asia-pacific/2487915.stm

Unnamed Author, "Jiang's stark warning over corruption" CNN, November 8, 2002, http://asia.cnn.com/2002/WORLD/asiapcf/east/11/08/chn.congress/index.html

Unnamed Author, "Kashmir killings rock hopes for peace", BBC, November 2, 2002, http://news.bbc.co.uk/2/hi/south_asia/2390459.stm

Unnamed Author, "Kenya missile attack sparks new urgency", CNN, December 4, 2002, http://asia.cnn.com/2002/WORLD/meast/12/03/missile.defense/index.html

Unnamed Author, "Kidnap victim's child pleads for visit", BBC, October 25, 2002, http://news.bbc.co.uk/2/hi/asia-pacific/2362053.stm

Unnamed Author, "Korean relatives reunited", BBC, April 29, 2002, http://news.bbc.co.uk/2/hi/asia-pacific/1957200.stm

Unnamed Author, "Koreans reunited with long-lost relatives", CNN, April 29, 2002, http://asia.cnn.com/2002/WORLD/asiapcf/east/04/29/korea.reunion/index.html

Unnamed Author, "Koreas clash in sea battle", BBC, June 29, 2002, http://news.bbc.co.uk/2/hi/asia-pacific/2073694.stm

Unnamed Author, "Kyrgyz Government resigns", BBC, May 22, 2002, http://news.bbc.co.uk/hi/english/world/asia-pacific/newsid_2001000/2001752.stm, and "Entire national government stands down", CNN, May 22, 2002, http://asia.cnn.com/2002/WORLD/asiapcf/central/05/22/kyrgyz.govt/index.html

Unnamed Author, "Kyrgyzstan says Chinese diplomat's death 'accidental'", BBC, July 4, 2002, http://news.bbc.co.uk/2/hi/asia-pacific/2082649.stm

Unnamed Author, "Lee Teng-hui accepts election blame", BBC, March 19, 2000, http://news.bbc.co.uk/2/hi/asia-pacific/682909.stm

Unnamed Author, "Live or Die: Tales of Human Tragedy From North Korean Famine Refugees in China", *Nightline*, aired June 10, 2002, http://abcnews.go.com/sections/nightline/DailyNews/northkorea020610_famine.html

Unnamed Author, "Major upsets in Kashmir poll", October 16, 2002, CNN, http://asia.cnn.com/2002/WORLD/asiapcf/south/10/10/kashmir.count/index.html

Unnamed Author, "Millionaire jailed in China", BBC, March 11, 2000 http://news.bbc.co.uk/2/hi/asia-pacific/673815.stm

Unnamed Author, "Missile talks between United States, North Korea end in stalemate", CNN, July 12, 2000, http://asia.cnn.com/2000/ASIANOW/east/07/12/nkorea.us/index.html

Unnamed Author, "Mother: United States Taliban fighter 'must have been brainwashed'", CNN, December 5, 2001, http://asia.cnn.com/2001/WORLD/asiapcf/central/12/03/ret.american.taliban/index.html

Unnamed Author, "N Korea 'may end' nuclear pact", BBC March 22, 2002, http://news.bbc.co.uk/2/hi/asia-pacific/1887593.stm

Unnamed Author, "N Korea 'will not end nuclear programme'", BBC, October 29, 2002, http://news.bbc.co.uk/2/hi/asia-pacific/2370345.stm

Unnamed Author, "N Korea confesses to kidnappings", BBC, September 17, 2002, http://news.bbc.co.uk/2/hi/asia-pacific/2262074.stm

Unnamed Author, "N Korea food aid 'misses target'", BBC, February 8, 2002, http://news.bbc.co.uk/2/hi/asia-pacific/1809287.stm

Unnamed Author, "N Korean food aid 'running out'", BBC, September 30, 2002, http://news.bbc.co.uk/2/hi/asia-pacific/2287988.stm

Unnamed Author, "N. Korea 'armed to the teeth'", CNN, August 29, 2002, http://asia.cnn.com/2002/WORLD/asiapcf/east/08/29/nkorea.us/

Unnamed Author, "N. Korea refuses to disarm" CNN, October 29, 2002, http://edition.cnn.com/2002/WORLD/asiapcf/east/10/29/nkorea.japan/

Unnamed Author, "New Axis of Evil?", World Net Daily, September 8, 2003, http://www.worldnetdaily.com/news/article.asp?ARTICLE_ID=34481

Unnamed Author, "New book claims CIA backed Pope, Solidarity", CNN, September 19, 1996, http://asia.cnn.com/US/9609/19/briefs/

Unnamed Author, "No more oil aid for N Korea", BBC, November 15, 2002, http://news.bbc.co.uk/2/hi/asia-pacific/2479141.stm

Unnamed Author, "North Korea pressed on South's missing", BBC, September 20, 2002, http://news.bbc.co.uk/2/hi/world/asia-pacific/2270222.stm

Unnamed Author, "North Korea's number two in Libya", BBC, July 14, 2002, http://news.bbc.co.uk/hi/english/world/middle_east/newsid_2127000/2127138.stm

Unnamed Author, "North Korean aid dries up", CNN, October 1, 2002, http://asia.cnn.com/2002/WORLD/asiapcf/east/09/30/nkorea.aid/

Unnamed Author, "North Korean test missile test flies over Japan into the Pacific", CNN, August 31, 1998, http://asia.cnn.com/WORLD/asiapcf/9808/31/nkorea.missile.02/index.html

Unnamed Author, "North Koreans 'forced to eat grass'", BBC, June 20, 2002, http://news.bbc.co.uk/2/hi/asia-pacific/2055658.stm

Unnamed Author, "North Koreans arrive in Seoul" BBC, June 24, 2002, http://news.bbc.co.uk/2/hi/asia-pacific/2061772.stm

Unnamed Author, "Nuclear deadlock at Japan-N Korea talks", BBC, October 30, 2003, http://news.bbc.co.uk/2/hi/world/asia-pacific/2374287.stm

Unnamed Author, "Obituary: Syria's shrewd master", BBC, June 10, 2000, http://news.bbc.co.uk/2/hi/middle_east/359051.stm

Unnamed Author, "Observances subdued 7 years after Tiananmen Square crackdown", CNN, June 4, 1996, http://asia.cnn.com/WORLD/9606/04/tianamen.anniv/

Unnamed Author, "Oil rebounds as Chavez returns", CNN, April 15, 2002, http://asia.cnn.com/2002/BUSINESS/04/15/oil.chavez/index.html

Unnamed Author, "Oil Shipments to N Korea frozen", CNN, November 15, 2002, http://asia.cnn.com/2002/US/11/14/nkorea.oil/index.html

Unnamed Author, "Out with the old: Taiwan Timeline: 1972-1986", BBC, undated, http://news.bbc.co.uk/hi/english/static/in_depth/asia_pacific/2000/taiwan_elections2000/1972_1986.stm

Unnamed Author, "Outrage over N. Korean admission", CNN, September 18, 2002, http://asia.cnn.com/2002/WORLD/asiapcf/east/09/18/nkorea.japan/index.html

Unnamed Author, "Pakistan explodes nuclear devices", CNN, May 28, 1998, http://asia.cnn.com/WORLD/asiapcf/9805/28/pakistan.nuclear.2/index.html

Unnamed Author, "Pakistan parties remain deadlocked", BBC, November 18, 2001, http://news.bbc.co.uk/2/hi/south_asia/2487801.stm

Unnamed Author, "Pakistan transfers troops to Kashmir", *Washington Times*, January 17, 2002, http://www.washingtontimes.com/world/20020117-32522280.htm

Unnamed Author, "Profile: General Pervez Musharraf", BBC, July 11, 2002, http://news.bbc.co.uk/2/hi/south_asia/1742997.stm

Unnamed Author, "Profile: Lal Krishna Advani", BBC, September 25, 2002, http://news.bbc.co.uk/2/hi/south_asia/2075803.stm

Unnamed Author, "Profile: Saddam Hussein", BBC, http://www.bbc.co.uk/bbcfour/documentaries/profile/saddam_hussein.shtml

Unnamed Author, "Putin Joins Bush vs. Saddam but Warns of Saudis, Pakistan", Newsmax, November 23, 2002, http://www.Newsmax/archives/articles/2002/11/22/153337.shtml

Unnamed Author, "Q&A: 'This Cold War Is Much More Dangerous'", *Business Week*, May 28, 2001, http://www.businessweek.com/magazine/content/01_22/b3734012.htm

Unnamed Author, "Radio threat to N Korea's grip on news", BBC, August 11, 2003, http://news.bbc.co.uk/2/hi/asia-pacific/3141331.stm

Unnamed Author, "Red Army families seek Japanese home", BBC, September 10, 2002, http://news.bbc.co.uk/2/hi/asia-pacific/2248787.stm

Unnamed Author, "Red Army members want talks", BBC, July 10, 2002, http://news.bbc.co.uk/2/hi/asia-pacific/2119696.stm

Unnamed Author, "Reporters see wrecked Buddhas", BBC, March 26, 2001, http://news.bbc.co.uk/2/hi/south_asia/1242856.stm

Unnamed Author, "Reports of Cuba shipments could hurt Sino-US ties", CNN, June 13, 2001, http://asia.cnn.com/2001/WORLD/asiapcf/east/06/12/china.cuba/index.html

Unnamed Author, "Rumsfeld Seeks Exit for Bosnia Mission", Newsmax, May 19, 2001, https://www.Newsmax/archives/articles/2001/5/18/171310.shtml

Unnamed Author, "Russia and China 'broke Iraq embargo'", BBC, December 19, 2002, http://news.bbc.co.uk/2/hi/europe/2591351.stm

Unnamed Author, "Russia and China urge Korea thaw", BBC, December 2, 2002, http://news.bbc.co.uk/2/hi/asia-pacific/2533533.stm

Unnamed Author, "S Korea leader sorry for summit scandal", BBC, February 14, 2003, http://news.bbc.co.uk/2/hi/asia-pacific/2760039.stm

Unnamed Author, "Sacked Chinese workers in mass rally", CNN, March 13, 2002, http://asia.cnn.com/2002/WORLD/asiapcf/east/03/13/china.unrest/index.html

Unnamed Author, "Saudi police 'stopped' fire rescue", BBC, March 15, 2002, http://news.bbc.co.uk/2/hi/middle_east/1874471.stm

Unnamed Author, "'Second suspicious ship' spotted off Japan", CNN, December 25, 2001, http://asia.cnn.com/2001/WORLD/asiapcf/east/12/23/japan.china.boat/index.html

Unnamed Author, "Secret paper shows China 'rift' over Tiananmen", CNN, April 23, 2001, http://asia.cnn.com/2001/WORLD/asiapcf/east/04/22/tiananmen.document/index.html

Unnamed Author, "Sen. Helms Targets China Export Waivers", CNN All Politics, June 11, 2002, http://asia.cnn.com/ALLPOLITICS/1998/06/11/helms/index.html

Unnamed Author, "Setback for North Korea trade zone", BBC, October 1, 2002, http://news.bbc.co.uk/2/hi/business/2289777.stm

Unnamed Author, "Sources: United States kills Cole suspect", CNN, November 5, 2002, http://asia.cnn.com/2002/WORLD/meast/11/04/yemen.blast/index.html

Unnamed Author, "Special Report: Showdown Iraq", CNN, http://asia.cnn.com/SPECIALS/2002/iraq/, History of Iraq Link, 1979 tab

Unnamed Author, Stratfor.com, as cited by World Net Daily, "China tests United States definition of terrorism", World Net Daily, December 17, 2001, http://wnd.com/news/article.asp?ARTICLE_ID=25727

Unnamed Author, "Sudan denies any links with Osama Bin Laden", Reuters via CNN, August 30, 1998, http://asia.cnn.com/WORLD/africa/9808/30/sudan.bin.laden/index.html

Unnamed Author, "Syria denies hiding Iraqi weapons", CNN, December 26, 2002, http://asia.cnn.com/2002/WORLD/meast/12/25/israel.syria/

Unnamed Author, "Taiwan president proclaims Americas tour a victory", CNN, June 5, 2001, http://asia.cnn.com/2001/WORLD/asiapcf/east/06/05/taiwan.president/index.html

Unnamed Author, "Taiwan presses for US arms sales", BBC, April 9, 2001, http://news.bbc.co.uk/2/hi/asia-pacific/1268316.stm

Unnamed Author, "Taiwan tripper may upset China", CNN, May 6, 2001, http://asia.cnn.com/2001/WORLD/asiapcf/east/05/06/taiwan.president.us.visa/index.html

Unnamed Author, "Taiwan voters defy China", BBC, March 19, 2000, http://news.bbc.co.uk/2/hi/asia-pacific/682137.stm

Unnamed Author, "Taiwan's Mixed Bag", ABC News, April 17, 2000, http://abcnews.go.com/sections/world/DailyNews/taiwan000417.html

Unnamed Author, "Taiwanese president leaves US", BBC, August 14, 2000, http://news.bbc.co.uk/2/hi/asia-pacific/828717.stm

Unnamed Author, "Taiwan's people begin historic vote", CNN, March 23, 1996, http://www-cgi.cnn.com/WORLD/9603/taiwan_elex/23/

Unnamed Author, "Taliban bars women aid drivers", CNN, June 1, 2001, http://asia.cnn.com/2001/WORLD/asiapcf/central/05/31/afghanistan.women/index.html

Unnamed Author, "Tensions ease after Taiwan election", CNN, March 24, 1996, http://www-cgi.cnn.com/WORLD/9603/taiwan_elex/day_after/

Unnamed Author, "The Consequences of Nuclear Tests in Eastern Turkestan", Citizens Against Communist Chinese Propaganda, http://www.caccp.org/et/cnt.html

Unnamed Author, "The First 1992 Presidential Debate: October 11, 1992", PBS, 2000, http://www.pbs.org/newshour/debatingourdestiny/92debates/1stprez2.html

Unnamed Author, "Tibet protesters target Chinese Embassy", BBC, October 7, 2000, http://news.bbc.co.uk/2/hi/asia-pacific/961104.stm

Unnamed Author, "Tibet sentences condemned", BBC, December 5, 2002, http://news.bbc.co.uk/2/hi/asia-pacific/2547357.stm

Unnamed Author, "Timeline: Afghanistan", BBC, October 31, 2002, http://news.bbc.co.uk/2/hi/south_asia/1162108.stm

Unnamed Author, "Timeline: Conflict over Kashmir", CNN, May 24, 2002, http://asia.cnn.com/2002/WORLD/asiapcf/south/05/24/kashmir.timeline/index.html

Unnamed Author, "Timeline: India", BBC, November 1, 2002, http://news.bbc.co.uk/2/hi/south_asia/1155813.stm

Unnamed Author, "Timeline: Iran", BBC, October 5, 2002, http://news.bbc.co.uk/2/hi/middle_east/806268.stm

Unnamed Author, "Timeline: Pakistan", BBC, November 21, 2002, http://news.bbc.co.uk/2/hi/south_asia/1156716.stm

Unnamed Author, "Timeline: Sudan", BBC, July 31, 2002, http://news.bbc.co.uk/2/hi/middle_east/827425.stm

Unnamed Author, "Timeline: Tensions on the Korean Peninsula", CNN, August 12, 2002, http://asia.cnn.com/2002/WORLD/asiapcf/east/08/12/korea.timeline/index.html

Unnamed Author, "Timeline: United Arab Emirates", BBC, March 19, 2002, http://news.bbc.co.uk/2/hi/middle_east/828687.stm

Unnamed Author, "Timeline: US-China relations", BBC, October 29, 2002 http://news.bbc.co.uk/2/low/asia-pacific/1258054.stm

Unnamed Author, "Timeline: Yemen", BBC, October 16, 2002, http://news.bbc.co.uk/2/hi/middle_east/country_profiles/1706450.stm

Unnamed Author, "UAE cuts ties with Taliban", CNN, September 23, 2001, http://asia.cnn.com/2001/WORLD/asiapcf/central/09/22/ret.afghan.taliban/index.html

Unnamed Author, "Uighur leader dies in Chinese custody", BBC, October 25, 2000, http://news.bbc.co.uk/2/hi/asia-pacific/990638.stm

Unnamed Author, "Uighur woman jailed over mailed newspapers" BBC, March 16, 2000, http://news.bbc.co.uk/2/hi/asia-pacific/679726.stm

Unnamed Author, "UN orders out inspectors", BBC, December 16, 1998, http://news.bbc.co.uk/2/hi/americas/235900.stm

Unnamed Author, "United States expanding war on terrorism", CNN, March 6, 2002, http://www.cnn.com/2002/US/03/01/ret.us.forces/index.html

Unnamed Author, "United States faces China hard sell on Iraq", CNN, September 13, 2001, http://asia.cnn.com/2002/WORLD/asiapcf/east/09/13/china.iraq.bush/index.html

Unnamed Author, "United States finds link between bin Laden and Cole bombing", CNN, December 8, 2000, http://asia.cnn.com/2000/US/12/07/cole.suspect/index.html

Unnamed Author, "United States national among Yemen dead", MSNBC, November 7, 2002, http://stacks.msnbc.com/news/830203.asp?cp1=1

Unnamed Author, "United States report slams China's terrorism war", CNN, March 5, 2002, http://asia.cnn.com/2002/WORLD/asiapcf/east/03/05/china.rightsreport/index.html

Unnamed Author, "United States resumes south China spying", CNN, May 29, 2001, http://asia.cnn.com/2001/WORLD/asiapcf/east/05/28/china.us.resume.spying/index.html

Unnamed Author, "United States: China has not slowed missile tech exports to Middle East", World Tribune.com, January 21, 2002, http://216.26.163.62/2002/ea_china_01_21.html

Unnamed Author, "United States: China separatists 'plotted embassy attacks'", CNN, August 30, 2002, http://asia.cnn.com/2002/WORLD/asiapcf/east/08/30/kyrgyz.china.terror/index.html

Unnamed Author, "US considers N Korea sanctions", BBC, April 26, 2003, http://news.bbc.co.uk/2/hi/asia-pacific/2977497.stm

Unnamed Author, "US diplomat visits China's Muslim area", BBC, December 18, 2002, http://news.bbc.co.uk/2/hi/asia-pacific/2586655.stm

Unnamed Author, "US frees missile-carrying ship", BBC, December 11, 2002, http://news.bbc.co.uk/2/hi/middle_east/2567225.stm

Unnamed Author, "US grants N Korea nuclear funds", BBC, April 3, 2002, http://news.bbc.co.uk/2/hi/asia-pacific/1908571.stm

Unnamed Author, "US lawmakers reassure India", BBC, November 9, 2002, http://news.bbc.co.uk/2/hi/south_asia/1644980.stm

Unnamed Author, "US lifts India and Pakistan sanctions", BBC, September 23, 2001, http://news.bbc.co.uk/2/hi/americas/1558860.stm

Unnamed Author, "US politicians support Chinese dissident", BBC, July 24, 2002, http://news.bbc.co.uk/2/hi/americas/849743.stm,

Unnamed Author, "US punishes Chinese firms", BBC, January 25, 2002, http://news.bbc.co.uk/hi/english/world/asia-pacific/newsid_1780000/1780998.stm

Unnamed Author, "US punishes firms over Iran ", BBC, July 4, 2003, http://news.bbc.co.uk/2/hi/business/3043498.stm

Unnamed Author, "US sanctions over China missile sales", BBC, September 1, 2001, http://news.bbc.co.uk/2/hi/americas/1521086.stm

Unnamed Author, "US waives China missile sanctions", BBC, November 21, 2000, http://news.bbc.co.uk/2/hi/americas/1034502.stm

Unnamed Author, "US warned over North Korea," BBC, February 23, 2003, http://news.bbc.co.uk/2/hi/asia-pacific/2789303.stm

Unnamed Author, "Video twist to Japan-China row", BBC, May 10, 2002, http://news.bbc.co.uk/2/hi/asia-pacific/1978817.stm

Unnamed Author, "Weapons inspectors leave after Butler report", CNN, December 16, 1998, http://asia.cnn.com/WORLD/meast/9812/16/un.iraq.01/index.html

Unnamed Author, "Where they stand on Iraq: Kuwait", CNN, December 20, 2002, http://asia.cnn.com/2002/WORLD/meast/12/19/sproject.irq.kuwait/

Unnamed Author, "Who is Osama Bin Laden?", BBC, September 18, 2002, http://news.bbc.co.uk/2/hi/south_asia/1551100.stm

Unnamed Author, "Yemen blasts spark terror fears", BBC, October 13, 2000, http://news.bbc.co.uk/2/hi/middle_east/970347.stm

Vernon, Wes, "Bush and Congress Push the 'Arm Saddam Act'", Newsmax, October 11, 2002, http://www.Newsmax/archives/articles/2002/10/10/193255.shtml

Waller, J. Michael, "Castro Offers Former Russian Spy Base to China", *Insight*, May 30, 2002, http://www.insightmag.com/main.cfm/include/detail/storyid/254144.html

Walsh, James, "Others Who Shaped 1998: Osama bin Laden", *Time Asia*, December 28, 1998, http://www.time.com/time/asia/asia/magazine/1998/981228/osama1.html

Warrick, Joby, "U.N. Nuclear Agency Says Iran Breached Agreements", *Washington Post*, June 7, 2003, p. A19

Weaver, Lisa Rose "China defends 'spy' jailing," CNN, February 11, 2003, http://edition.cnn.com/2003/WORLD/asiapcf/east/02/11/china.dissident/index.html

Windrem, Robert, "Death, terror in N. Korea gulag", MSNBC, January 15, 2003, http://www.msnbc.com/news/859191.asp?0cv=CA01

Wingfield-Hayes, Rupert, "The plight of North Korea's refugees", BBC, September 5, 2002, http://news.bbc.co.uk/2/hi/asia-pacific/2238894.stm

Wingfield-Hayes, "Where China stands on Iraq", BBC, October 11, 2002, http://news.bbc.co.uk/2/hi/asia-pacific/2319403.stm

Wu Guoguang, "The Sacrifice That Made a Leader", *Time Asia*, undated, http://www.time.com/time/asia/features/heroes/zhao.html

Yonhap News Agency, "NK-Iran in Arms Deal", reprinted by *The Korea Times*, August 6, 2003, http://times.hankooki.com/lpage/nation/200308/kt2003080615060211990.htm

Index

1991 Gulf War, 32
38th parallel, 48, 197
38th Parallel, 47
Abd al-Majid al-Khoei, 36
Abdulmejit, 133
Ablait Abdureschit, 151
Advani, 80, 265
Afghanistan, vi, vii, viii, xi, 1, 2, 3, 5, 6, 7, 8, 9, 14, 15, 16, 18, 20, 21, 22, 28, 35, 36, 40, 77, 78, 82, 83, 87, 89, 90, 92, 94, 95, 99, 102, 109, 114, 116, 117, 118, 122, 127, 135, 138, 140, 141, 143, 145, 155, 165, 170, 179, 187, 188, 190, 191, 193, 194, 201, 203, 208, 209, 213, 214, 222, 268
Agreed Framework, 56, 57, 59, 63, 69, 70, 71, 169, 199
Ahn Myong Jin, 50
AI, 136, 153
al Aqsa, 36, 153, 219
al Qaeda, v, vi, vii, x, xi, 1, 2, 3, 4, 6, 7, 8, 9, 10, 11, 12, 13, 14, 15, 16, 17, 18, 19, 20, 21, 23, 27, 28, 33, 36, 62, 77, 78, 79, 85, 87, 88, 89, 90, 93, 94, 95, 99, 101, 102, 110, 117, 118, 120, 121, 124, 128, 130, 136, 138, 142, 144, 145, 146, 155, 169, 193, 201, 202, 219, 222, 229, 248
al-Fatah, 101
Al-Zarqawi, 28
America, vi, ix, xii, 1, 2, 3, 5, 6, 7, 9, 11, 14, 21, 22, 31, 32, 47, 65, 73, 74, 85, 95, 104, 105, 118, 119, 122, 123, 124, 127, 129, 134, 154, 155, 157, 167, 169, 170, 177, 179, 181, 182, 183, 185, 187, 188, 191, 192, 195, 197, 198, 199, 201, 208, 209, 213, 218, 219, 220, 221
American, vi, vii, viii, x, xi, 1, 2, 3, 4, 6, 7, 10, 11, 13, 14, 15, 16, 17, 18, 19, 20, 22, 23, 24, 28, 29, 30, 31, 33, 34, 35, 37, 40, 42, 43, 44, 45, 46, 48, 51, 53, 57, 58, 62, 63, 65, 67, 71, 74, 77, 78, 79, 82, 83, 85, 87, 89, 90, 93, 94, 95, 98, 99, 101, 102, 104, 105, 106, 107, 108, 109, 110, 112, 114, 115, 116, 117, 118, 119, 120, 121, 122, 123, 127, 128, 135, 140, 141, 142, 143, 145, 146, 148, 153, 154, 157, 162, 165, 166, 167, 169, 171, 172, 174, 178, 179, 180, 182, 185, 187, 188, 189, 190, 191, 192, 193, 194, 195, 197, 198, 199, 200, 201, 202, 203, 206, 207, 209, 210, 211, 214, 215, 217, 218, 219, 220, 221, 225, 235, 240, 258, 287
Ansar al-Islam, 28
anti-American, viii, 6, 37, 44, 78, 90, 105, 115, 120, 145, 182, 188, 190, 192, 194, 209, 218
anti-Americanism, 23, 33, 34, 35, 38, 41, 46, 74, 105, 121, 129, 143, 188, 193, 195
Anti-Ballistic Missile Treaty, 106

anti-Communist, 31, 48, 71, 82, 122, 123, 134, 135, 139, 147, 166, 168, 175, 180, 181, 186, 197, 201, 202, 204, 205, 206, 207, 211, 212, 213, 216, 217
anti-rightist campaign, 54, 146, 178
Arafat, 36
Asia, vii, x, xi, xii, 4, 13, 16, 17, 18, 19, 20, 33, 40, 45, 54, 64, 67, 72, 73, 84, 85, 95, 97, 99, 111, 116, 118, 137, 163, 165, 166, 167, 177, 178, 179, 180, 181, 188, 192, 196, 204, 207, 209, 220, 224, 225, 226, 229, 236, 239, 241, 243, 247, 249, 272, 273
Asiaweek, 144
Askar Akayev, 113
Assad, 103
Australia, 96, 207, 234, 252
axis of evil, vi, viii, 20, 23, 24, 37, 39, 44, 45, 61, 63, 92, 124, 182, 195, 196, 205, 222
Ayatollah, 34, 36, 37
Azhar, 88
Azimbek Beknazarov, 113
Ba'ath Party, 25
Ba'athism, 32, 189, 190, 194, 216
Ba'athist, 22, 23, 24, 25, 26, 27, 28, 30, 32, 33, 37, 42, 43, 45, 60, 63, 101, 103, 104, 105, 118, 123, 129, 182, 190, 191, 194, 196, 203, 205, 214, 216
Baghdad, 28, 168, 214, 227
ballistic, 63
Bao, 159, 211, 212
Baren, 132
Bashar, 103
Bashar al-Assad, 104, 194, 216

BBC, viii, 29, 72, 133, 226, 232, 234, 242, 249, 251, 252, 253, 254, 255, 256, 257, 258, 259, 260, 261, 262, 263, 264, 265, 266, 267, 268, 269, 270, 271, 272, 273
Beijing, xi, 18, 40, 46, 54, 55, 67, 78, 101, 111, 112, 113, 130, 131, 132, 140, 146, 148, 149, 158, 160, 167, 168, 181, 183, 191, 200, 207, 211, 214, 216, 223, 237, 238, 241, 244, 246, 252
Beirut, 103
Belgrade, 189
Benazir Bhutto, 82
Berlin, 102
Bharatiya Janata Party, 79
Bhutto, 82
bin Laden, 1, 7, 9, 10, 11, 12, 78, 129, 138, 143, 155, 254, 270
biological weapons, 58
Bishkek, 139
BJP, 79, 83, 85, 89, 97
Blue House, 52
Bosnia, 109, 266
Bronson, 39, 104
Buddhist, 96, 128, 202
Bush, v, x, 15, 23, 38, 39, 40, 45, 57, 86, 98, 111, 142, 227, 238, 244, 252, 265, 272
Bush Administration, x, 15, 23, 38, 39, 40, 57, 98
Cacak, 213
Castillo, 170
Castro, 170
Central Asia, xi, 13, 16, 99, 177
Central Committee, 149
Central Military Commission, 16, 40, 158, 163, 215
Chang Wanquan, 151

Chavez, 170
Chechnya, 13, 111, 114, 153
chemical weapons, 58
Chemical Weapons Convention, 39
Chen, 169, 174, 175, 225
Chiang, 130
China Machinery and Electric Import and Export Company, 39
China National Electronics Import and Export Corporation, 39
Chinese Communist Party, v, 12, 104, 130, 151, 157, 163, 173, 213
Chinese people, xii, 131, 150, 151, 158, 160, 162, 168, 172, 176, 177, 186, 201, 211, 213, 216, 218, 221
Chosun Ilbo, 70
CIA, 10, 57, 59, 63, 193, 230, 256, 263
Clinton, 10, 11, 21, 57, 61, 84, 85, 86, 91, 93, 111, 168, 169, 233, 235, 251, 256
Clinton Administration, 38, 84, 169
CMC, 158, 163, 164, 165
Cold War I, 78, 108, 109, 178, 188
Cold War II, v, xii, xiii, 4, 20, 21, 22, 33, 38, 42, 43, 44, 46, 65, 74, 75, 78, 79, 93, 94, 95, 98, 99, 108, 109, 115, 119, 124, 145, 155, 157, 168, 185, 186, 187, 188, 193, 196, 200, 201, 204, 208, 210, 213, 214, 215, 216, 217, 218, 219, 220, 221, 222
Cole, 8, 120, 122, 267, 270

Communist China, v, vi, vii, viii, ix, x, xi, xii, 1, 2, 3, 4, 5, 6, 10, 11, 12, 13, 14, 16, 17, 18, 19, 20, 21, 22, 23, 24, 29, 30, 31, 32, 33, 34, 38, 39, 40, 41, 42, 43, 44, 45, 46, 48, 51, 52, 53, 54, 55, 56, 58, 59, 60, 62, 64, 65, 66, 67, 68, 69, 72, 73, 74, 77, 78, 79, 80, 81, 82, 83, 84, 86, 87, 88, 89, 91, 92, 93, 95, 96, 97, 98, 99, 100, 101, 102, 103, 104, 105, 106, 107, 108, 109, 110, 111, 112, 113, 114, 115, 117, 118, 119, 122, 123, 124, 128, 129, 131, 132, 133, 134, 135, 136, 137, 139, 141, 142, 144, 145, 146, 148, 150, 151, 152, 153, 154, 155, 157, 159, 160, 161, 163, 164, 165, 166, 167, 168, 169, 170, 171, 172, 173, 174, 175, 176, 177, 178, 179, 180, 181, 185, 186, 187, 189, 190, 191, 192, 193, 194, 195, 196, 198, 199, 200, 202, 203, 204, 205, 206, 207, 208, 209, 210, 211, 212, 213, 214, 215, 216, 217, 218, 219, 220, 221, 222, 287
corruption, 161
Craner, 142, 153, 210
Cuba, 170
Cultural Revolution, 54, 146, 160, 178
Dagestan, 114, 153
Dalai Lama, 96, 128, 147, 149, 165, 180, 211, 223, 257
Damascus, 194, 214
Delhi, 94, 225
democracy, xii, 14, 20, 31, 33, 37, 79, 82, 85, 93, 98, 103, 138, 143, 158, 174, 175, 176, 177,

180, 181, 189, 191, 192, 201, 202, 205, 206, 211, 215, 217, 218, 222
Democratic, 10, 47, 107, 168
Deng, 149, 150, 158, 159, 160, 163, 164, 165, 257
Die Zeit, 36
DMZ, 48
Donald McIntyre, 17
DPP, 174, 175
East Asia, xii, 91, 99, 180
East Turkestan, ix, x, 14, 15, 20, 31, 110, 112, 127, 129, 130, 131, 132, 133, 134, 135, 136, 137, 138, 139, 140, 141, 142, 143, 144, 145, 146, 147, 148, 149, 150, 151, 153, 154, 155, 166, 176, 180, 208, 209, 210, 211, 221, 222
East Turkestan National Congress, 138, 143
Eastern Europe, 145, 218
Economist Intelligence Unit, 96
El Al, 17
embassies, 7, 10, 46, 55
embassy, 55, 152, 271
engagement, vii, 38, 44, 57, 65, 74, 93, 96, 106, 107, 108, 109, 110, 114, 115, 118, 119, 123, 124, 148, 155, 167, 168, 182, 202, 207, 215, 217, 218, 219
EP-3, 171, 244
ETIM, x, 110, 128, 130, 139, 140, 141, 142, 146, 153, 154, 180, 210
ETU, 131, 133
Europe, 67, 68, 131, 145, 158, 188, 211, 213, 218, 252
falaqa, 25
Falun Gong, 136
FBI, 17, 225

former President Bush, 168
France, 142
Free Turkestan, 139
Gaddis, 162
Gadhafi, 64, 101, 102, 194
Gao, 134
George H. W. Bush, 167
Germany, 8, 218
Gladney, 139, 144
Gluckman, 144
Golan Heights, 103, 190
Gorbachev, 212
Great Britain, 30
great leap forward, 54, 146
Guangdong, 161, 212
Ha'aretz, 63
Hafez, 103
Hainan, 171
Hamas, 219
Harakat ul-Mujahideen, viii
Hayworth, 217
Hekmatyar, 35
Heliongjiang, 212
Hezbollah, 36, 43, 219, 232, 243
Hindu, 79, 83
Hollywood, 147
Hong Kong, 159, 160, 211, 220, 234, 241
hostages, 34, 35, 51, 114
Houston, 169
Hu, 104, 148, 157, 158, 164, 165, 215, 216, 217, 255
Hu Yaobang, 157, 158
Huawei Technologies, 3, 14, 29
human rights, 29, 65, 66, 71, 107, 128, 134, 138, 139, 142, 145, 153, 168, 208, 210, 251, 258, 287
Human Rights Watch, 145
Hussein, viii, 24, 25, 26, 27, 28, 32, 33

IAEA, 36, 57
Igor Ivanov, 15
Inchon, 47
India, vii, xii, 6, 62, 77, 78, 79, 80, 81, 82, 83, 84, 85, 86, 87, 88, 89, 90, 93, 94, 95, 96, 97, 98, 99, 165, 177, 179, 180, 181, 183, 186, 201, 202, 204, 211, 213, 218, 220, 224, 226, 242, 243, 244, 247, 249, 251, 258, 259, 260, 269, 271
International Atomic Energy Agency, 36, 57
Inter-Service Intelligence, 5, 88, 117
Iran, vi, vii, viii, ix, 4, 6, 16, 19, 20, 23, 24, 26, 27, 34, 35, 36, 37, 38, 39, 40, 41, 42, 43, 44, 45, 60, 62, 63, 64, 101, 103, 105, 115, 116, 117, 118, 122, 124, 129, 169, 182, 188, 190, 192, 193, 195, 199, 200, 203, 208, 214, 216, 222, 230, 231, 235, 242, 248, 253, 258, 260, 269, 271, 272, 273
Iraq, vi, vii, viii, x, 12, 15, 22, 23, 24, 25, 26, 27, 28, 29, 31, 32, 33, 34, 35, 37, 42, 43, 45, 60, 62, 63, 64, 101, 103, 104, 105, 114, 115, 116, 117, 118, 119, 122, 123, 124, 129, 140, 142, 153, 182, 187, 188, 190, 191, 192, 194, 195, 196, 203, 205, 208, 213, 214, 216, 222, 223, 224, 235, 236, 237, 238, 240, 243, 249, 253, 254, 256, 266, 267, 270, 272, 273
Ishihara, 63, 204
ISI, 5, 88, 117
Islam, 6, 7, 27, 28, 35, 42, 116, 127, 128, 132, 135, 137, 139, 143, 146, 147, 154, 186, 208, 209
Islamic Republic, 23, 26, 34, 38, 40, 192, 193
Islamism, 189
Israel, 36, 41, 78, 79, 85, 86, 95, 98, 103, 104, 153, 165, 195, 201, 202, 216, 235, 247, 251, 255
Jaish-i-Muhammad, 88
Japan, xii, 37, 47, 49, 50, 51, 55, 56, 58, 59, 60, 61, 64, 67, 68, 69, 71, 72, 96, 162, 165, 166, 177, 178, 180, 186, 189, 191, 198, 204, 205, 207, 213, 218, 220, 233, 237, 260, 263, 264, 266, 272
Jeffrey Goldberg, 28
Jenkins, 51
Jesse Helms, 152
Jiang, 4, 5, 16, 40, 67, 142, 148, 164, 165, 168, 192, 215, 217, 233, 237, 240, 241, 250, 251, 260
Jiang Zemin, 5
jihad, 209
John Adams, 154
John Walker Lindh, viii, 77, 89
Kabul, x, 2, 3, 4, 6, 9, 14, 15, 16, 17, 18, 19, 35, 94, 191, 193, 214, 255
Kadeer, 133, 134
Kadish, 61
Kashmir, viii, 62, 77, 78, 79, 80, 82, 83, 85, 87, 88, 89, 90, 93, 94, 95, 96, 99, 101, 115, 183, 191, 201, 224, 227, 248, 249, 260, 262, 265, 268
Kazakhstan, xi, 111
KEDO, 57
Kennedy, 86

Khatami, 37, 40
Khomeni, 34
Kim Dae-jung, 69, 70
Kim Il-sung, 47
Kim Jong-il, 46, 49, 50, 52, 53, 56, 65, 68, 69, 71, 72, 198
Koizumi, 50, 72
Korea, ix, 37, 45, 46, 47, 49, 50, 51, 52, 53, 55, 56, 57, 60, 61, 63, 64, 67, 69, 71, 72, 73, 74, 91, 92, 121, 180, 196, 197, 198, 199, 200, 204, 205, 226, 227, 228, 231, 235, 236, 250, 256, 257, 258, 262, 263, 264, 265, 266, 271, 273
Korean War, 47, 48, 70, 150, 162, 197, 225
Kosovo, 109
Kurds, 26, 27
Kuwait, 26, 32, 120, 272
Kyrgyzstan, x, xi, 89, 111, 112, 113, 139, 141, 253, 261
Lam, 5, 12, 15, 40, 67, 111, 141, 237, 238, 239, 240, 241
Lanzhou Daily, 135
Lebanon, 23, 35, 103, 195, 232, 256
Ledeen, 65, 120, 242
Lee, 66, 173
Li Peng, 159
Li Qianyuan, 151
Li Shaomin, 134
Libya, vi, vii, ix, 62, 64, 101, 102, 105, 123, 129, 169, 186, 193, 194, 199, 214, 222, 245, 252, 263
Lioyang, 212
Liu Dongdong, 151
Liyang Chemical Equipment Company, 39
Lockerbie, 101, 102

London Daily Telegraph, 12
MacArthur, 47, 48, 191
madrassas, 5
Mahatma Gandhi, 79
Mahjar, 25
mainland, 166, 171, 173, 174, 176, 177, 206, 213
Mao, 48, 81, 131, 146, 150, 158, 160, 162, 178, 181, 197, 234
Marines, 35
Marxism, 150
Massoud, 8, 9
Mazar-e-Sharif, 5, 9, 89
MFN, 167
Michael Kopetski, 107
Middle East, vi, 23, 32, 33, 35, 40, 41, 42, 52, 62, 63, 74, 78, 99, 103, 105, 122, 124, 147, 182, 193, 248, 270
Middle Kingdom, 173
military, vii, viii, x, xi, 2, 4, 5, 7, 11, 14, 15, 16, 19, 23, 24, 25, 26, 29, 30, 35, 38, 39, 40, 42, 45, 46, 53, 63, 65, 69, 73, 74, 78, 79, 80, 81, 82, 83, 85, 86, 87, 88, 89, 91, 92, 95, 96, 97, 99, 103, 105, 106, 107, 108, 109, 112, 113, 115, 116, 119, 122, 123, 133, 134, 149, 151, 159, 163, 164, 165, 166, 167, 169, 170, 171, 177, 179, 180, 185, 187, 190, 191, 192, 194, 195, 196, 198, 201, 203, 206, 213, 214, 215, 216, 217, 218, 220, 231, 255
Milosevic, 189, 213, 246
missiles, viii, 2, 3, 10, 17, 21, 31, 37, 39, 61, 62, 63, 64, 65, 92, 99, 102, 106, 112, 115, 117, 121, 122, 169, 171, 174, 175, 176, 183, 214, 231, 232, 260

Moscow, 111, 112, 114, 181, 212
Most Favored Nation, 217
mujahedin, 6, 82, 116, 146, 209
Mullah Omar, viii, 4, 8, 35, 222
Musharraf, 78, 80, 85, 88, 89, 90, 93, 94, 95, 99, 115, 265
Muslim, ix, x, 7, 20, 77, 78, 79, 85, 90, 102, 112, 127, 132, 137, 143, 148, 152, 154, 186, 194, 209, 233, 247, 255, 271
National Review Online, 65
nationalism, 33, 42, 145, 150, 151, 162, 163, 178, 181, 189, 192, 216
Nationalists, 174
NATO, xi, 112, 238, 245
New Delhi, 86, 87
New Party, 175
New York City, v, 94, 101
New York Post, 63
New Yorker, 28, 232
Newsweek, 122
Nixon, 78
Nobel Peace Prize, 70
Non-Proliferation Treaty, 56, 57, 58, 169
Norinco, 41
North Atlantic Treaty Organization, xi, 111, 112
North Korea, vi, vii, viii, ix, 37, 44, 45, 46, 47, 48, 49, 50, 51, 52, 53, 54, 55, 56, 57, 58, 60, 61, 62, 63, 64, 65, 66, 67, 68, 69, 70, 71, 72, 73, 74, 81, 91, 92, 99, 101, 105, 115, 121, 129, 169, 183, 186, 195, 196, 197, 198, 199, 200, 204, 213, 214, 219, 222, 225, 230, 231, 234, 236, 243, 244, 248, 249, 252, 262, 263, 266, 272, 273, 287

Northern Alliance, 6, 8, 9, 13, 16, 17, 78, 83, 87, 114, 117, 201, 203, 204, 214, 235
Northern Limit Line, 70
nuclear weapons, vi, viii, 23, 30, 32, 37, 38, 56, 57, 58, 59, 60, 61, 62, 65, 66, 71, 83, 84, 91, 92, 96, 131, 195, 198, 199, 200, 214, 215, 219
Osama, v, x, 1, 2, 3, 5, 6, 7, 8, 9, 11, 12, 13, 20, 28, 33, 35, 77, 85, 94, 102, 105, 111, 117, 127, 128, 130, 135, 139, 143, 144, 146, 169, 193, 194, 214, 222, 267, 272
Osama bin Laden, v, x, 1, 3, 5, 6, 7, 9, 11, 12, 13, 20, 28, 33, 35, 77, 85, 94, 102, 105, 111, 117, 127, 128, 130, 135, 139, 143, 144, 169, 193, 194, 214, 222, 272
OTF, 130, 134, 140
PA, 145, 153
Pakistan, vi, vii, viii, ix, x, 2, 3, 5, 6, 9, 10, 13, 14, 16, 17, 18, 19, 60, 62, 63, 64, 77, 78, 79, 80, 81, 82, 83, 84, 85, 86, 87, 88, 89, 90, 91, 92, 93, 94, 95, 96, 99, 115, 116, 118, 120, 121, 129, 165, 169, 179, 182, 183, 193, 201, 202, 204, 209, 219, 228, 229, 231, 235, 236, 241, 242, 257, 259, 260, 264, 265, 269, 271
Palestine, 127
Palestinian Authority, 36
Pan American Flight 103, 194
Park, 52
Patriotic Union of Kurds, 28
Pearl Harbor, 1
Pelosi, 217

Pentagon, v, 1, 3, 12, 21, 30, 92, 127, 231, 244
People First Party, 175
People's Republic, v, vi, vii, viii, ix, x, xi, xii, xiii, 2, 3, 4, 6, 10, 11, 12, 13, 14, 15, 16, 17, 18, 19, 20, 21, 22, 23, 24, 29, 30, 31, 34, 38, 39, 40, 41, 42, 43, 44, 46, 47, 48, 52, 54, 55, 59, 60, 62, 65, 67, 73, 78, 81, 82, 84, 86, 91, 93, 96, 97, 98, 99, 100, 101, 104, 105, 106, 108, 109, 110, 111, 112, 113, 114, 115, 117, 119, 122, 123, 124, 127, 129, 131, 132, 134, 135, 136, 137, 138, 139, 140, 142, 143, 147, 148, 149, 152, 154, 155, 157, 158, 159, 161, 163, 164, 166, 167, 168, 169, 170, 171, 172, 173, 177, 178, 179, 180, 181, 182, 189, 191, 192, 194, 195, 200, 202, 203, 204, 205, 207, 208, 210, 211, 213, 214, 215, 217, 218, 219, 222
Permanent Normal Trade Relations, 217
Persian Gulf, 26, 120
PetroChina, 102
PHALCON, 86
Philippines, 96, 127, 178, 201, 207
PLA, 108
plutonium, 58
PNTR, 106
Poland, 199, 211, 220, 223
Politburo Standing Committee, 149
Pomfret, 143
President Bush, vi, xii, 21, 23, 24, 34, 39, 40, 85, 86, 114, 140, 142, 167, 193, 195, 206, 218, 248
PUK, 28
Pyongyang, 46, 47, 48, 54, 59, 61, 62, 67, 69, 72, 205, 214, 249
Qiao Liang, 11
Ramadan, 137
Reagan Administration, 167
refugees, 53, 54, 55, 66, 254, 255, 273
Reporters Without Borders, 135
Republicans, 147
reunification, xii, 70, 163, 166, 174, 175, 177, 186, 189, 196, 197, 198, 199, 204
Roh, 71
Rohrbacher, 217
Ronald Reagan, 34, 221
Rumsfeld, 30, 225, 231, 266
Russia, xi, 13, 31, 60, 78, 83, 96, 111, 112, 113, 114, 115, 119, 123, 142, 153, 170, 179, 180, 186, 203, 204, 219, 252, 259, 266
Saddam, viii, 14, 20, 23, 24, 25, 26, 27, 29, 30, 31, 32, 34, 63, 118, 140, 182, 188, 190, 191, 214, 216, 222, 223, 231, 251, 265, 272
Saddam Hussein, viii, 14, 20, 23, 24, 25, 26, 27, 29, 30, 31, 32, 34, 63, 140, 182, 188, 214, 216, 222, 223, 251, 265
Sankei Shimbun, 37, 64
Saudi Arabia, vii, 6, 10, 116, 117, 118, 119, 120, 122, 124, 182, 208, 209, 213, 219
SCO, xi, 111, 112, 113
Scud, 62, 63, 64, 121, 205, 242
Scuds, 62, 63, 121, 227

Security Council, 14, 24, 30, 31, 47, 114, 140, 142, 153, 247
Seoul, 48, 198, 226, 263
Shah, 38
Shanghai, 160
Sharif, 82
Shelton, 86
Shenyang, 69
Shenzhen, 160, 211
Shiite, 6, 35, 36
Sinuiju, 68
South China Sea, 171
South Korea, 37, 46, 48, 49, 51, 55, 56, 59, 64, 67, 68, 69, 70, 71, 72, 96, 166, 180, 186, 196, 197, 198, 204, 207, 213, 220, 257
Soviet Union, 6, 33, 44, 46, 47, 49, 52, 67, 82, 83, 93, 105, 108, 109, 130, 157, 158, 167, 179, 202, 209, 212, 214, 220, 221
Soviets, v, 9, 48, 78, 82, 158, 179, 211
Special Forces, 214
Spratly, 178
starvation, 52
Stratfor, 138
Sudan, 1, 6, 7, 36, 102, 105, 123, 193, 194, 199, 222, 250, 254, 257, 267, 269
Sunni, 6
sunshine, 69, 70, 71
Sverdlovsk, 213
Syria, vi, vii, ix, 62, 64, 103, 104, 105, 123, 129, 169, 186, 190, 193, 194, 199, 200, 214, 216, 219, 222, 225, 264, 267
Taepodong, 60, 61, 63, 64
Taiwan, xii, 10, 14, 31, 33, 42, 65, 67, 96, 106, 107, 112, 130, 151, 152, 163, 165, 166, 169, 172, 173, 174, 175, 176, 177, 178, 180, 181, 186, 189, 203, 204, 205, 206, 207, 210, 213, 217, 218, 220, 221, 224, 231, 232, 252, 255, 257, 260, 264, 267, 268
Taiwan Solidarity Union, 176
Taiwanese, 136, 151, 173, 174, 175, 176, 177, 180, 181, 189, 206, 268
Tajikistan, xi, 15, 111, 112
Taliban, vi, viii, x, xi, 1, 2, 3, 4, 5, 6, 7, 8, 9, 10, 11, 12, 13, 14, 15, 16, 17, 18, 19, 20, 21, 35, 40, 62, 77, 78, 83, 87, 88, 89, 90, 92, 94, 95, 99, 101, 114, 117, 118, 120, 127, 129, 135, 143, 169, 170, 182, 188, 191, 193, 201, 214, 219, 222, 224, 225, 231, 232, 234, 246, 248, 255, 262, 268, 269
Tang Jiaxuan, 15
Taz, 29
terrorism, vii, xi, xiii, 2, 5, 11, 15, 20, 23, 29, 34, 43, 44, 45, 49, 56, 62, 67, 74, 78, 82, 83, 85, 93, 94, 100, 101, 110, 115, 121, 122, 123, 129, 135, 136, 138, 139, 140, 142, 144, 146, 150, 151, 153, 154, 155, 172, 182, 185, 187, 193, 194, 195, 196, 200, 201, 207, 209, 215, 221, 222, 227, 254, 259, 267, 270
terrorist war, v, vi, vii, xiii, 2, 4, 7, 21, 22, 43, 44, 46, 74, 79, 89, 93, 94, 99, 105, 110, 119, 124, 129, 154, 155, 157, 176, 183, 185, 188, 194, 195, 201,

203, 207, 208, 209, 210, 215, 216, 218, 219, 221, 222
terrorists, v, vi, vii, viii, x, xii, 1, 4, 8, 11, 17, 20, 21, 22, 23, 36, 37, 43, 45, 49, 56, 60, 62, 65, 66, 77, 79, 82, 85, 88, 90, 91, 93, 95, 99, 101, 103, 110, 114, 117, 122, 128, 129, 135, 136, 138, 139, 140, 141, 142, 145, 147, 153, 154, 182, 183, 185, 186, 189, 190, 194, 196, 198, 199, 201, 209, 214, 215, 219, 220, 221, 222
Terrorists, v, xii, 77, 90, 229, 233
The Japan That Can Say "No", 204
The New Republic, 94
Tiananmen Square, xii, 132, 149, 157, 158, 159, 163, 165, 167, 216, 220, 256, 264
Tibet, ix, 93, 96, 131, 136, 137, 147, 148, 149, 165, 166, 176, 180, 210, 211, 216, 221, 222, 223, 252, 268
Tibetan government-in-exile, 180, 202
Tikrit, 214
Time Asia, 141
Tokyo, 63, 72, 204
tributyl phosphate, ix, 59, 60
Truman, 47
Turkey, 85
U.S.S. Cole, 7, 11, 62, 120
U.S.S.R., 67, 179
Uighurs, ix, x, 112, 127, 128, 130, 131, 132, 133, 138, 139, 142, 144, 145, 146, 147, 148, 155, 166, 180, 186, 208, 239
UN, 24, 27, 29, 31, 32, 47, 48, 141, 142, 247, 270

United Arab Emirates, vii, 6, 10, 116, 120, 122, 182, 213, 219, 257, 269
United Kingdom, 25, 79, 223, 251
United Nations, 3, 14, 24, 30, 31, 47, 54, 63, 103, 140, 141, 173, 247
United Nations High Commissioner for Human Rights, 137
United States, v, vi, vii, viii, x, xi, xii, 1, 2, 3, 4, 5, 6, 7, 9, 10, 11, 12, 13, 14, 15, 16, 17, 18, 19, 20, 21, 22, 24, 26, 30, 31, 32, 33, 34, 35, 36, 37, 38, 39, 40, 41, 42, 43, 44, 45, 47, 48, 49, 53, 56, 58, 59, 60, 61, 62, 63, 64, 65, 66, 67, 68, 69, 71, 72, 74, 77, 78, 79, 81, 82, 83, 84, 85, 86, 87, 89, 91, 92, 93, 94, 95, 98, 99, 100, 101, 102, 104, 105, 106, 108, 109, 110, 111, 112, 114, 116, 118, 119, 120, 121, 122, 123, 124, 127, 128, 130, 134, 136, 138, 140, 141, 142, 143, 144, 145, 146, 152, 153, 154, 155, 157, 158, 159, 163, 165, 166, 167, 168, 169, 170, 171, 172, 173, 174, 177, 178, 179, 180, 181, 182, 183, 185, 186, 187, 188, 189, 190, 191, 192, 193, 194, 195, 196, 197, 198, 200, 201, 202, 203, 205, 206, 207, 208, 209, 211, 213, 214, 215, 216, 217, 218, 219, 220, 221, 222, 226, 229, 230, 232, 234, 235, 236, 238, 239, 240, 241, 243, 244, 245, 246, 249, 251, 252, 255, 259, 260, 262, 267, 270, 271, 287

United States Armed Forces, 108
University of Aeronautics and Astronautics, 101
Unrestricted Warfare, 11, 12, 242
uranium, viii, ix, 24, 36, 38, 57, 59, 71, 92, 203
Urumqi, 131, 134, 256
Ustad Khalil, 4, 18
Uzbekistan, xi, 15, 89, 111, 112, 179
Vajpayee, 80, 83, 85, 86, 89
Vietnam, 96, 165, 178, 259
Vollertsen, 52, 53
Wahhabism, 116, 143, 146
Wahhabist, 6, 35, 117, 120, 191
Wall Street, 98
Walpole, 57
Wang Bingzhang, 152
Wang Lequan, 151
Wang Xiangsui, 11
war on terror, v, vi, vii, xi, xii, 2, 4, 5, 13, 15, 18, 21, 30, 34, 43, 44, 65, 74, 75, 77, 79, 87, 89, 92, 93, 95, 99, 100, 113, 122, 124, 125, 129, 145, 153, 154, 155, 157, 170, 176, 180, 182, 183, 185, 186, 187, 193, 200, 201, 208, 209, 210, 213, 214, 215, 217, 222
Washington, v, vi, 14, 15, 16, 19, 28, 29, 39, 40, 47, 71, 82, 83, 86, 88, 92, 111, 113, 114, 119, 144, 152, 202, 223, 224, 225, 226, 227, 228, 229, 230, 231, 232, 234, 235, 236, 237, 242, 243, 244, 245, 246, 247, 248, 249, 250, 251, 252, 253, 254, 255, 265, 272
Washington Post, 143
Washington Times, 14, 16, 29, 39, 144, 224, 227, 228, 229, 230, 231, 232, 234, 236, 237, 243, 244, 247, 248, 249, 251, 252, 254, 255, 265
Washington, D.C., v, vi
weapons of mass destruction, viii, 24, 27, 32, 63, 73, 74, 103, 104, 183, 192
West Bank, 23, 153
Western Europe, 170
WFP, 53
White House, 52
Wolf, 107
World Trade Center, v, viii, 1, 2, 3, 5, 11, 12, 18, 21, 77, 92, 114, 117, 127, 135
World Trade Organization, 107
World War II, v, 47, 79, 109, 130, 150, 162, 173, 178, 188, 189, 191
Xiamen, 161, 212, 248
Xinhua, 3, 12, 135
Xinjiang, ix, 15, 31, 66, 110, 111, 127, 130, 137, 141, 148, 149, 151, 166, 208, 226, 237, 239
Yang Bin, 68
Yang Xiaofeng, 135
Yekaterinaburg, 213
Yeltsin, 213
Yemen, vii, 62, 63, 74, 116, 120, 121, 122, 123, 124, 182, 213, 219, 227, 231, 269, 270, 272
Yining, 133
Yokota, 50
Yongbyon, 58
Yonhap, 37, 64, 273
Yugoslavia, 189, 199, 213, 246
Zhao, 157, 158, 159, 164, 211
Zhongnanhai, 12
Zhongxing Telecom, 14
Zhou Shengtao, 151
Zhu Rongji, 5, 175

ZTE, 29

Zulfikar Ali Bhutto, 82

A Note on the Author

D.J. McGuire is the co-Chairman and President of the <u>China e-Lobby</u>, an organization he co-founded in 2000, dedicated to exposing the abuses of human rights, threats to American security, and attacks on general decency committed by Communist China, and to influencing United States policy to ensure these egregious acts do not go unopposed. He has founded, written, and published three weekly e-mail/internet publications of the China e-Lobby: *Update* since April 2000, *The Week's Links* since July 2000, and *The North Korea Report* since April 2002. He still writes and publishes all three to this day.

Prior to the China e-Lobby, Mr. McGuire was active in Republican politics at the local level for a dozen years. He was also on the editorial staff of the *Remnant*, the independent student newspaper at the College of William and Mary, from 1990 to 1993. He holds a Master's in Economics from Georgetown University (1999) and a Bachelor's in Economics from the College of William and Mary (1994).

Printed in the United States
1438000001B/147